Shine Bright 2de va te permettre d'approfondir ta connaissance du monde anglophone et de progresser en anglais grâce à **des supports authentiques** et des **outils innovants** tels que live!.

Apprends en agissant avec Shine Bright 2de

La première partie de ton manuel est constituée de **20 dossiers (*Files*)** ancrés dans la thématique centrale du programme de seconde : **« L'art de vivre ensemble ».**

Chaque dossier est construit autour d'une **problématique adossée à l'un des huit axes du programme**, laquelle est affichée sur la double page d'ouverture. Tu verras parfois un second axe signalé en-dessous : il s'agit d'un axe « mineur » qui pourra être abordé à travers certains documents ou pages spécifiques.

Grâce à **des documents variés** et **porteurs de sens** (vidéo, audio, textes littéraires et journalistiques, supports iconographiques, etc.) et à **des activités de difficulté progressive**, tu construiras les compétences culturelles et linguistiques nécessaires à la réalisation de la tâche finale.

Apprends en te cultivant avec Shine Bright 2de

À travers les pages ***Explore***, les 20 *Files* du manuel te feront découvrir la diversité du monde anglophone : du quartier de Harlem à la campagne anglaise, en passant par la Nouvelle-Zélande et le Kenya, c'est un véritable tour des pays anglophones qui t'est proposé !

Les pages ***Test your culture*** te mettront à l'épreuve de façon ludique pour te permettre de vérifier que les connaissances culturelles sont bien assimilées.

Apprends en variant les outils avec Shine Bright 2de

Nous proposons **une palette d'outils diversifiés** afin que ce manuel s'adresse à tout type d'élève.

Ainsi, **des parcours différenciés** sont proposés pour l'étude de certains documents et la réalisation de certaines tâches intermédiaires (***Your task***).

Tu pourras aussi développer tes compétences linguistiques et langagières.

- Pour la grammaire (***Boost your English***), des infographies et des tutos vidéos t'aideront à comprendre et à maîtriser les outils linguistiques nécessaires pour bien comprendre et t'exprimer. Ces outils sont complétés par un précis grammatical en fin de manuel.
- Pour le vocabulaire, tu auras à disposition des cartes mentales récapitulatives pour chaque dossier, associées à des activités interactives via live! LEXIQUIZ.
- Enfin, des rubriques dédiées à la méthodologie, conçues de manière très visuelle, t'accompagneront dans la réalisation des tâches : la rubrique ***Yes you can!*** dans les pages ***Final task*** et les pages ***Strategies*** à la fin de ton manuel.

Nous avons eu à cœur de te proposer des chemins vers la réussite et te souhaitons un voyage culturel et linguistique enthousiasmant avec Shine Bright 2de

Les auteurs

À la découverte de ton manuel

Les pictos de ton manuel

Compréhension orale

Compréhension écrite

Expression orale en interaction

Expression écrite

Expression orale en continu

Expression écrite en interaction

MÉDIATION Médiation écrite ou orale

WB → p. 4 Renvoi au *workbook*

STRATEGIES Renvoi aux pages de méthodologie en fin de manuel

PRÉCIS Renvoi au précis grammatical en fin de manuel

Pump it up! Renvoi au cahier de langue *Pump it up!*

Nathan live! VIDÉO Vidéo accessible via Nathan live ou dans ton manuel numérique

Nathan live! MP3 Audio accessible via Nathan live, sur le site compagnon lycee.nathan.fr/shine-bright2 ou dans ton manuel numérique

Nathan live! LEXIQUIZ Des activités pour mémoriser le vocabulaire

Pour découvrir et comprendre

Dans ton manuel, chaque chapitre comporte plusieurs pages de documents pour découvrir la langue et les différents aspects de la thématique culturelle.

À quoi sert la double page d'ouverture ?

- Elle te permet de découvrir la problématique de l'unité à travers des **documents courts** et un **travail collaboratif**.

Comment fonctionnent les autres pages de documents ?

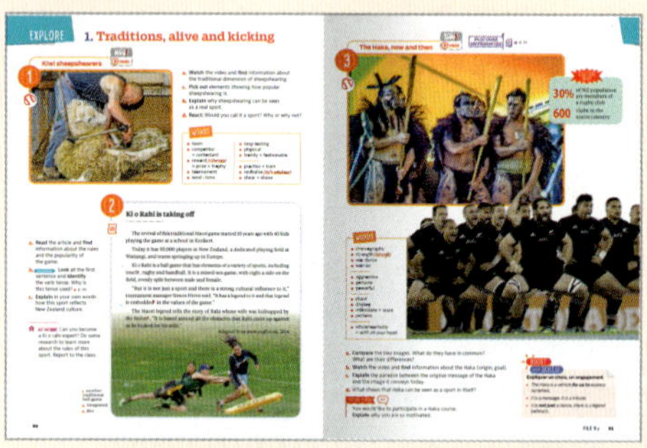

- Chaque page ou double page ***Explore*** traite un des aspects de la problématique de départ à travers **plusieurs documents authentiques**. Elle propose **des activités de réception, de production et de médiation**.
- Le picto PARCOURS DIFFÉRENCIÉS WB → p. 4 t'indique les documents qui font l'objet de parcours de compréhension plus ou moins guidés dans ton ***workbook***.
- La rubrique ***Your task*** te propose une tâche à réaliser à la suite de l'étude d'un document. Deux ***Ways*** sont parfois présentés afin de te donner le choix. Une boîte ***Boost your skills*** t'aidera à améliorer ta production.
- La rubrique ***At home*** te donne des pistes pour approfondir à la maison.

Comment fonctionnent les *Snapfiles* ?

- Ces chapitres **plus courts** te feront découvrir une thématique culturelle à travers une suite de documents et **une tâche à réaliser au fur et à mesure de l'étude des documents**.

Pour maîtriser la langue et préparer la tâche finale

Quels outils sont à ta disposition pour progresser ?

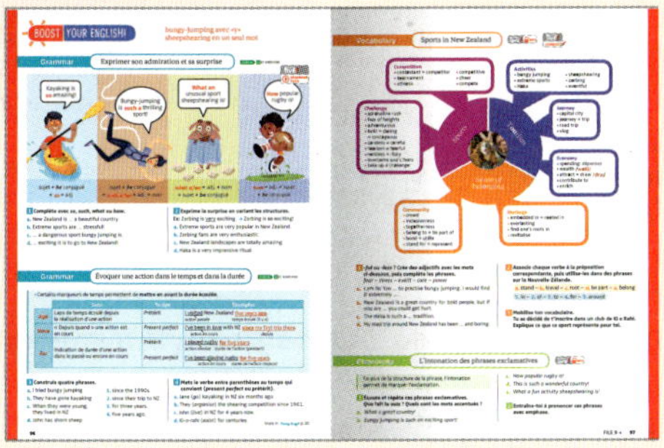

- Tu disposes de plusieurs outils pour consolider ta maîtrise de la grammaire anglaise :
  - Tu es plutôt visuel(le) ? Les **infographies** sont faites pour toi.
  - Tu es plutôt auditif(ve) ? Les ***Grammar tuto*** seront ton outil de prédilection.
- Le lexique de chaque unité n'aura plus de secret pour toi grâce aux **cartes mentales de vocabulaire**, aux **activités de mémorisation** sur Nathan live! LEXIQUIZ et à celles de **manipulation** dans le manuel.
- Savoir prononcer et écrire correctement est essentiel pour se faire comprendre : les activités de la rubrique ***Phonology*** ou ***Spelling*** t'y aideront.

Pour progresser et t'évaluer

Es-tu joueur ?

Si c'est le cas, les pages ***Test your culture*** vont te plaire ! Elles te permettront de faire le point sur tes connaissances culturelles.

Quels autres outils peux-tu utiliser dans ton manuel ?

À la fin de ton manuel, tu disposes de pages qui te seront utiles tout au long de l'année :

- Les pages ***Strategies*** te fournissent des outils méthodologiques.
- Le précis grammatical vient compléter les pages ***Boost your English*** de chaque chapitre et te propose des exercices supplémentaires.
- Le ***Lexique*** répertorie les mots les plus importants étudiés dans les *Files*.

À quoi servent les pages *Final task* et *Test your skills* ?

Ces pages sont l'aboutissement de ton travail sur l'ensemble de l'unité.

Elles te permettront de montrer que tu as compris les enjeux de la problématique, assimilé les éléments culturels et appris à manipuler les outils linguistiques nécessaires pour t'exprimer (***Final task***) ou pour comprendre (***Test your skills*** et grille d'auto-évaluation dans le *workbook*).

La rubrique ***Yes you can*** sera un guide précieux pour t'accompagner dans ta production finale.

Et en dehors du manuel ?

Pour progresser et consolider tes connaissances grammaticales, lexicales et phonologiques, tu peux utiliser le cahier ***Pump it up! English language 2de*** : il s'appuie sur les contenus thématiques et lexicaux de ton manuel pour te permettre de poursuivre l'étude de la langue **en contexte.**

SOMMAIRE

● Axe majeur
● Axe mineur

modern
family

SOMMAIRE

MPOSSIBL
BURGER!*
"Made entirely of

SOMMAIRE

RÉPARTITION DES *FILES* PAR AXES DU PROGRAMME

BIENVENUE AU LYCÉE

VOTRE ANNÉE DE SECONDE

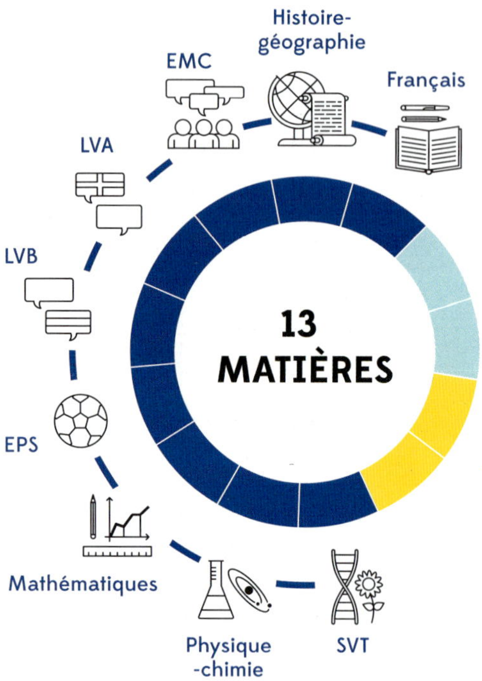

Les 13 matières qui animeront toute votre année

Celles que vous connaissez

Deux nouveautés — SES ; SNT (Sciences numériques et Technologie)

Deux optionnelles — À choisir parmi des enseignements généraux ou technologiques

- Un accompagnement personnalisé tout au long de l'année
- Des heures réservées pour préparer votre orientation

www.orientation-lycees

Préparez vos choix pour la Première

LA VOIE TECHNOLOGIQUE

Les séries technologiques sont organisées autour de grands domaines de connaissances appliquées aux différents secteurs d'activités et proposent l'étude de situations concrètes.

LA VOIE GÉNÉRALE

Un tronc commun et trois enseignements de spécialités qui ouvrent des horizons. Un choix très ouvert : vous poursuivrez deux de ces spécialités en Terminale.

www.horizons2021.fr

Votre Bac démarre dès la Première

BULLETINS

Vos bulletins scolaires de Première et de Terminale seront pris en compte dans la note finale.

ÉPREUVES

En Première et en Terminale, vous serez évalué en contrôle continu dans votre lycée. Vous passerez aussi des épreuves nationales.

GRAND ORAL

Une nouvelle épreuve pour tous en Terminale.

Construisez votre parcours professionnel

VOUS

- Explorez le monde professionnel.
- Découvrez les formations du Supérieur.
- Interrogez-vous sur vos centres d'intérêt et vos atouts.

VOTRE LYCÉE

- Bénéficiez de l'accompagnement personnalisé et des Semaines de l'orientation.
- Adressez-vous à votre professeur principal, aux psychologues de l'éducation nationale (au lycée ou au CIO).

LES OUTILS NUMÉRIQUES

Posez directement vos questions aux conseillers ONISEP sur la plate-forme gratuite et personnalisée Mon Orientation.

www.monorientationenligne.fr

AUTOUR DE VOUS

Journées portes ouvertes, Salons, stages d'immersion, visites d'entreprise...

Retrouvez tous les liens utiles pour votre orientation sur le site nathan.fr/orientation

DEMAIN, LA PREMIÈRE

Deux voies d'orientation s'offrent à vous

Le conseil de classe du 3e trimestre étudiera votre choix et le chef d'établissement prendra une décision.

UN BACCALAURÉAT GÉNÉRAL

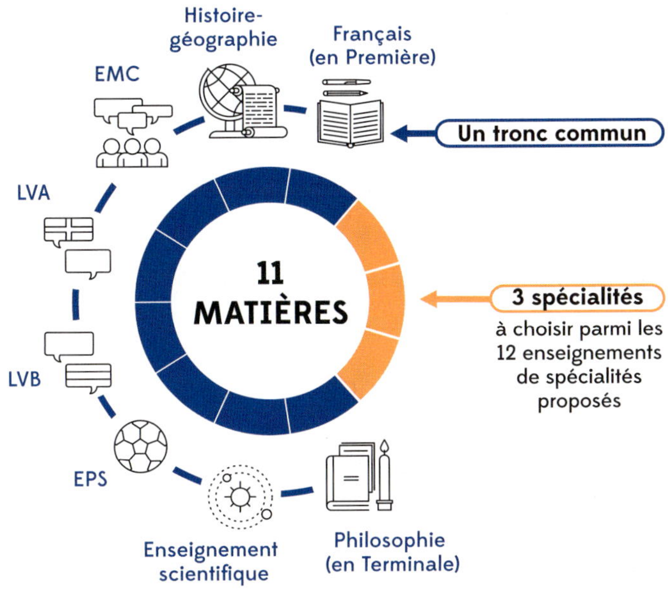

12 enseignements de spécialités

- Histoire-géographie, géopolitique et sciences politiques
- Langues, littératures et cultures étrangères
- Sciences de la vie et de la Terre
- Sciences économiques et sociales
- Mathématiques
- Numérique et sciences informatiques
- Humanités, littérature et philosophie
- Sciences de l'ingénieur
- Littérature, langues et cultures de l'Antiquité
- Physique-chimie
- Arts
- Biologie-écologie *(dispensé en lycées agricoles)*

Découvrez les horizons que vous ouvrent vos choix d'enseignement de spécialités *www.horizons2021.fr*

UN BACCALAURÉAT TECHNOLOGIQUE

Disciplines communes à tous les Baccalauréats technologiques (sauf TMD) avec des programmes adaptés à chaque série.

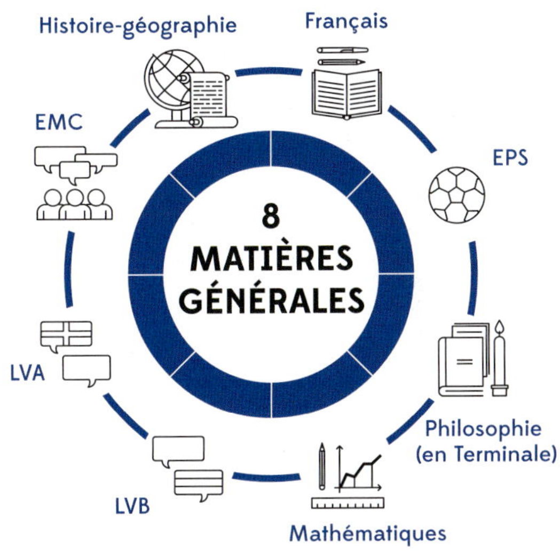

8 séries technologiques

- STL laboratoire
- TMD musique, danse
- STD2A design, arts appliqués
- STMG management, gestion
- ST2S santé, social
- STAV agronomie et vivant
- STHR hôtellerie, restauration
- STI2D industrie, développement durable

Nathan onisep

Test

QUEL EST MON TYPE DE MÉMOIRE ?

Tout le monde est capable d'apprendre ! Il est utile pour cela de trouver les bonnes méthodes et de créer les bons outils. Fais ce test pour mieux te connaître et identifier quel(s) type(s) de mémoire te correspondent.

Légende

- Ça me correspond tout à fait ▸ 4 points
- Ça me correspond un peu ▸ 3 points
- Ce n'est pas vraiment moi ▸ 2 points
- Ça ne me correspond pas du tout ▸ 1 point

1. Je dessine des schémas, des cartes mentales, des affiches pour m'aider à mémoriser.
2. Je me souviens mieux de ce que je lis que de ce que j'entends.
3. Quand j'apprends du vocabulaire, je me répète la définition dans ma tête.
4. Pour mobiliser une information, je me souviens surtout des pages du manuel ou de mon cahier qui y sont consacrées.
5. Je comprends mieux les consignes orales que les consignes écrites.
6. Je préfère lire une histoire que l'entendre.
7. J'apprends mieux un mot si je l'écris plusieurs fois.
8. Je comprends mieux quand je lis ma leçon à voix haute.
9. Je me souviens mieux des repères ou des règles en les répétant.
10. J'apprends mieux quand je marche ou que je fais tourner un objet dans mes mains.
11. Quand je relis ma leçon, il me vient beaucoup d'images du cours.
12. J'aime construire des choses et bricoler.
13. Je comprends mieux les explications sous forme de tableau ou de schéma.
14. Pour retrouver une information, je me souviens surtout de ce que je faisais au moment de l'apprendre.
15. Pour retrouver une information, je me souviens surtout de ce qu'a dit mon professeur à ce sujet.

Résultats

Tes résultats peuvent être proches dans deux colonnes, ce qui signifie que tu combines plusieurs types de mémoire !

A	B	C
Additionne le nombre de points obtenus aux questions :	Additionne le nombre de points obtenus aux questions :	Additionne le nombre de points obtenus aux questions :
2 4 6 11 13	3 5 8 9 15	1 7 10 12 14

Si ton score de la **COLONNE A** est le plus élevé : tu as plutôt une **mémoire visuelle**.
Si ton score de la **COLONNE B** est le plus élevé : tu as plutôt une **mémoire auditive**.
Si ton score de la **COLONNE C** est le plus élevé : tu as plutôt une **mémoire corporelle**.

LA MÉMOIRE VISUELLE

Avoir une mémoire visuelle signifie que tu retiens mieux ce que tu lis, vois ou écris. Tu photographies mentalement les pages de tes cahiers, le tableau…

Tes outils

- Soigne ton travail, la présentation de tes cours pour que tes cahiers ou tes classeurs soient agréables à regarder.
- Utilise tout ce qui peut marquer ta mémoire visuellement : couleurs, schémas, mise en page…
- Surligne ou souligne des mots, des phrases, des terminaisons, etc., ou utilise des codes couleurs.

LA MÉMOIRE AUDITIVE

Avoir une mémoire auditive signifie que tu retiens mieux ce que tu entends. Tu comprends et mémorises mieux lorsque tu lis des informations à voix haute et que tu les reformules avec tes propres mots.

Tes outils

- Écoute bien en classe et révise en oralisant : lis tes cours à voix haute, mais aussi les consignes des exercices, le vocabulaire que tu veux apprendre, etc. Tu peux aussi t'enregistrer, puis écouter l'enregistrement plusieurs fois pour bien mémoriser les informations importantes.
- Tu peux également travailler en duo ou en groupe : échangez des questions, reformulez ensemble ce que vous avez compris.

LA MÉMOIRE CORPORELLE

Avoir une mémoire corporelle signifie que tu retiens mieux en bougeant, en faisant des mouvements. Tes sensations et tes émotions jouent un rôle important dans le processus de mémorisation.

Tes outils

- Privilégie les activités de manipulation, les jeux et l'écriture pour apprendre.
- Rédige des fiches de révision, des listes de mots, des résumés très courts.
- Utilise un des murs de ta chambre pour installer un tableau blanc (ou des feuilles de papier) : cela te servira à faire des listes, à faire des schémas, à organiser tes idées.
- Identifie les mouvements qui te permettent de mieux te concentrer (marcher, faire bouger un objet dans tes mains…) et fais-les lorsque tu révises.

EXPLORE

2. Gentrification

The corner of 125th Street and Malcolm X Boulevard

1 "The Times They Are A Changin'"

The first time Camilo José Vergara pointed his camera at the corner of 125th Street and Malcolm X Boulevard, it was 1989.

The Whole Foods Market[1] opened in 2017 and, to be fair, will surely bring fresher produce and better meat to a neighborhood where such things can be scarce[2]. (At prices, however, that many residents cannot pay.) New construction is not inherently bad just because it is new. But here, as in so many other places, an interesting building that was very much anchored[3] in its time and place has given way to one that is very much not.

Christopher BONANOS, *nymag.com*, 2017

1. An American supermarket chain known for its organic products
2. rare 3. *ancré*

2

https://www.nytimes.com

The end of black Harlem?

By MICHAEL HENRY ADAMS, author of *The End of Black Harlem*, 2016

I have lived in Harlem for half my life – 30 years. I have seen it in all its complexities: a cultural nexus[1] of black America, the landing place for Senegalese immigrants and Southern transplants, a home for people fleeing oppression and seeking[2] opportunity. Harlem is the birthplace of so much poetry and music and beauty, but in the eyes of many who have never set foot here, it has long been a swamp[3] of pain and suffering. It is also changing, rapidly. [...]

But when we friends gather at a restaurant [...], we are every color, every race, every age, identity and class. In the moment, laughing, drinking and dancing together, it seems marvelous. This Harlem, this is what New York is supposed to look like, to be like. Only, most of us know that our fun times together are doomed[4].

1. centre 2. looking for 3. *marais* 4. *condamnés*

Focus on Doc 1 or 2.

PARCOURS DIFFÉRENCIÉS WB → p. 5

Doc 1

a. Comment on the evolution of the building.

b. Read the text and **say** what is positive and negative about the arrival of Whole Foods Market in Harlem.

c. Comment on the conclusion.

Doc 2

a. Read the text and **pick out** elements showing the complexity of Harlem.

b. GRAMMAR **Focus** on: *"It is also changing, rapidly"* (l.8). **Comment** on the use of *be* + V-*ing*. ► p. 24

c. Explain what the author fears.

YOUR TASK

DIFFÉRENCIATION

You are a journalist from Harlem.

WAY 1 One of the historical buildings in your neighbourhood is going to be replaced by a supermarket. **React** in a post.

WAY 2 **Write** a report on how things evolve in Harlem.

WORDS

- org**a**nic food: *aliments bio*
- pr**e**judice /'prɛdʒʊdɪs/: *préjugés*
- hist**o**rical ≠ m**o**dern, brand new
- ev**o**lve: *évoluer, changer*
- repl**a**ce

BOOST YOUR SKILLS!

Témoigner d'une évolution

- *It* ***is** also **changing**, **rapidly**.*
- *It **has given** way to...*

3. Harlem success stories

live! MP3 PARCOURS DIFFÉRENCIÉS WB → p. 6

1 I got nervous before I cooked for President Obama

a. **Listen** to the recording and **give information** about the man (name, country of origin, job).

b. **Explain** how the Red Rooster restaurant reflects Harlem's culture.

c. **Make a list** of the man's achievements.

2

kibonen.ny • Follow

It is throwback[1] every day. Humble beginnings at my little store in Harlem. I felt so achieved as I walked into this place every day. Today the dream is bigger and better and finer.
I love what I do and what it represents to humanity, to the #cameroonian girl, to the #african girl and to the #dreamer #africanfashiondesigner #fromafricafortheworld #fromafricatotheworld #fromafricatonewyork #humblebeginnings

frifavour inspiring

bandykiki ❤️

ddtalks Every accomplished dream, no matter how big, has a beginning. You have earned your stripes sis 😘. #megasizedinfluencer

stephamy22 Just love this 😭❤️

whitebirchcraftco You are so pretty! Keep up your great work! Girl power! 😘

1. *souvenir*

WORDS

- achiever
- success ≠ failure
- wardrobe: *garde-robe*

- charismatic
- influential /ɪnflu'enʃəl/
- inspiring
- impressed
- impressive

- praise ≠ criticise
- inspire

a. **Look** at the picture and **comment** on Kibonen's clothes and attitude.

b. **Guess** where she is. Then **read** the text and **check** your hypotheses.

c. GRAMMAR **Observe** these words: *bigger*, *better*, *finer*. **Comment** on their form.
PRÉCIS 8

d. **Focus** on the hashtags. **Say** what information they give about Kibonen and her goals.

YOUR TASK
Read the comments and analyse them.
Then, **write** your own.

BOOST YOUR SKILLS!

Faire l'éloge de quelque chose ou de quelqu'un

- *It may seem like Marcus Samuelsson* ***was born to*** *cook.*
- ***The biggest hits*** *on Red Rooster's menu include...*
- *Today the dream is* ***bigger and better and finer****.*
- *You have* ***earned your stripes****.*

AT HOME Find a success story from Harlem and present it to the class. Talk about the links between this person and Harlem.

4. Community life

1

https://www.harlem.projectplay.us

THE ASPEN INSTITUTE
PROJECT PLAY

Ibrahim Cisse is a vibrant, confident sixth-grader. But when he moved to East Harlem from the Ivory Coast four years ago, he was a wide-eyed 8-year-old boy who knew no one and spoke little English. It was Ibrahim's passion for soccer that pushed him to play at his local park and join the afterschool sports program. Although his new friends spoke different languages, Ibrahim saw cultural and linguistic differences as opportunities, not barriers. "I like to talk to people and learn from them," he said. "You can learn a lot from people who are different from you."
The city program provides[1] him and hundreds of other kids with a safe place to meet and play and offers academic tutoring and mentoring opportunities as well. Ibrahim's transformation from isolated outsider to child athlete, peer mentor and community ambassador has made him wise[2] beyond his years. "People need to start realizing that there is no difference between us – white or any other color," he said. "We are all the same. We need to listen to each other and respect each other."

ABOUT US >

Rule number one to get kids active through sports: Ask Kids What They Want. Who better to know their experiences than kids themselves? To mobilize around growing the quality and quantity of youth sports in East Harlem, youth must have a platform for their voices to be heard as a part of the decision-making process.

1. offers **2.** *sage*

a. Read the article, **find** out who Ibrahim Cisse is, and **say** what difficulties he faced when he moved to Harlem.

b. Explain how the afterschool sports programme helped him.

c. Compare how Ibrahim was when he arrived and how he is today.

d. Describe what Project Play does for young people like Ibrahim.

WORDS

- food stall
- purpose = aim
- solidarity
- traditional /trə'dɪʃənəl/
- welcoming

- charming
- culturally diverse
- delicious
- open-minded
- discover
- improve
- support: *soutenir*
- taste

2

https://www.116thstfestival.com

Celebrating 34 years

Event-goers from around the country are expected to gather at this year's festival, which anticipates more than 200,000 guests. People of all ethnicities and backgrounds are welcome to join in the fun, learn about Hispanic culture, and enjoy a family-friendly outing.

The 116th Street Festival started in 1985 as "Abrazo Fraternal" and has grown to encompass[1] 20 blocks, and on the day of the festival, people for miles will hear the sounds of Hispanic and various musics and smell the aromas of mouthwatering Hispanic dishes. The famous festival continues to bring an economic advantage to the neighborhood as well as offer a communal atmosphere for Hispanics and anyone who wishes to learn more about the fun-loving culture that boasts[2] decadent music, food, and more.

The 116th Street Festival offers various performances, new and classic Hispanic foods, and a fun, electrified atmosphere.

116th Street Festival
34TH ANNIVERSARY
2019
ABRAZO FRATERNAL DEL BARRIO FOUNDATION

1. include **2.** show off

a. Focus on the name and logo of the website. What kind of event is it? **Guess** what the two countries represented are.

b. Read the document and **explain** what the festival is about and who it is open to.

c. Explain what the neighbourhood and the visitors can benefit from this festival.

d. Find examples showing how diversity is a key element of the festival.

AT HOME Go on the Festival's official website and find ideas of activities to do there.

HOW TO PLAY "KNOW YOUR WAY ROUND HARLEM"

TEST YOUR CULTURE

Play in groups of two to four pupils. Start with a capital of three tokens.

Walk around Harlem and answer the questions to test your knowledge about the neighbourhood.

If you answer correctly, you may collect your tokens.

If you cannot answer correctly, you lose the number of tokens that the question is worth.

The group with the most tokens wins a meal at Red Rooster!

GAME ON!

1 Harlem is located...
– in the northern part of Manhattan.
– in the western part of the Bronx.
– in the southern part of Brooklyn.

(1) (1)

2 The Harlem Renaissance is known for...
– rock music.
– jazz music.
– rap music.

(1) (1)

3 Dizzie Gillespie was...
– a singer.
– a musician.
– a painter.

(1)

4 Langston Hughes's poems dealt with...
– discrimination.
– nature.
– war.

(1) (1)

10 The 116th Street Festival celebrates...
– African-American culture.
– Hispanic culture.
– Asian culture.

(1) (1)

9 What is Project Play?
– An association created to build houses for young orphans.
– An association to promote sports in the neighbourhood.
– An association for young people to learn how to play jazz.

(1) (1)

5 What is gentrification?
– It is when men behave like gentlemen.
– It is when a neighbourhood becomes richer.
– It is when a neighbourhood becomes more violent.

(1)

8 What is Kibonen's goal?
– To have one million followers on Instagram.
– To bring American fashion to Cameroon.
– To make Cameroon's fashion known throughout the world.

(1) (1) (1)

7 El Barrio is the nickname of...
– Harlem.
– West Harlem.
– East Harlem.

(1)

6 Chef Marcus Samuelsson is famous because...
– he fought against segregation.
– he cooks dressed up as a rooster.
– he appears on the TV show "Top Chef".

(1) (1)

BOOST YOUR ENGLISH!

Grammar — Évoquer des faits présents

PRÉCIS 12 ET EXERCICES

Pour évoquer des faits, des généralités ou des habitudes, on utilise le **présent simple**, souvent avec des adverbes de fréquence tels que *often, always, sometimes, never*, etc.
Pour décrire des faits actuels ou en cours, parler d'un événement imminent, attirer l'attention sur quelque chose, on utilisera le **présent en *be* + V-*ing***.

live! GRAMMAR TUTO

HABITUDES, GÉNÉRALITÉS | **ACTION EN COURS** | **FUTUR PROCHE** | **ATTIRER L'ATTENTION, FAIRE UN COMMENTAIRE**

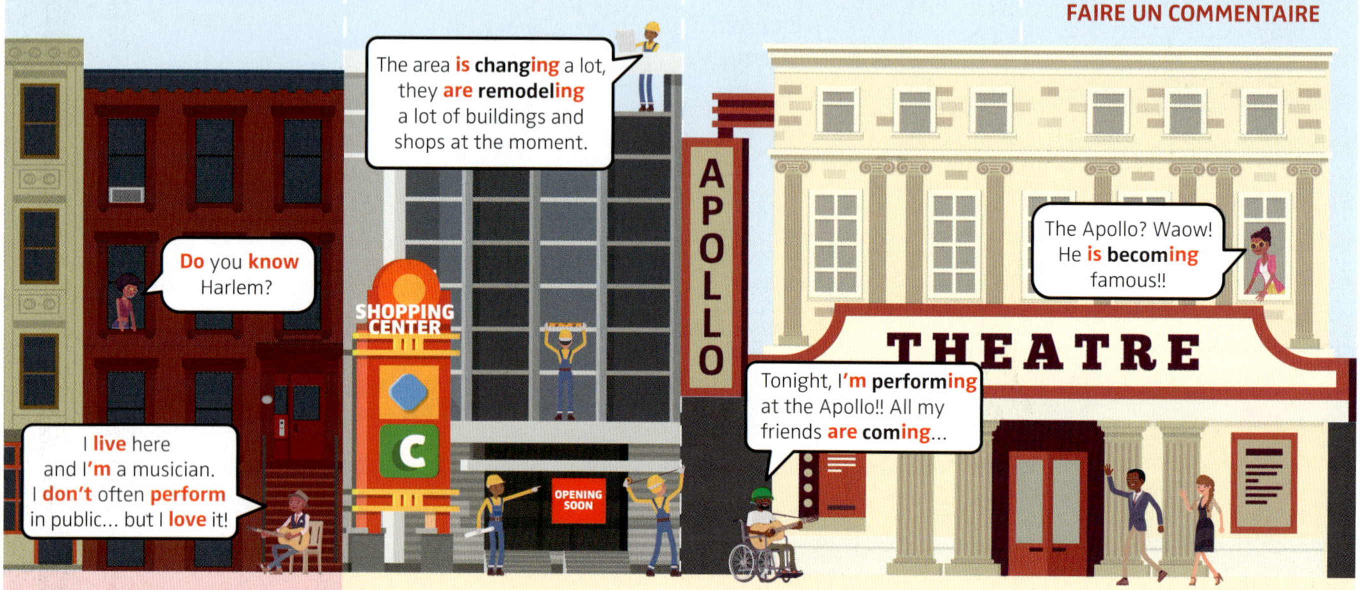

Présent simple
Auxiliaire : do/does ou don't/doesn't
Attention au s à la 3e pers. du sing.

Présent be + V-ing
Auxiliaire : be au présent

1 Complète ces phrases avec les éléments suivants.

but today | **more and more** | **nowadays** | **every year** | **usually**

a. ..., many Manhattanites are settling down in Harlem.
b. She ... takes the subway to work, ... she's walking to see the changes in her neighbourhood.
c. They are being ... disrespectful to Harlemites!
d. ..., Project Play helps kids who love sports.

2 Mets les verbes au présent simple ou au présent en *be* + V-*ing* selon le sens.

a. She (*feel*) so proud of being a Harlemite.
b. These days, the area (*evolve*) and (*change*).
c. Usually, I (*not / oppose*) gentrification, but I (*not / like*) the changes they (*make*) in Harlem.
d. (*you / buy*) an appartment in Harlem? You're right. This is the perfect moment to do so.

3 Mets ces phrases au présent simple ou en *be* + V-*ing* selon le sens. Attention au sujet et à la forme demandée entre parenthèses.

a. She (*help*) young people succeed thanks to her association. (affirmative)
b. Harlemites (*be enthusiastic*) about change? (interrogative)
c. I (*know*) Harlem very well. (négative)
d. You (*come*) to the 116th Street Festival? (interrogative)
e. At the moment, at school, we (*study*) poems by African-American writers. (affirmative)
f. Kibonen (*live*) the dream! (affirmative)

4 Tu es guide touristique à Harlem. Prépare ta présentation à l'écrit :

– donne des généralités sur le quartier ;
– présente un lieu célèbre et son histoire ;
– décris les habitudes des habitants ;
– évoque les changements actuels.

More in *Pump it up!* p. 18-21

Vocabulary — Harlemite and proud

live! MP3 — live! LEXIQUIZ

Acting for change

Problems
- equality ≠ inequality
- issue = subject
- segregation
- strength ≠ weakness
- defiant ≠ submissive

Actions
- association
- event
- solidarity
- argue = debate
- defend a cause
- have an impact on = influence
- support: *soutenir*

History in stone

Landmarks
- borough
- brownstone building
- city centre (UK) / center (US)
- gentrification
- neighbourhood (UK) / neighborhood (US)
- brand new
- historical
- modern

Legacy
- heritage
- famous ≠ unknown
- celebrate
- evolve: *évoluer, changer*
- pay tribute to
- remember
- replace

Art
- band: *groupe*
- literature /'lɪtrətʃər/
- mural
- poetry /'poʊətri/
- stanza: *strophe*
- street art
- bright ≠ dark
- colourful (UK) / colorful (US)
- huge = very large

Success stories
- achiever
- success ≠ failure
- charismatic
- influential /ɪnflu'enʃəl/
- impressive
- praise ≠ criticise

1 **Associe chaque mot à sa definition.**

mural – achiever – borough – gentrification – stanza

a. a person who has success
b. a group of lines in a poem
c. one of the five districts of New York City
d. making a neighbourhood more attractive for middle-class inhabitants
e. a piece of art executed directly on a wall

2 **Complète ces phrases avec les mots de la liste.**

celebrates – influential – neighbourhood – colourful – inequalities – huge

a. Harlem is a ... of Manhattan.
b. A lot of associations fight against social ... .
c. Every year, the 116th Street Festival ... Hispanic culture.
d. When you walk around Harlem, you can see ... ... murals.
e. The Harlem Renaissance was a very ... artistic movement.

Phonology — La prononciation des graphies <a> et <i>

live! MP3 More in *Pump it up!* p. 76-77

Les graphies <a> et <i> ne se prononcent pas toujours de la même manière en anglais.

/æ/ cat	/ə/ admit	/ɒ/ watch	/ɔ:/ talk	/ɑ:/ car	/eɪ/ face	/eə/ care

/ɪ/ live	/ai/ alive	/ɜ:/ third

1 **Écoute et répète ces mots : concentre-toi sur la prononciation de la lettre <a>. Puis classe-les selon leur prononciation.**

artist – gentrification – flat – bar – association – walk – Harlem – satchel – mural – what

2 **Écoute et répète ces mots : concentre-toi sur la prononciation de la lettre <i>. Puis classe-les selon leur prononciation.**

history – innovate – village – entire – refurbish – bird – defiant – pride

FINAL TASK

Write a short poem about Harlem and recite it.

To celebrate the 100th anniversary of the Harlem Renaissance, associations from the neighbourhood are organising a poetry competition. Take part in this competition: write a short poem to celebrate Harlem, then recite it in front of the jury.

1. **Choose** an aspect of Harlem: history, famous person, landmark, community spirit, art, success story.
2. **Think** of the message you would like to convey through your poem.
3. The element you have chosen will be the speaker of your poem: **imagine** what he/she/it would say and take notes.
4. **Write** your poem, **sharing** your impressions and feelings.
5. **Learn** your own poem by heart, then **recite** it in class.

YES YOU CAN! Write a poem and recite it

POINT DE VUE

Décide qui parle dans ton poème : une personne, un groupe, un objet, un bâtiment ?

"I am the darker brother."

SUJET

Choisis le thème de ton poème et le message véhiculé. Tu peux évoquer les difficultés, l'évolution et les solutions trouvées.

"They send me to eat in the kitchen
When company comes,
But I laugh,
And eat well,
And grow strong."

PROSODIE

La poésie permet beaucoup de liberté. Essaie d'inclure des rimes, des répétitions, des allitérations.

"I, too, sing America.
[...]
I, too, am America."

FIGURES DE STYLE

Enrichis ton poème avec des métaphores, des comparaisons, des images. Fais allusion aux cinq sens : sons, couleurs, odeurs, etc.

"grow strong"
"how beautiful I am"

DÉCLAMATION

Écoute à nouveau le poème de Langston Hughes page 19.

Puis récite ton poème en mettant bien le ton, en faisant attention à l'intonation, aux mots accentués et au rythme des phrases. Sois dynamique et convaincu(e).

STRATEGIES Enrichir son vocabulaire p. 218

AUTO-ÉVALUATION
WB → p. 7

Compréhension de l'oral — Comprendre un reportage

A tour of East Harlem

Nathan live! MP3

A2
1. **Watch** the video and **give** two other names for "East Harlem".
2. **Explain** why Harlem has more than just one name.

B1
3. **Say** who founded the Museo Del Barrio and when.
4. **Explain** what the goal of the Museo Del Barrio is.

B1+
5. **Give** information about Tito Puento (date of birth, achievements) and **say** how the city of New York paid tribute to him.

Compréhension de l'écrit — Comprendre un article de journal

https://www.huffingtonpost.com

Making films in and about Harlem

By Stacy Parker Le Melle 01/24/2017

I recently had the opportunity to talk with filmmaker Nadhege Ptah about her experiences as both an independent filmmaker and a local mom in Harlem. I first saw her short film *Dodo Titi* in 2016 and was impressed by the poignant way she told the story of a Black nanny[1] who felt that her employers valued the family dog more than her.

How has Harlem inspired you as an artist?
Harlem has a bold and spicy flavor[2] filled with electrical energy of entertaining people. As an actor and writer it's a great place to watch and study, it fuels the creative juices. Also, the legacy, history, and memories still linger[3] with the elders in the community, like my former neighbor who passed[4] and shared personal stories of his friendship with Malcolm Little before he became Malcolm X. One can't learn that from the history books.

What are your homelands? How does "home" figure into your work?
I was born in America, but raised culturally by my parents' homeland in Haiti. So, I experienced being in between two culturally different homelands. I was navigating the African-American experience with a Haitian upbringing. My inner world of imagination was home for me, it allowed me to feel safe, create my own and be accepted without having to prove my allegiance in language, music, food, etc.

A2
1. Before your read the text, **say** what type of document this is.
2. **Focus** on the first paragraph. **Identify** who "I" and "she" refer to. **Find** their respective jobs.
3. In the movie *Dodo Titi*, who do the employers prefer: their pet, or their employee? **Justify** with a quote from the text.

B1
4. **Explain** what Nadhege Ptah has learnt from the inhabitants of Harlem.

B1+
5. **Explain** how Nadhege Ptah's bicultural identity has influenced her work.

1. *nounou*
2. *saveur*
3. stay
4. die

1. Becoming part of a community

1

live! MP3

Charlotte has just arrived at her new high school.

Moving schools wasn't easy, but I was feeling quietly confident. I was doing everything right – pristine[1] uniform, neat hair, plus I was running wonderfully early. [...]

The first thing I noticed, as I climbed the infinite steps, was that none of the students [...] were wearing the uniform. I frowned. They were asking for detention.

I sat down, opened my bag and pulled out a science textbook. I had science first, so I wanted to prepare. I flipped through[2] the perfect pages, savouring the sanitary smell of printer ink.[3]

When the bell rang half an hour later, I placed the book back in my bag and stood up. The quadrangle was now teeming with[4] students. I paused. None of them were wearing the uniform; I looked like a unicorn among horses. [...]

The second bell had rung well before I located my classroom. I opened the door prudently, an apology on my lips.

"I'm really sorry I'm late, I––" My words were drowned out by a torrent of laughter emanating from the students. A man in a T-shirt and shorts stood behind the lab bench that served as a teacher's desk. [...]

"I think you have the wrong school," he said. "City Girls Grammar is about 2 k's[5] that-a-way." He pointed a finger out the window then looked back down at his paper.

"I don't think *you* understand. I'm the new student. Charlotte Georgina Underwood."

Keely Brown, *A New Type of Education* in *My First Lesson: Stories Inspired by Laurinda*, 2016

1. *impeccable*
2. turn
3. *encre*
4. *grouille de*
5. kilometres

a. **Read** the text and **pick out** information about Charlotte.

b. **Describe** the other pupils. **Compare** Charlotte with them. ▸ p. 36

c. **Say** how the teacher reacts to Charlotte's appearance. **Explain** why.

d. **Explain** how Charlotte deals with the situation. What do you think of her attitude?

2 The boarding experience

live! VIDÉO

PARCOURS DIFFÉRENCIÉS WB → p. 8

a. **Look** at the picture: Where are the pupils and what are they doing? **Imagine** what they may like about this place.

b. **Watch** the video and **say** how the pupils feel about boarding.

c. **Give your opinion.** Would you like to be a boarder? Why?

3 OUR HOUSE SYSTEM

'Every person, every classroom, every day.'

The House System is a foundation tradition that over the school's history has been a highly effective way to foster[1] student wellbeing, social growth and school connectedness.

STAND TOGETHER WE ARE UNITED

BANJO

Named for the great Australian bush poet, Banjo Paterson

COLOR: Orange – the name of Paterson's birthplace

LEGACY: creativity, determination, success

MASCOT: Brumby – strength and freedom

CHARITY: Beyond Blue[2]

WITH STRENGTH AND UNITY WE BUILD CHAMPIONS

STYNES

Named for the great Irish-born Australian football player, charity worker and writer, Jim Stynes

COLOR: Purple – a combination of Melbourne Football Club's red and blue; ambition, power, independence

LEGACY: success, virtue, courage, overcoming

MASCOT: Shark – forward moving, master of survival, symbol of life, power, instinct

CHARITY: The Royal Children's Hospital

BRAVE IN OUR ACTIONS, SELFLESS IN OUR APPROACH

JACKMAN

Named for the great Australian performing artist, Hugh Jackman

COLOR: Blue – loyalty, wisdom

LEGACY: confidence, intelligence, faith, integrity

MASCOT: Wolf – strength, nobility, loyalty, familial tie (also for Jackman's wolverine role)

CHARITY: Fred Hollow's Foundation[3]

TOGETHER WE SOAR TO VICTORY

FREEMAN

Named for great Australian Olympian, Cathy Freeman

COLOR: Red – connecting indigenous and modern

LEGACY: speed, strength, life, love, standing out from the pack

MASCOT: Peregrine Falcon – powerful, determined, focused, success, victory, rising above

CHARITY: Autism Spectrum Australia

1. encourage 2. focuses on mental health issues 3. focuses on vision problems

sthelena.vic.edu.au

a. Look at the brochure and **focus** on the mascots. What values do you think they represent?

b. Read the House descriptions. How can they create a community spirit between pupils?

c. Give your opinion. Which House would you like to join? Why?

YOUR TASK (DIFFÉRENCIATION)

You are the school captain of a boarding school.

WAY 1 **Write** a post on the school website to present a new house.

WAY 2 **Write** a short article for the local newspaper to share your experience of the house system.

BOOST YOUR SKILLS!

Comparer à des éléments connus

- *It's **similar to** junior high school.*
- *It's **kind of / pretty much like** belonging to a family at school.*
- *It **reminds me of** the Houses in* Harry Potter.
- *It's a **more effective** way to foster student wellbeing.*

GRAMMAR p. 36

WORDS

- bond = link
- fellow pupil = schoolmate
- legacy
- motto
- role model
- values /'vælju:z/
- banded together = united
- long-lasting
- blend in = integrate = fit in
- engage in + V-ing = get involved in
- foster /'fɒstə/ = cultivate
- pass on = transmit

2. Personal development

1

PARCOURS DIFFÉRENCIÉS WB → p. 9

School Captains 2018

Claudia and Sami

In your role as School Captains, what is important to you?

As School Captains, it is vital we represent our fellow students' interests, ideas and endeavours[1]. Student voice is extremely important to both of us, and our school. As leaders we believe the ability to share, create and connect is integral for not only student development, but the growth of our amazing school community as a whole.

To be a leader is to inspire, and we aim to be more than just Captains, but role models and friends for every member of our diverse College family.

What do you bring to the role?

Our commitment to service and our passion for helping others has guided us both through life, and now we hope to share these qualities with our peers[2]. Over our five years at College, we have developed a strong understanding of others and an ability to empathise with a variety of people.

We aren't all born leaders, leaders grow, and we aim to encourage these values throughout the lives of all students, whether it be in competition, academic endeavour, creativity or personal challenges.

What do you find special about the College?

Our Year 12 motto – 'Alone we are strong, together we are stronger' – stems from[3] what we love the most about College. The school's close-knit community and strong relationships are what we find truly special. The accepting and inclusive nature allows a variety of people to come together, thrive[4] and feel a sense of belonging like no other.

www.hamiltoncollege.vic.edu.au

1. efforts 2. schoolmates 3. come from 4. *s'épanouir*

a. Read the text and **say** who Claudia and Sami are.

b. Find elements in the text which show that they take their role to heart.

c. Describe the impact of their actions both on the school community and on themselves.

d. Compare the role of pupil representatives in France with that of Claudia and Sami.

2 Debating

Nathan live! VIDÉO

a. Watch the video and **say** why Johanna's parents encouraged her to talk in public when she was a child.

b. Give Johanna's reasons for choosing her school activity.

c. Pick out two advantages she sees to debating.

d. Explain the link between debating and Johanna's future job.

3

https://www.high-school-australia.com

Highschool Australia

Home | Program | High School Australia | Testimonials | All Programs | About Us

SURF AND SCHOOL ON THE SUNSHINE COAST

Isabel wrote after her return to Germany in January 2019:

Hello, my name is Isabel, I'm 15 years old and I was in Australia from July to December 2018 at the Kawana Waters State College on the Sunshine Coast.
I chose this school because it has the most appealing surfing program and I always wanted to learn how to surf. […]

In my first week of school, my school had organised a camp, where we all got to know each other quickly. There were many tasks that could only be done through teamwork. That was a lot of fun and we all got close very soon. In school, the Australians were very intrigued – Which country do you come from, where is that – they showed great interest.
Then the day began, in a much nicer way than in Germany. I had optional subjects such as dance, snorkelling[1] or cooking, because here you come into contact with classmates very quickly, and after school we went to the beach or into the shopping centre. Time passed by fast. Once a week I had surfing lessons and on the weekend there were a lot of parties.
The school offers trips to Sydney, the Great Barrier Reef where you can see turtles, sharks and dolphins up close, or the Outback[2].

1. *plongée avec masque et tuba*
2. remote, arid and unpopulated area

INTERNATIONAL STUDENT CARD

First Name: Isabel
Age: ....
Country of origin: ....
School: ....
School location: ....
Valid from .... to ....

a. Read Isabel's testimony. **Copy** and **fill in** Isabel's international student card details.

b. Explain what makes Isabel's school so attractive.

c. GRAMMAR **Look** at that sentence, "*Then the day began, in a much nicer way than in Germany*" (l.12). How is the comparative form constructed? What does it express? p. 36

DIFFÉRENCIATION

YOUR TASK

You are going to spend a semester in Kawana Waters State College and you have to choose your optional subject.

WAY 1 **Talk** with a senior student on Open Day to discover a class.

WAY 2 **Discuss** your class options with a teacher.

WORDS

- resolution = perseverance
- boring = uninteresting
- challenging
- fulfilling = rewarding /rɪ'wɔːdɪŋ/
- eager to = keen to
- excel in = be very good at
- perform well
- succeed in + V-ing
- take a subject = follow a course

BOOST YOUR SKILLS!

Exprimer ses préférences

- *Surfing is certainly* ***the most*** *appealing programme for me.*
- ***The greatest*** *thing about debating is that you develop lasting skills.*
- *Snorkelling is undoubtedly* ***the most inspiring*** *subject.*

GRAMMAR p. 36

EXPLORE

3. Getting involved

1 Fighting bullying

Nathan live! VIDÉO

PARCOURS DIFFÉRENCIÉS WB → p. 10

a. **Look** at the pupil and **imagine** what the main message of this video is.

b. **Watch** the video and **explain** why and how the pupils are fighting bullying.

c. **In your opinion**, how can it make a difference?

CULTURE SPOT

In Australia, **Dreamtime** refers to the Aboriginal (or Indigenous) stories and beliefs.

2 Standing as One

Nathan live! VIDÉO

a. **Watch** the video and **pick out** the clip's messages.

b. **Read** the article and **find** who created the video. **Explain** why.

c. **Say** why it is important that the students take part in this type of project.

YOUR TASK

Write an email to *tweeddailynews.com* to present a school project you are involved in.

Kingy students' powerful message goes viral

Indigenous Kingscliff High School students recently worked with the not-for-profit multimedia company One Vision Productions to create a powerful music video, *Standing as One*. The clip was posted online just two days ago and has already been viewed more than 40,000 times. It explores the void between the world of the Dreamtime and modern, consumerist societies.

One Vision Productions director Mark Robertson welcomed the success of the clip: "This clip is a testament[1], that when youth are empowered to have a voice, the strength of perception of our next generation is highlighted. The success of this video will empower these young people and give them so much confidence. They will realise the impact they can have as future leaders."

Liana TURNER, *tweeddailynews.com.au*, 2017

1. *témoignage*

BOOST YOUR SKILLS!

Expliciter ses idées

- ***What I mean is,*** *the whole community also benefits from this project.*
- ***In other words,*** *being a part of this project has been truly beneficial.*

WORDS

- initiator /ɪnˈɪʃieɪtə/
- role-model

- gratifying
- selfless = altruistic
- worthwhile /wɜːθˈwaɪl/: *qui en vaut la peine*

- contribute to + V-ing
- denounce /dɪˈnaʊns/
- get involved: *s'engager*
- make a difference = make things change
- take a stand = give one's opinion
- volunteer for

TEST YOUR CULTURE

HOW TO PLAY "BECOME A SCHOOL CAPTAIN"

Play in groups.

You are running for school captain.

To be elected, you need to be qualified by each House.

Visit each House, where the house leader will ask you three questions. If you get at least two answers right, the House will qualify you.

The first pupil to be qualified by all six Houses wins the title!

GAME ON!

KOOKABURRA

1 What is a school day divided into?

2 Who is at the head of a school?

3 What do you call a school for both boys and girls?

PLATYPUS

4 How old are Year 10 pupils?

5 What is a government school?

6 Name three subjects specific to high school in Australia.

BLACK SWAN

7 What is a boarding school?

8 Why do some teens need to go to boarding school in Australia?

9 What do you call the communities within a school?

KOALA

10 Name a competition you can participate in as a pupil.

11 Who created *Standing as One*?

12 Name one way for a school to contribute to a cause.

POSSUM

13 What skills, other than physical, can you develop in surfing classes?

14 What do you call school leaders?

15 What is the nickname of Australia?

TASMANIAN DEVIL

16 What do you call your last tests in high school?

17 What big event takes place in Year 12?

18 Give one role you can be elected to in an Australian school.

BOOST YOUR ENGLISH!

Grammar — Qualifier et comparer

1 Placer les adjectifs dans le bon ordre

PRÉCIS 7 ET EXERCICES

- En anglais, les adjectifs se placent avant le nom qu'ils qualifient : *a **multicultural** school.*
- Lorsque plusieurs adjectifs se suivent, il faut les placer dans un ordre précis : quantité, appréciation ou jugement, taille, âge, forme, couleur, origine, matière (du plus subjectif au plus factuel) : *an international professional school*

« *professional* » est factuel car il définit le type d'école, « *international* » est plus subjectif.

1 Complète chaque phrase avec les adjectifs entre parenthèses dans le bon ordre.

a. I went to a(n) (*traditional* / *high* / *amazing*) school.

b. In Australia, I had to wear a (*cotton* / *blue* / *short-sleeved*) shirt at school.

c. Anna was my (*young* / *charismatic* / *Aboriginal*) roommate.

2 Utilise ces mots pour former des groupes nominaux avec deux adjectifs ou plus.

school – multicultural – welcoming – experienced – students – young – captains – engaged – friendly – Australian – foreign

More in ***Pump it up!*** p. 10

2 Comparer des éléments entre eux

PRÉCIS 8 ET EXERCICES

Nathan live! GRAMMAR TUTO

COMPARATIFS

Her school bag is **bigger** and **heavier than** his.

adjectif court — *adjectif court terminé par y*

But she is **more muscular than** him.

adjectif long

He is **as hard-working as** her.

School assembly is **less boring than** I thought.

This bag is **not as full as** this one.

SUPERLATIFS

This is **the kitschest** bag I've ever seen!

adjectif court

To me, Australian schools are **the most appealing**

adjectif long

and **the least stressful** ones.

adjectif long ou court

3 Complète avec les adjectifs entre parenthèses au superlatif.

a. Brisbane is (*big*) city this girl has ever been to.

b. Debating is (*exciting*) activity you can try when you suffer from asthma.

c. The (*important*) feature when you are a school captain is to be a leader.

d. This House is (*respected*) one in the school!

4 Choisis un adjectif parmi la liste pour comparer les éléments entre eux en respectant les indications.

varied – ambitious – exciting – tiring

a. Subjects in Australian schools / in French schools >

b. Visiting Sydney / discovering the Outback =

c. The Stynes House / the Banjo House >

d. Debating / learning how to surf <

More in ***Pump it up!*** p. 16

Vocabulary — High-school spirit in Australia

live! MP3 · live! LEXIQUIZ

Places
- boarding school
- hallway /ˈhɔːlweɪ/ = corridor
- school grounds = campus
- school hall: *salle polyvalente*

People
- classmate
- headmaster / headmistress = principal
- junior ≠ senior pupil
- leader
- roommate
- school captain = head boy / head girl (GB)
- staff

Everyday life · Community · Calendar

Activities
- attend a workshop
- compete with sb
- develop skills
- learn (about)
- meet up with
- practise /ˈpræktɪs/ + V-ing
- participate in = take part in (a race, a challenge)
- study
- take an exam

Relationships
- friendly = welcoming
- united = connected
- bond = become friends
- join (a club/house)
- integrate = blend in
- socialise = meet people

Daily routine
- assembly
- lunch time
- period: *heure de cours*
- recess = break
- timetable = schedule
- be on time
- start at ≠ finish at

Year highlights
- excursion /ɪkˈskɜːʃənz/ = field trip
- formal = prom (USA)
- apply for = submit an application for
- graduate = pass the final exams /ɪɡˈzæmz/
- obtain a high school certificate = get a certificate of education

1 Associe chaque début de phrase à la fin qui convient.

a. Our champions proudly compete
b. Everybody takes part
c. All pupils can practise
d. Anybody may apply
e. House leaders meet up

1. every Friday.
2. for surf classes.
3. in volunteer work.
4. with other schools.
5. debating.

2 Complète chaque phrase avec l'un des deux mots.

hall / *hallway*
a. At school, lockers are often located in a … .
b. Pupils gather regularly in the … for assembly.

learn / *teach*
c. At school, they … you many different things.
d. When you go on field trips, you … about the environment.

pass / *take*
e. At the end of the school year everybody … exams.
f. You get congratulated when you … an exam.

Spelling — Le doublement des consonnes

live! MP3 More in *Pump it up!* p. 78-79

En anglais, on double la consonne finale lorsqu'on ajoute *-ed*, *-ing*, *-er*, *-est* ou *-y* à la fin d'un mot qui se termine par « **consonne, voyelle, consonne** » (sauf avec *w* et *x*) :
stop → *stopped* → *stopping* • *sun* → *sunny* • *fit* → *fitter* mais *fitness*

1 Ajoute les suffixes suivants à ces verbes.

help – snow – cheat – chat – run – fix – cancel – read

-ed · -ing

2 Forme un ou deux mots à partir de ces adjectifs.

big – eventual – flat – hot – practical – fat

-er · -est · -y

FINAL TASK

Post an article on the school website about your exchange experience.

You are spending a school year as a senior pupil in Australia. Before you return home, post an article on the school website about your experience there.

1. **Choose a high school in Australia in the File or on the internet.**
2. **Prepare a detailed account of your experience. Take notes about:**
   – the school's organisation and how things work there,
   – how this school compares with your own school,
   – what you liked about this school and how you related to the school community,
   – the benefits of experiencing high school in Australia (spirit, self-development, individual and collective values, etc.) and how you see yourself now.
3. **Write your article for the school website.** Make it sound great so as to encourage other students to experience high school in Australia too!

YES YOU CAN! Write an appealing article

TITRE
Donne un titre accrocheur à ta page.

INTRODUCTION
Mets la phrase d'introduction en caractères gras et/ou en couleur.

PARTAGE
Donne la possibilité à tes lecteurs de partager ton article sur les réseaux sociaux.

Highschool stralia

Home | Program | High School Aus a | Testimonials | All Programs | A ut Us

SURF AND SCHOOL ON THE SUNSHINE COAST

In my first week of school, my school had organised a camp, where we all got to know each other quickly. There were many tasks that could only be done through teamwork. That was a lot of fun and we all got close very soon. In school, the Australians were very intrigued – Which country do you come from, where is that – they showed great interest.
Then the day began, in a much nicer way than in Germany. I had subjects such as dance, snorkelling[1]

ILLUSTRATION
Illustre ton article avec une photo qui reflète un moment clé de ton expérience.

STRUCTURE
Fais des paragraphes pour rendre ton article plus clair.

STRATEGIES Développer une idée à l'écrit P. 219

Compréhension de l'oral — Comprendre un reportage

The Plain English Speaking Award

Nathan live! VIDÉO

A2 **1.** What is the Plain English Speaking Award (PESA)?

A2+ **2.** **Give** the level of education and age of the participants.

3. How many stages can you go through if you participate in PESA?

B1 **4.** Who decides on the topic? **Give details** about the selection criteria.

B1+ **5.** **Say** how Luke Macaronas felt as a participant. **Explain** why.

Compréhension de l'écrit — Comprendre les réactions de personnages de fiction

Big Chook and Roland listen to their principal during assembly.

"Welcome back for term two everyone," the principal began. "Term one went very well I think and I hope that you will all make term two even bigger and better than term one."

His speech just rambled on and on, Big Chook mused[1], trying hard to keep listening.

"This term we have our fundraising[2] event, the King of the Mountain. So, let's all dig deep[3] and better than last year's final fundraising amount," the principal said, walking over to a side table covered by a large white sheet.

Big Chook sat up and moved to the edge of his seat, wondering what was going to be unveiled.

The principal removed the sheet, revealing two large trophies. "I was so impressed with last year's results that this year I decided to award your hard work. One trophy will be awarded to the person who collects the most donations and the second will be for the person who wins the King of the Mountain race."

Big Chook's eyes locked onto the large gold fundraiser trophy and for a moment, he actually thought he was drooling[4].

Roland saw his friend's hungry eyes and smiled with amusement at his desire. "You know, you should win both of them."

M. R. DEGUARA, *The Neverland of Highschool (The Adventures of Big Chook, Book 2)*, 2015

A2 **1.** Who are Big Chook and Roland?

2. **Say** what Big Chook and Roland are doing there.

A2+ **3.** **Explain** in your own words what the King of the Mountain (l.6) is, and why there are two trophies.

B1 **4.** **Give** two reasons why the principal has decided to award trophies.

B1+ **5.** **Explain** the two friends' reactions.

1. reflect, think
2. *collecte de fonds*
3. try hard, give a lot
4. *baver*

EXPLORE

1. Mysteries and pranks

1 Desperately seeking Sue

A cryptic[1] message spotted in a field in Oxfordshire has had curious social media users – and police – searching for a mystery "Sue". In a picture tweeted by the National Police Air Service (NPAS), the letters SUE **X** could be seen etched[2] into the field in Tetsworth, near Thame in Oxfordshire. Police encouraged social media users to spread the message "far and wide" to track down Sue. For two days, she kept officers guessing.

Twitter users were coming up with their own conclusions.

14:07, UK, 2017

1. enigmatic 2. *tracées*

Anna Lockwood

Alien invasion or sneaky piece of marketing? Some conspiracy theorists may wonder #WhoisSue after farmer's message in a field goes viral: theguardian.com/uk-news...

3:57 PM – Nov 18, 2017

The farmer probably spelled the letters out by spraying weedkiller on the field.

Pete
@PeteCoe74

You're sure it's not an advert for a local law firm?

5:57 PM – Nov 2, 2017

dylan godfroy
@dylangodfroy532

Nope, could be a loved one of that person trying to get in on google maps to show how much they love her maybe?

1:35 AM – Nov 3, 2017

Peter Mendell
@PSPandaBear

She must be a pilot.

8:20 AM – Nov 3, 2017

a. **Look** at the picture and **explain** why it went viral.

b. **Read** the article and **determine** the role of the police.

c. GRAMMAR **Read** the tweets and **pick out** ways to express probability and certainty.
PRÉCIS 22

d. **Rephrase** the different hypotheses. **Imagine** others.

WORDS

- bias /'baɪəs/ = viewpoint
- breaking news
- miscellaneous news: *faits divers*
- relevance: *pertinence*

- dumbfounded dʌm'faʊndɪd = astonished
- flabbergasted = very surprised
- puzzled = intrigued

- cover
- report
- testify
- witness

2 Mystery in an eerie village

Nathan live! VIDÉO

PARCOURS DIFFÉRENCIÉS WB → p. 12

Yet another mystery in Oxfordshire

A new mystery has gripped the Oxfordshire settlement after a series of odd white markings started appearing on its pavements. Initially, panic spread. Locals feared the arrows and crosses could be a burglars' "Da Pinchi[1] Code" left outside homes. What followed was a flurry[2] of frantic messages left online. On the "Spotted: Kidlington" page, one poster worried that there had been "a few break-ins[3] where these marks are" and another reported markings after they found some behind their house.

Worried residents even made several calls to Thames Valley Police.

www.telegraph.co.uk/news, 2016

1. pinch = *voler* 2. *une vague de* 3. burglaries

BOOST YOUR SKILLS!

Faire des hypothèses et exprimer la probabilité

- *They **may** be following Harry Potter's trail.*
- *He **might have** want**ed** to discover a typical village.*
- ***Perhaps** she want**ed** to disappear.*

Exprimer la certitude

- *She **must** be a newcomer in the village.*

PRÉCIS 22

a. **Watch** the video and **take notes** on the mystery (what happened and where).

b. **Pick out** the journalist's explanations for the presence of these tourists. Which one do you find the most convincing?

c. **Read** the article and **identify** the second mystery.

d. **Give** the local people's reactions in both cases and **explain** the contrast with the tourists' attitude.

e. PHONOLOGY **Pronounce** these words: *started – fascinated – gripped – feared – worried – determined – followed – spotted*. What forms are used to tell these stories? p. 52

YOUR TASK

DIFFÉRENCIATION

WAY 1 You work for Kidlington's local newspaper. **Prepare a few questions** to ask people about what happened in their village.

WAY 2 You work for a radio and you have been asked to deal with countryside mysteries. **Prepare the script** for a radio spot, starting with *"British villages are not such quiet places..."*

EXPLORE

2. Such a quiet village?

1

live! MP3

Griselda Clement, the Vicar's wife, is organising a tea party at the vicarage of Saint Mary Mead. She and her husband are discussing who they are going to invite.

"My duty," said Griselda, "my duty as the Vicaress. Tea and scandal at four-thirty."

"Who is coming?"

Griselda ticked them off[1] on the fingers with a glow of virtue on her face.

"Mrs Price Ridley, Miss Wetherby, Miss Hartnell, and that terrible Miss Marple."

"I rather like Miss Marple," I said. "She has, at least, a sense of humour." [...]

"She's the worst cat in the village," said Griselda. "And she always knows every single thing that happens – and draws the worst inferences from it."

"I wonder what we shall have for tea," said Griselda, seating herself on my writing-table. "Dr. Stone and Miss Cram, I suppose, and perhaps Mrs Lestrange. By the way, I called on her yesterday, but she was out. Yes, I'm sure we shall have Mrs Lestrange for tea. It's so mysterious, isn't it, her arriving like this and taking a house down here, and hardly ever going outside it? Makes one think of detective stories. You know – *'Who was she, the mysterious woman with the pale, beautiful face? What was her past story? Nobody knew. There was something faintly sinister about her.'* I believe Dr. Haydock knows something about her."

"You read too many detective stories, Griselda," I observed mildly.

Agatha CHRISTIE,
The Murder at the Vicarage, 1930

1. count one by one

a. Look at the map of Saint Mary Mead and **say** why Miss Marple's house is well-located.

b. Read the text and **find** the Vicaress's favourite activity. Why does she say: *"My duty"* (l.1)?

c. Focus on the enumeration of people: Why do people gossip about Miss Marple and Miss Lestrange?

d. GRAMMAR **Observe** the structure of the narration: **say** who is talking and what tense is used. PRÉCIS 13

e. Comment on *"You read too many detective stories, Griselda"* (l.19).

CULTURE SPOT

Miss Marple is a fictional old lady who lives in the village of Saint Mary Mead and spends her time solving crimes as an amateur detective.

AT HOME Find information on other famous British detectives. You may look for fictional characters from novels, movies or TV series.

A map of Agatha Christie's Miss Marple's Saint Mary Mead

2

PARCOURS DIFFÉRENCIÉS WB → p. 13

Nathan live! MP3

Agatha Raisin, a newcomer in the village of Carsely, has taken part in a quiche competition. Mr. Cummings-Browne, her neighbour, died in the night, and Agatha is suspected of having poisoned him with her quiche. Bill, the local policeman, has come to tell her about the case.

Agatha asked all about the case, all the details she had not asked before. M. Cummings-Brown had been found dead in the morning. Then why, asked Agatha, had Mrs. Cummings-Browne gone straight up to bed?

"Oh, that was because her husband was usually late, drinking at the Red Lion." [...]

"Anyway, how did you guess I never cooked that quiche? For you did, you know, even before I baked[1] one."

"The minute I saw there wasn't a single baking ingredient in the kitchen, I was sure," he laughed. "I asked you to make one to be absolutely sure. You should have seen your face!"

"Oh, very funny."

He looked at her curiously. What an odd[2] woman she was, he thought. Her shiny, well-groomed hair was not permed but cut in a sort of Dutch bob[3] that somehow suited her square, rather truculent[4] face. Her body was square and stocky and her legs surprisingly good. "What," asked Bill, "was so special to a recently ex-high-powered businesswoman like yourself about winning a village competition?"

"I felt out of place," said Agatha bleakly[5]. "I wanted to make my mark on the village."

He laughed happily, his eyes closing into slits. "You've just done that. Mrs. Cummings-Browne knows now you cheated and so does Fred Griggs, the local bobby, and he's a prize gossip."

Agatha felt too humiliated to speak. So much for her dream home. She would need to sell up. How could she face anyone in the village?

M.C. BEATON, *Agatha Raisin and the Quiche of Death*, 1992

1. cook in an oven 2. strange 3. *coupe au carré*
4. aggressive, bad-tempered 5. *d'un air sombre*

WORDS

- **e**vidence
- g**o**ssip
- s**u**spect
- w**i**tness

- gu**i**lty
- qu**i**et = p**ea**ceful
- rough = unfr**ie**ndly

- susp**e**ct
- t**e**stify

a. **Look at** the photo and **imagine** who these people may be.

b. **Read** the text and **explain** how the policeman found out Agatha was not the murderer.

c. **Explain** Agatha's reasons for taking part in the competition.

d. **Go** to *lyceen.nathan.fr/shine-bright2* and **watch** the trailer. **Explain** why Agatha decided to inquire into the murder.

YOUR TASK

The police interrogated Agatha. **Write** a report summarising her situation: **describe** the context and **explain** the facts.

BOOST YOUR SKILLS!

Résumer une situation

- *The victim* ***had been found dead in the morning.***
- *Why* ***hadn't he gone*** *straight to bed?*
- ***The minute she saw...***
- ***She felt too humiliated to...***

BOOST YOUR ENGLISH!

Grammar — Évoquer des faits passés, émettre des hypothèses

1 Exprimer des faits passés

PRÉCIS 13 ET EXERCICES

live! GRAMMAR TUTO

Prétérit simple	Prétérit en *be* + V-*ing*	Alternance des deux prétérits

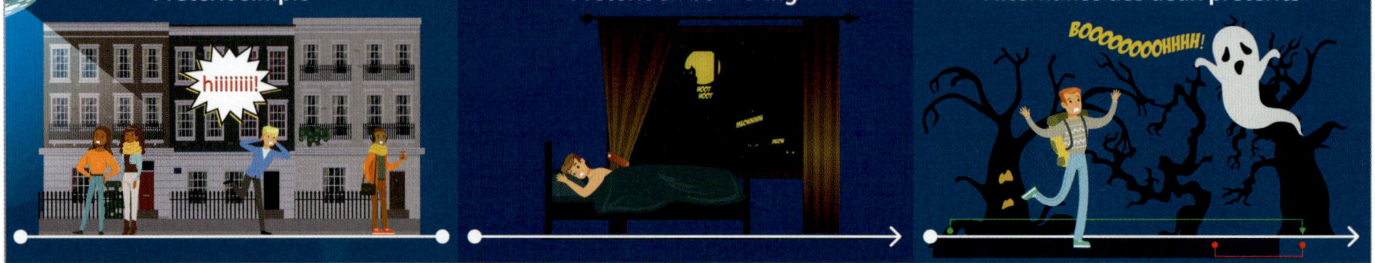

Spooky things **happened** in Manchester last week. Some people **saw** or **heard** weird things, but others simply **didn't notice** anything. → *On reste factuel.*	Last night, I **was lying** in my bed **while** an owl **was hooting** and cats **were meowing**... That **was** so scary... → *On zoome sur la description de la scène, le déroulement des faits.*	I **was walking** in the woods when a ghost **appeared**! → *Une action en cours est interrompue par une autre plus soudaine.*

1 Recopie et mets les verbes au prétérit simple ou au prétérit en *be* + V-*ing*.

Last Sunday, I (*visit*) a small village in England when I (*get*) the feeling it was a haunted place. I (*be*) scared, but I (*decide*) to learn more, so I (*go*) into a pub. There, some villagers (*have*) a roast, others (*talk*) and some (*watch*) a football game on TV. One of them suddenly (*turn*) round and (*look*) at me with an evil look on his face. I (*panic*) and (*run*) out of the pub. As I (*run*) as fast as I could, I suddenly (*wake*) up!! It (*be*) just a dream!

2 Rédige un rapport de police à partir de ces notes en choisissant la forme du prétérit qui convient.

The neighbours: play chess / not see anything
The victim's wife: watch TV / hear footsteps
The postman: deliver letters in the neighbourhood / see muddy footprints
The victim's children: walk the dog / not at home

More in ***Pump it up!*** p. 22-25

2 Émettre des hypothèses

PRÉCIS 22 ET EXERCICES

Pour **émettre des hypothèses sur des faits révolus ou à venir**, on utilise des **modaux** qui expriment notre **degré de certitude** :

Attention ! **Verbe** suivant un modal = **invariable**

DU PLUS CERTAIN must • could • may • might **AU MOINS CERTAIN**

Modaux + *have* + V-*en* = référence à des faits révolus	**Modaux + base verbale = référence à des faits à venir**
*The murderer **must have used** poison.* → Je suis quasiment sûr que cela s'est produit.	*There **could be** new evidence on the crime scene.* → Il y a des chances que cela soit le cas.
*Somebody **might have seen** the murderer.* → Il y a peu de chances que cela se soit produit.	*The police **may find** the murderer soon.* → J'estime qu'il y a des chances pour que cela se produise.

3 Reformule ces hypothèses avec des modaux.

a. I'm sure Jack killed his parents!
b. Maybe they are going to tell the truth... Who knows?
c. Is the quiche the weapon? Possibly...
d. I doubt the victim called the police.

4 Lis ces tweets, puis émets des hypothèses sur les circonstances de ces canulars, les réactions des gens, etc.

"No UFO! Just an old tractor, flashlights and a good deal of imagination! Found some clues, we'll soon find the prankster!"

"There's no such thing as a ghost in the village! A few old sheets, spooky music and a full moon did the trick. Looking for more clues."

More in ***Pump it up!*** p. 39-43

Vocabulary — Mystery in the countryside

Nathan live! MP3 — Nathan live! LEXIQUIZ

Crime scene

Investigation
- clue
- corpse = dead body
- evidence
- forensic /fə'rɛnsɪk/
- investigation = inquiry
- theft /θɛft/ = burglary
- handcuff
- interrogate

Suspect
- culprit /'kʌlprɪt/
- guilty
- shocked
- testify /'tɛstɪˌfaɪ/
- witness

Ghosts

Apparitions
- bogey = demon /'bəʊgɪ/
- bogeyman: *croquemitaine*
- nightmare
- phantom
- shade = shadow

Fear
- awe /ɔː/: *terreur*
- shivers of fear
- appalling = terrifying = frightening
- bloodcurdling
- eerie = creepy /'kriːpɪ/
- evil /'iːvəl/
- hair-raising
- livid
- get goosebumps

Actions
- sight
- sound
- feel
- freeze
- sense

Noises
- cry
- footstep
- rattling
- screech = yell
- squeak = creak: *grincer*

Village life

Places
- alley
- churchyard
- lane
- market place
- town hall
- narrow
- remote = isolated = withdrawn /wɪð'drɔːn/

Events
- church service
- competition
- exhibition
- attend
- get lost
- stroll = roam /rəʊm/
- wander

1 Complète les adjectifs avec les terminaisons appropriées (*-ed* ou *-ing*).

a. My neighbour is confus… . She has been robbed by a frighten… man.

b. This investigation was exhaust… but fascinat… . The culprit was someone unexpect… .

c. I am puzzl… by this appall… ghost story.

d. Villages are not bor… . There are so many surpris… people and stories.

2 Tu as passé une nuit dans un hôtel hanté. Raconte ton expérience sur ton blog en utilisant le vocabulaire de la carte mentale.

Spelling — La ponctuation du dialogue

Nathan live! MP3

- En anglais, il n'y a pas de tiret dans un dialogue, uniquement des **guillemets**. On ferme les guillemets avant chaque verbe introducteur, par exemple : "I was sure," he laughed.
- Note que les guillemets anglais s'écrivent **" "** (hauts et sans espaces) alors qu'en français, ils s'écrivent **« »** (bas et avec espaces).

1 Réécris ce passage en le transformant en dialogue et en ajoutant la ponctuation.

Jane had never been there before. The woman who welcomed her asked her if she had had a nice journey and if she wasn't too tired. Jane thanked her and told her with a smile how nice the village was and how she was glad to be there.

2 Remets les mots dans l'ordre pour faire des phrases. Attention à placer correctement la ponctuation.

a. *haunted / He / live / do / village / you / a / her / asked / ? / " / " / in / ,*

b. *quiche / said / I / she / didn't / the / cook / ! / " / " / ,*

c. *" / " / I / appalling / had / never / such / nightmare / have / an / , / explained / she / .*

d. *? / asked / , / did / churchyard / the / He / visit / you / me / " / "*

FINAL TASK

Participate in a creative writing competition about "Mystery in the village".

You want to enter a short story competition which is being organised in a British village. You first have to send an extract from your story, including a dialogue. If you are selected, then you will have to send the whole story. Be creative!

1. **Choose the mystery** you want to write about (crime, ghost, prank, etc.). **Find a title** for your story.
2. **Use your imagination and decide on:**
   – the situation, time, location, weather, etc. in order to set the atmosphere,
   – the characters. Remember, two of them will be discussing something,
   – the plot.
3. **Write a short introduction** to present the situation.
4. **Write** the extract from your story including **narrated parts and a dialogue**.

YES YOU CAN! Write a mystery story

INTRODUCTION

Fais un court résumé de la situation.

Agatha Raisin, a newcomer in the village, has taken part in a quiche competition.

DIALOGUES

Ajoute une interaction entre les personnages présents pour rendre l'ensemble plus vivant.

"Anyway, how did you guess I never cooked that quiche? For you did, you know, even before I baked one."

"The minute I saw there wasn't a single baking ingredient in the kitchen, I was sure."

RECIT

Commence par la narration au passé. Les passages racontés permettent de faire évoluer l'action, de décrire ce que font les personnages, de préciser leurs émotions. Utilise le prétérit et le *past perfect* pour le récit.

Agatha ***asked*** *all about the case, all the details she* ***had*** *not* ***asked*** *before.*

Utilise le passif pour entretenir le mystère.

He ***had been found*** *dead in the morning.*

PONCTUATION

Dans ton dialogue, pense à utiliser des guillemets et à ne pas mettre de tiret.

Les verbes introducteurs (*say, ask, wonder, explain,* etc.) sont souvent au prétérit. En anglais, on peut mettre le sujet avant ou arès le verbe.

"I felt out of place," ***said Agatha*** *bleakly. "I wanted to make my mark on the village."*

She said*, "You've just done that."*

LEXIQUE

Exprime les sentiments en utilisant un lexique approprié : ici, la honte.

"I ***felt out of place,****" said Agatha bleakly. [...] Agatha felt* ***too humiliated*** *to speak [...] How could she* ***face anyone*** *in the village?*

STRATEGIES Enrichir son vocabulaire P. 218

AUTO-ÉVALUATION
WB → p. 15

TEST YOUR SKILLS

Compréhension de l'oral — Comprendre un reportage

Pengersick Castle

A2
1. Where is Pengersick Castle?
2. What kind of events take place there?

A2+
3. **List** the ghosts that have been spotted in and around the castle.
4. **Pick out** the job of most of the ghosts, **explain** why they had *"treasures"*.

B1
5. Many people reported seeing ghosts around the castle. **Explain** the journalist's point of view.

Compréhension de l'écrit — Comprendre un article d'investigation

Lucifer over Lancashire!

It was the setting for one of England's most infamous witches' covens[1].

So the discovery of a mummified cat sealed into the walls of a 17th century cottage was yesterday described by historians as "spellbinding[2]".

The unfortunate animal – associated with witches for centuries – was apparently buried alive to protect the inhabitants from evil spirits.

The discovery was made by water engineers on a construction project. The building contained a sealed room, with a mummified cat bricked into the wall.

Simon Entwistle, an expert on the Pendle witches, said: "In terms of significance, it's like discovering Tutankhamun's tomb. The building is in remarkable condition. You can walk through it and get a real sense that you're peering into the past. Even before we discovered the building, there were lots of jokes from the lads about broomsticks[3] and black cats. The find has really stunned us all."

The Pendle witchcraft saga began in March 1612 when local woman Alizon Device was accused of bewitching a pedlar[4] for some metal pins.

Branded a witch, she in turn accused a neighbouring family of involvement in black magic, and after the Good Friday[5] gathering, eight women and two men were hanged as witches.

Archaeologist Frank Giecco said: "It's like discovering your own little Pompeii. We rarely get the opportunity to work with something so well preserved."

www.dailymail.co.uk, 2011

1. *sabbat de sorcières* 2. fascinating 3. *manches à balai* 4. *colporteur* 5. *Vendredi Saint*

A2
1. **Explain** what the engineers discovered.
2. Why were they "stunned" by their discovery?

B1
3. **Pick out** details about the discovery and **explain** its origin.
4. **Say** if this discovery is part of a legend or of something real.

B1+
5. **Focus** on the comparison between this discovery and Pompeii. **Explain** it.

EXPLORE

1. The American (family) dream

1 How my American Dream is different from my parents'

https://www.fastcompany.com

GEN Z (AGES 7—23)

"I think that for my parents' generation the American Dream guaranteed having a house, children, and a long-term career. I think of the American Dream as having a nation that works for everyone from all social and economic backgrounds."

23-year-old product designer from Minneapolis

MILLENNIALS (AGES 24–37)

"My parents wanted to have a steady job in the city, have a nice house and some kids, and eventually retire[1] on the lake in New Hampshire. I don't want to have children or get married soon. We're in like $70,000 of student loan debt[2] total. How are we supposed to save up[3] for a ceremony, a down payment on a house, all that stuff? I feel people my age haven't been given the economic opportunities our parents have. My American Dream is paying off my student loans."

25-year-old marketing associate from Newton, Massachusetts

GEN X (AGES 38–56)

"I believe the American Dream today is to simply survive. I cannot afford[4] to raise children and care for my parents at the same time."

38-year-old business analyst from Washington, D.C.

1. *prendre sa retraite* 2. *endettement lié à un prêt étudiant* 3. *économiser* 4. have enough money

a. Look at the picture and **read** the testimonies. **Identify** what the "American Dream" meant for these people's parents.

b. Explain what today's generations aspire to.

c. GRAMMAR **Rephrase** the underlined part of the sentence with a determiner: *"I think that for my parents' generation..."* What is the apostrophe used for? ► p. 64

d. Explain why the younger generations' dreams differ from their parents'.

WORDS

- bond /bɑːnd/: *lien*
- expectations: *attentes*
- financial burden: *poids financier*
- job insecurity
- personal fulfilment = satisfaction

- downhearted = discouraged
- hopeless ≠ hopeful

- successful
- uncertain
- unrealistic

- challenge = question
- live up to: *être à la hauteur de*
- put off: *remettre à plus tard*
- succeed /səkˈsiːd/ = achieve something

2. Modern families

1

a. **Look at** the *Modern Family* family tree and **explain** how the characters are related.

b. VOCABULARY **Observe** these compound adjectives: *"sword-fighting, poetry-loving."* **Explain** what they mean. PRÉCIS 7

c. **Explain** what is "modern" about this family.

2

A team of two

Nathan live! VIDÉO

PARCOURS DIFFÉRENCIÉS

WB → p. 16

WORDS

- **fa**ther-in-law /lɑː/: *beau-père (par alliance)*
- step**fa**ther: *beau-père (dans une famille recomposée)*
- team sp**i**rit
- ec**lec**tic = di**verse** /dɪˈvɜːs/ (US), /daɪˈvɜːs/ (UK)
- **fran**tic = **ve**ry **bu**sy
- gr**ou**nd**break**ing = revol**u**tionary
- tough /tʌf/ = **dif**ficult
- **try**ing = de**man**ding
- uncon**ven**tional = un**u**sual
- break the mould
- break up = **se**parate
- **mar**ry ≠ di**vorce** **some**one

a. **Watch** the video and **introduce** the family.

b. **Explain** what can make their situation difficult.

c. SPELLING **Observe** and **explain** the underlined word: *"We're <u>gonna</u> be there for each other."* ► p. 64

d. **Explain** how this family structure has strengthened their bonds.

BOOST YOUR SKILLS!

Présenter des personnages et une situation

- ***Being*** *a single dad... The boy***'s** *dad... for* ***each other****...* ***both****...* ***together****...*
- ***usually****...* ***always****...* ***whenever****...*

YOUR TASK

Present this family situation on a talk show on single-parent families. **Explain** why they were chosen.

3. Happy apart, back together

1

PARCOURS DIFFÉRENCIÉS WB → p. 17

Nathan live! MP3

"This is really nice," their dad said, looking around Pound Hall 913 and setting a laundry basket full of shoes and books on Cath's mattress[1].

"It's not nice, Dad," Cath said, standing bored by the door. "It's like a hospital room, but smaller. And without a TV."

"You've got a great view of the campus," he said.

Wren wandered over to the window. "My room faces a parking lot."

"How do you know?" Cath asked.

"Google Earth."

Wren couldn't wait for all this college stuff to start. She and her roommate – *Courtney* – had been talking for weeks. Courtney was from Omaha, too. The two of them had already met and gone shopping for dorm-room stuff together. Cath had followed them and tried not to pout[2] while they picked out posters and matching desk lamps.

Cath's dad came back from the windows and put an arm around her shoulders. "It's gonna be okay," he said.

She nodded[3]. "I know."

"Okay," he said, clapping. "Next stop, Schramm Hall. Second stop, pizza buffet. Third stop, my sad and empty nest."

"No pizza," Wren said. "Sorry Dad. Courtney and I are going to the freshman[4] barbecue tonight." She shot her eyes at Cath. "Cath should go, too."

"Yes pizza," Cath said defiantly.

Her dad smiled. "Your sister's right, Cath. You should go. Meet new people."

"All I'm going to do for the next nine months is meet new people. Today I choose pizza buffet."

Wren rolled her eyes.

"All right," their dad said, patting Cath on the shoulder. "Next stop, Schramm Hall. Ladies?" He opened the door.

Cath didn't move. "You can come back for me after you drop her off[5]," she said, watching her sister. "I want to start unpacking."

Wren didn't argue, just stepped out into the hall. "I'll talk to you tomorrow," she said, not quite turning a look at Cath.

"Sure," Cath said.

Adapted from Rainbow ROWELL, *Fangirl*, 2013

1. *matelas*
2. *faire la moue*
3. *faire oui de la tête*
4. first-year student
5. *déposer*

WORDS

- **co**nfident: *sûr de soi*
- self-rel**i**ant /selfrɪ'laɪənt/ ≠ dep**e**ndent (on)
- str**e**ssless ≠ str**e**ssful
- w**o**rrying ≠ reass**u**ring

- compl**ai**n ab**ou**t
- leave the f**a**mily nest
- supp**o**rt: *soutenir*
- take care of = to look **a**fter

a. Read the text and **identify** the situation (characters, place, action).

b. Compare Cath's attitude to Wren's.

c. GRAMMAR *"Courtney and I* ***are going to*** *the freshman barbecue"* (l.19). **Explain** the use of the present continuous in this sentence.
► p. 64

d. Comment on the father's attitude and feelings. **Explain** what this new situation means to him.

YOUR TASK

In pairs, **act out** a scene between a parent and his/her teenager son or daughter on his/her first day at a new school.

BOOST YOUR SKILLS!

Parler de projets

- *We* ***are going to*** *the freshman barbecue.*
- ***First, ... Second, ... Third, ... Next, ...***
- ***After / Before*** *you drop me off...*
  After / Before dropping *me off...*
- *I'm* ***excited****... I* ***can't wait for****...*

GRAMMAR p. 64

2 The pros and cons of multigenerational living

Source: visual.ly/community

"It's bad for two reasons. One, for the economy. Because millennials are living with their parents longer, they are postponing[1] making those big decisions that include house ownership, getting married, having children, other things which are a boon[2] to the economy. But also in terms of character, it is in taking these lessons, in which you learn from taking risks, failing[3], messing up[4], that you learn when you get up on your own and to deal with it without having mum and dad to go back to. —Kirsten

"They get the type of jobs that don't pay enough to actually pay the bills. This economy is crushing them. I actually have a dear friend who lives with her parents and she's used it to build a house-cleaning business. It's booming. And I think that the other positive side of it is her relationship with her parents is great, she's got that multigenerational input[5], family wisdom, family strength, and that's really an important thing for the body politic to understand."—Gillian

Fox News Live

1. *remettre à plus tard* 2. something helpful 3. not succeed 4. make mistakes 5. *apport*

a. Read the infographic and **define** the term *"multigenerational living"*.

b. Identify the reasons why more American millennials live in multigenerational houses.

c. Comment on the pros and cons of multigenerational living.

WORDS

- advantage ≠ drawback
- boundary = limit
- disagreement
- the elderly = seniors
- four-generation house
- in the short ≠ long run
- lack of: *manque de*

- economic: *qui a trait à l'économie*

- economical = money-saving
- nosy = intrusive
- quiet ≠ noisy
- shared ≠ separate

- get along with
- move back
- quarrel = argue: *se disputer*
- work out: *fonctionner*

3 Multigenerational households

Nathan live! VIDÉO

a. Watch the video and **find out** what is unusual in this household.

b. Explain how space is organised in each house.

c. PHONOLOGY **Focus** on the pronunciation of <th> in this sentence: *"You would think this home was no different than any other home."* In which cases can the sound <th> be clearly heard? ► p. 65

BOOST YOUR SKILLS!

Évaluer les pour et les contre d'une situation

- *More millennials **are living** with their parents.*
- ***In fact,... actually... but also...***
- ***Provided that... Unless... If...***
- ***On the one hand... On the other hand... And yet,...***

YOUR TASK

Write a post on a forum discussion: *"Would you live in a multigenerational household?"*

WAY 1 **Explain** why you would like to live in a multigenerational household (or not).

WAY 2 **Discuss** the pros and cons of living in a multigenerational household.

EXPLORE

4. Keeping the family spirit alive

1 Teens teaching seniors

Nathan live! VIDÉO

WORDS

- social media
- tool: *outil*

- eager to = willing to
- rewarding = gratifying
- useful ≠ useless

- be on your own
- get up to date
- please someone
- pass on = transmit

2 Intergenerational learning

Nathan live! VIDÉO

Focus on Doc 1 or 2. PARCOURS DIFFÉRENCIÉS WB → p. 18

a. **Watch** the video and **identify** what the project is about.

b. **Explain** how this project benefits seniors.

c. **Discuss** how this experience is also beneficial to the teenagers and to the children.

YOUR TASK

In groups of three: one of you is the grandchild, the other two are the grandparents. The grandchild tries to **convince** his/her grandparents to take part in a similar intergenerational project.

BOOST YOUR SKILLS!

Défendre un projet

- *There is something* ***extra*** *going on here.*
- *That's* ***really*** *cool... It* ***makes me feel*** *good, happy.*
- ***It's an opportunity...***
- ***More than we even expected...***
- *That connection* ***will last forever.***

TEST YOUR CULTURE

HOW TO PLAY "FAMILY CHALLENGE"

Play in pairs. The younger player starts.

You live in a multigenerational household. How much do you know about each generation living under your roof?

Choose a room and answer a question about a generational issue. A room can't be chosen twice. If you answer correctly, you can move on to another room of your choice. If not, skip your turn until the next round.

The player with the most correct answers wins a family trip!

GAME ON!

THIRD FLOOR

Children's bedroom
Name one difficulty millennials face today.

Children's play area
Give two reasons why more Americans live in multigenerational houses today.

Grandchildren's bedroom
Give one advantage of an intergenerational project involving young children.

Bathroom
Give one challenge of living in a single-parent family.

SECOND FLOOR

Leisure room
What is "modern" about the family in the sitcom *Modern Family*? Give three elements.

Parents' master suite
Give three components of the "American Dream" for past generations.

Dining room
Name an American family tradition.

Kitchen
What do Americans traditionally eat for Thanksgiving?

FIRST FLOOR

Senior Suite

Sitting room
Suggest an intergenerational project involving seniors.

Bedroom
Say why young people sometimes go back to live with their parents at the end of their studies.

Garage
Give one advantage of leaving the family nest.

Kitchen
Give the names of two American series dealing with family life.

BOOST YOUR ENGLISH!

Grammar — Évoquer des faits à venir

PRÉCIS 17 ET EXERCICES

Nathan live! GRAMMAR TUTO

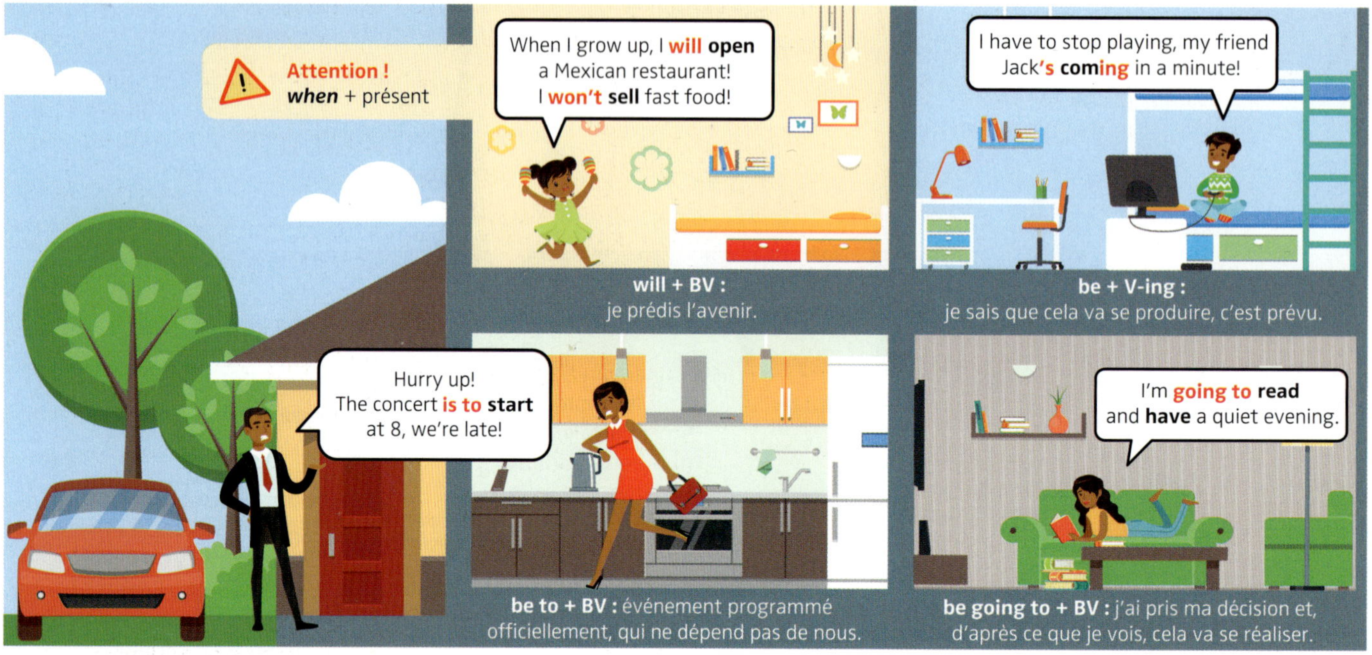

1 Complète ces propos en mettant les verbes à la forme qui convient pour exprimer des faits à venir.

The whole family (*come*) for Thanksgiving this year! Grandpa Jim and Nanna Kate (*arrive*) on Wednesday, their plane (*land*) at 9pm. We (*cook*) our favorite Thanksgiving dessert: pecan pie! Dad (*buy*) the turkey and decorate the house. You (*all / help*) me. Jack, you (*share*) your room with your cousins. Jess, (*you / do*) tonight? Nothing? Come and help me, we (*make*) a list of everything we need!

2 Tu es promoteur immobilier. Rédige un paragraphe pour ton site web afin de faire la publicité d'un quartier dédié aux maisons multigénérationnelles.

Mets en avant la date d'ouverture du quartier, les aménagements prévus, les avantages, ce que les gens pourront faire dans ce nouveau quartier, etc.

More in *Pump it up!* p. 36

Grammar — Les pronoms

PRÉCIS 9 ET EXERCICES

Les pronoms personnels	
• Les **pronoms personnels sujets** sont : *I, you, he/she/it, we, you, they.* • Ils remplacent un nom en position sujet : *Jack has two children, **he** is a happy dad.*	• Les **pronoms personnels compléments** sont : *me, you, him/her/it, us, you, them.* • Ils remplacent un nom en position complément (après le verbe) : *Jack has two children, he loves **them**.*

Les pronoms possessifs
• Les **pronoms possessifs** sont : *mine, yours, hers/his/its, ours, yours, theirs.* • Ils sont l'équivalent de « le mien », « la sienne », « le vôtre », ou de « à moi », à « toi », etc. *These two lovely children are **mine**.* (= *my children* les miens, à moi) → *mine* évite la répétition de *children* *This is not my problem, it's **yours**.* (= *your problem* le tien, à toi) → *yours* évite la répétition de *problem*

3 Remplace chaque GN souligné par un pronom.

a. I live with my parents but not in their house. <u>My parents and I</u> live in <u>my house</u>.

b. <u>Bob</u> has four children. <u>The four children</u> are teens, and help <u>Bob</u> with the housework.

c. *Modern family*? My mother loves <u>that series</u>. The characters are fun and <u>the characters</u> make <u>Mom</u> laugh. What about <u>your mother</u>?

d. This house is <u>my sister's house</u>, and that one is my brother's. <u>My brother and my sister</u> are next-door neighbours!

More in *Pump it up!* p. 12

Vocabulary — The American family

live! MP3 — live! LEXIQUIZ

Traditions
- pursuit /pə'sjuːt/ of happiness
- reunion = gathering
- eager to
- comply with = conform to
- gather = come together

Household
- close ≠ distant relative
- extended family
- nuclear family
- single-parent family

Ties
- close-knit: *soudé*
- break free
- bring up
- look after
- provide care for
- stick together
- support: *soutenir*

Generations
- baby-boomers
- millennials
- pensioner
- seniors = the elderly

Family members

Relationships

Generation cohabitation

Difficulties
- isolation
- misunderstanding
- rivalry /'raɪvəlri/
- cope with = handle
- depend on
- make ends meet
- overcome: *surmonter*
- split up = break up

Places
- college = university
- high school
- multigenerational house
- nursery school = pre-school
- retirement /rɪ'taɪrmənt/ home

Benefits
- sense of fulfilment
- meaningful (experience)
- aim at/for
- destigmatise
- enhance = improve
- foster = promote
- make connections with
- result in

Methods
- be involved in
- carry out = implement a programme (UK) / program (US)
- interact with
- pass on (knowledge)
- share
- stimulate

1 **Complète les phrases avec les prépositions qui conviennent :** *in – on – with – to.*

Families are eager ... live together ... share expenses. Grandparents can connect ... their grandchildren and millennials can better cope ... financial anxiety. The success of multigenerational living depends ... compromises and cooperation. These living arrangements generally result ... stronger bonds between generations.

2 **Trouve un synonyme pour chaque verbe.**

conduct – raise – separate – take care of – transmit

3 **Écris un email à un directeur de maison de retraite pour présenter ton projet intergénérationnel. Utilise les mots suivants :**

retirement home – implement – involve – interact with – enhance

Phonology — La prononciation du <th>

live! MP3

Le **<th>** est spécifique à l'anglais et sa prononciation pose parfois problème car ce n'est ni un /s/ ni un /z/. Selon les cas, il se prononce /ð/ (comme dans *these*) ou /θ/ (comme dans *this*).

1 **Écoute et répète ces mots en te concentrant sur la prononciation du <th>.**

Thanksgiving – father – without – there – through – thick

2 **a. Écoute et répète les mots suivants, puis classe-les selon leur prononciation : /ð/ ou /θ/.**

think – other – nothing – weather – earth – them – their – north

b. Classe les mots ci-dessus dans un tableau (/ð/ ou /θ/).

FINAL TASK

Present and defend an intergenerational project to get funds.

You live in an American city which offers grants to community-based projects that involve younger and older people. You are invited to present and defend your project to the city council.

1. **Think up an intergenerational project:**
   – identify the issue you want to address in your community,
   – describe a social, cultural or educational activity that can involve younger and older generations,
   – give details about the number of participants, the meeting place, and the resources you need,
   – explain what can be achieved through your project,
   – find a name for your project.
2. **Organise your notes** to make sure your presentation is as clear as possible.
3. **Present and defend your project: be convincing!**

YES YOU CAN! Defend a project with enthusiasm

1 INTRODUCTION

Présente-toi brièvement.
Explique pourquoi tu veux mener ce projet (utilise des anecdotes, des questions ouvertes, des citations).

When they learn the technology aspect, they can connect again.

2 PRÉSENTATION

Parle clairement et distinctement.
Structure ton propos et donne-lui du rythme.

*...the **pure, authentic connection** that this experience provides for the children...*

CONVAINCRE

Accentue les mots importants.

*And it's not **boring** at all. And it **is**!*

Pose des questions rhétoriques.

*You don't already have a Facebook, **right**? **No**? Okay.*

Fais référence à des faits d'actualité ou à des statistiques.

A lot of the seniors, their reason for joining the club is because...

Some teenagers think seniors are ... but they're not all like that.

3 CONCLUSION

Rappelle les idées clés de ton projet.
Exprime ton intime conviction, partage ton ressenti.

I learn a lot, too.

Remercie ton auditoire.

LANGAGE CORPOREL / GESTUELLE

Tiens-toi droit(e) et souris. Regarde ton auditoire.
Utilise tes gestes pour appuyer tes propos (par exemple lève l'index pour appuyer une idée importante).
Tu peux bouger et te déplacer dans la salle, mais sans jamais tourner le dos à ton auditoire.

STRATEGIES Faire une présentation orale P. 215

AUTO-ÉVALUATION
WB → p. 19

TEST YOUR SKILLS

Compréhension de l'oral — Comprendre un reportage

live! MP3

In pursuit of the American Dream

A2 **1. Watch** the video and **pick out** basic information about the Levin family (parents and children).

B1 **2.** What is Michael Levin's conception of the American Dream?

3. What does Suzanne Levin wish for her children?

B1+ **4. Explain** why the Levin family embodies the American Dream.

Compréhension de l'écrit — Comprendre un article de presse

Not a "Modern Family" at all

ABC's hit series *Modern Family* has returned to the air for its second season.

It's the "modern" elements of the Modern Family that you're supposed to notice right away. The family patriarch, Jay, has divorced his children's mother and is married to a much younger Colombian woman named Gloria. Gloria has her own son from a previous marriage, Manny. Jay's own children – Claire and Mitchell – are grown and have households of their own. Claire is married with three children. Mitchell, who is gay, lives with his partner Cameron and their adopted Vietnamese daughter, Lily.

And yet I'm struck[1], over and over again, by how unmodern – or at least how atypical, by contemporary American standards – this family is.

To begin with, the entire family lives in the same town. There's a lot of "day-to-day grandparenting," precisely the kind of grandparenting that few American children ever experience.

Moreover, in each of the (very well-appointed[2]) households there is at least one parent who stays home with the children. This is in stark contrast to the contemporary reality, in which families with one "stay-at-home" parent are a distinct minority.

Even if we regard the family on *Modern Family* merely as an ideal, we have to recognize that it is an ideal that is becoming out-of-reach[3] for more of us all the time.

www.frontporchrepublic.com, 2010

A2 **1. Read** the article. **List** the characters and **recap** the family relationships.

B1 **2.** What are the specificities of this family? **Pick out** three elements from the text.

3. According to the author, does this family reflect Americans' reality? **Explain** why.

B1+ **4.** What does the author want to denounce in this article? **Justify** your answer.

1. *frappé*
2. *bien équipées*
3. *hors d'atteinte*

4 Select a film for the film club

A boy inadvertently breaks three important rules concerning his new pet and unleashes a horde of malevolently mischievous monsters on a small town.

Teenager Marty McFly accidentally travels back in time to 1955. He puts his own existence at risk when he meets his future mother who falls in love with him.

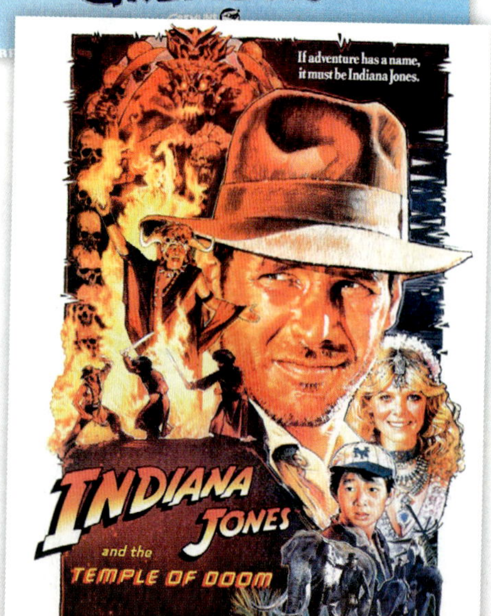

In North India, desperate villagers ask archaeologist Indiana Jones to find a mystical stone and rescue their children.

1985: the year of the teen movie

Generations of Americans can still remember a time when parents and their kids could go to the multiplex and enjoy original youth-oriented films that weren't either animated, part of a billion-dollar superhero franchise, or adaptations of young adult novels. While elaborate, big-budget movies like the *Hunger Games* series and Marvel films might be creative and loaded with special effects, they don't compare to the youth movies produced during the 1980s: a decade that saw an extraordinary crop of pictures whose like hasn't been seen since.

1985 marked the zenith for films aimed at younger audiences: *Ghostbusters*, *Indiana Jones and the Temple of Doom*, and *Gremlins*. This trend peaked the following year, which saw a hodgepodge[1] of cult classics and smash hits such as *Back to the Future* and *the Goonies*.

Back to the Future, directed by Zemeckis, still hasn't lost its luster[2]. In the *New York Times'* 1985 review of the film, critic Janet Maslin rewarded the director for his audacity. "Inventiveness" is the key word when it comes to analyzing why the film was such hit. "Ultimately, that's what made the movie successful, because it was a little bit edgy[3], but it was done in a fun way."

Adapted from *www.theatlantic.com*, 2015

1. *méli-mélo* 2. *éclat* 3. *audacieux*

WORDS

- adventure film
- blockbuster
- comedy
- cult movie
- entertaining
- humorous
- innovative
- mainstream
- prolific
- visionary
- end well

a. **Look** at the posters and **read** the plots. What genres do these films belong to?

b. **Explain** what was special about youth films in the 80s.

STEP 4 WB → p. 65

Choose the film you would screen at the film club. **Write** a pitch explaining why it could appeal to teenagers.

5 Create The 80s Trivia

Doc 1

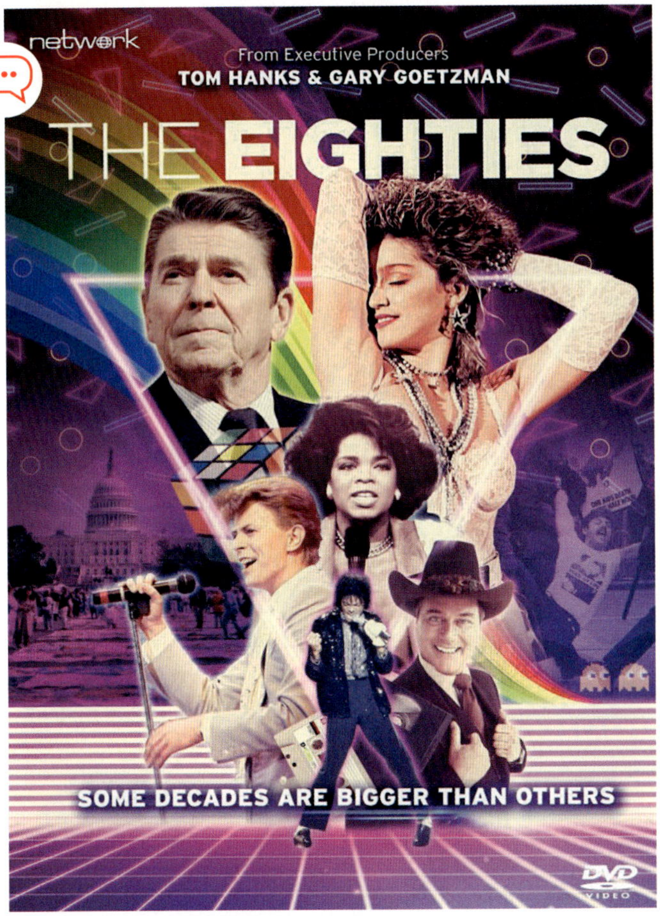

a. Look at the poster. **Say** what elements of pop culture you can recognise and what you know about them.

b. Read Doc 2 and **explain** why *Dallas* and "Thriller" have been so influencial.

c. Explain what phenomenon *Baby Boom* portrays.

STEP 5 WB → p. 65

In pairs, **create** a trivia (quiz) about the 80s. **Ask** your questions to another pair of pupils and **answer** theirs. The pair who **answer** the most questions win the game!

AT HOME Watch the video on *lyceen.nathan.fr/shine-bright2* to learn more about US pop culture in the 1980s.

BOOST YOUR SKILLS!

Organiser un programme

- *The day* ***starts with***...
- ***Then****, some young people can go to...*
- ***Meanwhile****, some others can go to...*
- ***Afterwards****, they can...*

Doc 2

TV SERIES

Who Shot J.R.? and *Dallas* were hugely popular worldwide, and it is estimated that 83 million people tuned in for "the revelation". It changed TV forever. Suddenly, Hollywood realized they could use cliffhangers[1] to keep viewers buzzing about their shows even in the off-season.

Adapted from *today.com*

MUSIC

On December 2, 1983, Michael Jackson's "Thriller" music video premiered on MTV and launched a dance craze, a red-jacket fashion, and more pricey and ambitious videos. Do you know what happened when that video came out on TV? The No. 1 selling album in the world, already out for a year, tripled its sales.

Adapted from *billboard.com*

CINEMA

Baby Boom portrays the glorious 80s: a synth-pop opening theme song, complete with keyboards and saxophone, women wearing sneakers and power suits (with shoulder pads), and yuppie[2] couples. It was in 1987 when Diane Keaton power-walked her way through the story as a killer corporate consultant with the nickname of "the Tiger Lady." The film's narrator tells the audience that "the working woman is a phenomenon of our time."

Adapted from *vice.com*

1. *épisode à suspense*
2. young urban professional

WORDS

- be comp**o**sed of = be made up of
- entert**ai**n = am**u**se
- hold an ev**e**nt = **o**rganise

FINAL STEP

MÉDIATION

Write a programme for The 80s Cruise's youth tour and present it.

a. Read the notes you have taken.

b. Make a one-day schedule with events and activities.

c. Present it to the director: STRATEGIES p. 215

- **explain** the ambiance that must be created on the cruiser,
- **mention** activities and events the Cruise cannot do without and explain why,
- **comment** on things which might attract teenagers because they are linked to today's society and culture.

EXPLORE

1. A multicultural legacy

1 Generation gap

live! VIDÉO

a. Watch the film extract and **give** two reasons why Yemi and his mum are arguing.

b. Say why Yemi might not be happy with his brother's arrival.

c. Explain his mother's viewpoint.

d. Describe the family's situation and **discuss** the importance of family solidarity here.

2

PARCOURS DIFFÉRENCIÉS WB → p. 20

Conflict between cultures can be positive

Two years ago I started writing a two-part serial called *Second Generation* for Channel Four. I set it in east London around the Bengali community where I grew up. Inevitably, it has flashes of autobiography, but perhaps more importantly, it has stories – stories that I have seen, stories that I have heard, stories that I know and stories that I have made up knowing they could happen. All of these stories start with the journey that brought our parents to this country. In my mind these families were pioneers, coming to an unknown and often hostile land with suitcases full of hopes and dreams and very little else.

With *Second Generation* I wanted to write something truthful – not something representative. My reason for making this distinction is that as second-generation Asians we have gone past representation. Asians have changed British culture in the 35-40 years we have been here. Our parents brought not only a culture but a system of values – hard work, respect for elders, strength of the family unit, irrevocable belief in education, acute business acumen[1] – that enabled them to flourish in a foreign environment and eventually change that environment from within.

Neil BISWAS, *theguardian.com*, 2003

▲ Neil Biswas poses with the Arts Council award at the South Bank Show Awards on January 23, 2007, in London

1. *un grand sens des affaires*

a. Read the article and **give** basic information about *Second Generation* (type of project, location, characters).

b. Explain why this title is well-chosen.

c. GRAMMAR **Look** at the tense used three times on lines 12 to 15 ("*My reason* [...] *have been here*"). **Explain** why it is used. ► p. 80

d. Comment on the links the author makes between generations of immigrants and British identity.

3

In some ways I felt a lot older than I was. I always considered myself mature for my age, especially compared with the other kids in my class. My theory was that it was because I had quite a lot of responsibility at home and had to be "sensible"[1] most of the time. I didn't get the space to behave like a spoilt[2] baby at home – I had to do my bit, especially as the only girl! I remember complaining to Hoyo[3] once about how all my friends got to do absolutely nothing at home and never had to worry about cleaning or looking after younger nephews and nieces. She gave me a funny look then.

"Safia, do you know how easy you have it here compared to back home in Somalia?"

I had heard this speech before.

"By the age of 11, I was cooking meals for the family and, as you know, your auntie was married by the time she was your age!"

Married? At my age? No way! Hoyo took one look at my horrified face and laughed:

"Don't worry, Safia," she giggled, "I'm not planning to marry you off just yet... You still need to learn to make *anjero*!"[4]

At that we both laughed. There was one thing that Hoyo wanted me to have almost more than anything else: a good education.

Na'ima B. ROBERT, *From Somalia with Love*, 2009

▲ Learning how to cook anjero

1. reasonable 2. *gâté* 3. mother, in Somali 4. a Somalian type of pancake

a. Read the text and **pick out** information about Safia (approximate age range, origin, family members).

b. Compare Safia's life experience with her classmates'.

c. PHONOLOGY **Read** the question *"Safia, do you know* [...]" (l.14-16) aloud, focusing on intonation. **Explain** your choice of intonation. ▸ p. 81

d. Explain why Safia's mother thinks her daughter is lucky.

YOUR TASK

In pairs, **act out** a scene inspired by *From Somalia with Love*, in which Safia and one of her brothers talk about how they want to bring up their children and why.

BOOST YOUR SKILLS!

Parler de son expérience personnelle

- *I **felt a lot older** than I was.*
- *I **always considered** myself **mature**.*
- ***My theory was** that it was because **I had quite a lot of** responsibility.*

WORDS

- clash = conflict
- plan (for the future)
- upbringing = education
- determined = resolute
- grateful = thankful
- narrow-minded ≠ open-minded
- trapped ≠ free
- be denied access to
- blame sb for sth = reproach sb with / for sth
- boost = encourage
- bring up
- improve sth = make sth better
- move on: *passer à autre chose*
- raise: *élever*
- succeed ≠ fail

EXPLORE

2. Mother tongues

1

PARCOURS DIFFÉRENCIÉS WB → p. 21 live! MP3

Grapes in My Father's Yard[1]

I love English,
I love my language too
And I love to see my children speak my language,
I thank my mum for my mother tongue [...]
I used to watch blooming[2] grapes
in my father's yard,
I used to listen to my father's song [...]
I want to say I am lost between grammars
I pretend to laugh at the jokes that I don't understand
I feel at home when I hear my great grand-father's tongue
Strange voices in Gujurati give comfort.
Strange voices in Kurdish give comfort.
Strange Polish voices give comfort. [...]
I want to belong

Astrid, Mihaela, Anokhee, Rangin, Anwar, Dilo, and Shirin, "Grapes in My Father's Yard", *www.storyingsheffield.com*

1. garden
2. *en fleurs*

a. Read and **listen** to the poem. What information do we get about the poets?

b. Explain how the poets consider England and the English language.

c. Say how they relate to their countries of origin.

d. GRAMMAR **Observe:** *"I used to listen to my father's song"* (l.7). What verb form does the speaker use to evoke the past? What impression is conveyed?

e. Say what the *"grapes in my father's yard"* evoke in the speaker's mind.

WORDS

- belonging: *appartenance*
- double culture /'kʌltʃə/
- fondness: *attachement*
- loss: *perte*
- nostalgia
- native
- traditional
- conjure up = bring to mind
- send back to (the past)
- suppress: *refouler*

2

After my Polish grandmother died, I did not speak her native language for 40 years

As a child I spoke Polish beautifully, thanks to my grandmother. While my mother went out to work, my grandmother, who spoke no English, looked after me, teaching me to speak her native tongue.

When I was five, Babcia died. In shock, I refused to speak Polish until I saw Babcia again. I never spoke Polish, never ate Polish food nor visited Poland. My childhood was gone and almost forgotten.

Then in 2004, more than 30 years later, things changed again. A new wave of Polish immigrants had arrived and I began to hear the language of my childhood all around me – every time I got on a bus. The language sounded so familiar yet somehow distant. I began to write a novel about a fictional Polish family and, at the same time, decided to enroll at a Polish language school.

And strangely, in my language classes, I still had my accent and I found words and phrases would sometimes come unbidden[1], long lost speech patterns[2] making a sudden reappearance. I had found my childhood again.

Adapted from Joanna CZECHOWSKA, *theguardian.com*, 2009

1. unexpectedly 2. sentence constructions

a. Read and **find** information about Joanna's origins and family.

b. Say when and why Joanna stopped speaking Polish, and when she decided to speak Polish again.

c. Explain what memories Polish represents for her.

YOUR TASK

In pairs, **act out** an interview with Joanna Czechowska.

BOOST YOUR SKILLS!

Exprimer la dualité

- *We continued **but** the language did not return.*
- ***Despite** the efforts of my father, ...*
- *So familiar **yet** somehow distant.*

3. Interculturally-connected

live! VIDÉO

1 Passing on the cultural heritage

WORDS

- customs
- mediator /miːdɪeɪtə/
- translator

- bilingual /baɪ'lɪŋgwəl/
- intercultural
- proficient = very competent
- self-confident ≠ self-conscious

- be fluent in = speak fluently

2

www.childrenssociety.org.uk

Children breaking down the language barrier

When families migrate to Britain, parents often find it hard to engage with many aspects of society. Children who attend school or have been learning English in their home country often master the new language before their parents or other family members. Also, it is easier for younger people to integrate with a new community. As a result, the role of interpreter or mediator often falls to the children. They have to deal with a variety of situations: they have to translate medical information when their parents go to the doctor, they have to translate their teachers' messages, they also have to do the shopping in local shops, and even communicate with the social services.

This role as interpreter can make the children feel frustrated or embarrassed. Also, they sometimes have to miss school in order to attend appointments with their parents. Their situation of responsibility sometimes gives them authority over the parent.

It is not good practice to expect young carers to interpret for other family members, particularly when it involves someone with an illness. Parents should be aware that children should not have to interpret medical information or be involved in social or legal procedures.

Focus on Doc 1 or 2.

PARCOURS DIFFÉRENCIÉS WB → p. 22

Doc 1

a. Watch the beginning of the video and **say** what advice is given to parents.

b. Watch the rest of the video and **explain** what parents can do to pass on their traditions and customs to their children.

Doc 2

a. Read the text and **explain** what problems an immigrant family can face.

b. Explain what children of immigrant parents sometimes have to do and why.

Docs 1 and 2

c. Explain the assets and difficulties met by people coming from a multicultural family.

YOUR TASK

As a social worker, **record** a message to parents of multicultural families to give them ideas of activities for their children to discover their two cultures.

BOOST YOUR SKILLS!

Expliquer ce que l'on peut faire ou doit faire pour aider quelqu'un

- *You **can** celebrate certain customs.*
- ***The thing to do** is to explore…*
- *You **must** tell your children their family history.*
- *They **have to** translate their teachers' messages.* PRÉCIS 20 21

EXPLORE

4. Love, pride and gratitude

1 THE DAY I MADE IT

ROUBEENA SHAMTALLEE had just graduated from the university of Edinburgh. She asked to be photographed outside the School of Literature and Cultures with her mother Shamima, her father Zyad, her little sister Zeenat and her teacher Marjorie (in blue). I asked Shamima whether she was proud of her daughter. You can guess her answer. Roubeena and Zeenat were born in London and their parents in Bangladesh. Shamima thinks her daughters had more opportunities than she did and that they will change the world.

KINGSTON MACABETU was laughed at by his teachers when he said he was going to be a top City lawyer[1]. Now he has a law degree[2] from London University and is a trainee[3] at a large City law firm. His mother Maryam is a nurse; she is Kingston's great supporter even if she was taken aback[4] at her son's career choice. Kingston's father Joss is Anglo-Nigerian. Maryam is very proud of her son but does not want to claim too much credit for his hard work and achievements. "He was born under a lucky star."

Inspired by photographer Bill Knight's exhibition, *Where I Come From*, 2017

1. *avocat(e).* 2. diploma 3. *stagiaire* 4. surprised

a. Look at the two photos and **guess** the theme of the photo exhibition.

b. Read the presentations. **Find** basic information about the people in the photos and the event.

c. SPELLING **Observe** this adjective: *Anglo-Nigerian.* **Explain** how the adjectives of double nationalities are formed.

d. Compare the situations of Roubeena and Kingston.

e. Account for the parents' feelings and reactions.

2 7 things you'd know if you grew up with immigrant parents

Nathan live! VIDÉO

a. Watch the video, **find** the topic of conversation and **define** its tone.

b. Pick out examples of embarrassing situations.

c. GRAMMAR **Focus** on the questions and answers. What do you notice about the prepositions? ► p. 80

YOUR TASK

DIFFÉRENCIATION

WAY 1 **Write** a text message to your parents to say why you are proud of them and of who you are.

WAY 2 **Write** a letter to your parents, saying that you are grateful even if you sometimes feel embarrassed. **Give** examples and anecdotes.

WORDS

- cliché
- stereotype

- awkward
- reluctant = unwilling

- annoy
- express gratitude
- hold in respect
- look up to sb
- owe sth to sb

BOOST YOUR SKILLS!

Exprimer son embarras, sa fierté et sa gratitude

- *I was **feeling like**... / **ashamed of**... / **embarrassed by**... / It was **so embarrassing**...*
- *I am **so proud of**...*
- *I am **so thankful** / **grateful** to my parents for... / I **want to thank** you for teach**ing** me...*

HOW TO PLAY "COMMUNITY MAGAZINE EDITOR"

Play in pairs.

You are launching a new magazine. Be the first to link each statement (*number*) to the appropriate person or character (*letter*) to complete your articles and beat the competition to the magazine stands.

TEST YOUR CULTURE

GAME ON!

1 "There was one thing that Hoyo wanted me to have almost more than anything else: a good education."

2 "Bengali families were pioneers."

3 "You can be born and raised here, like I was, while still being in touch with your culture."

4 "College? I don't think I'm gonna go back."

5 "As a child I spoke Polish beautifully."

6 "What's great is you've got here three, four generations celebrating Diwali in the Square."

7 FATHER and SON CLASH: "You have all the opportunities we never ever dreamed of!"

8 "Asians have changed British culture in the 35-40 years we have been here."

9 "My childhood was gone and almost forgotten – more than 30 years later, things changed again."

BOOST YOUR ENGLISH!

Grammar — Lier passé et présent

PRÉCIS 14 ET EXERCICES

live! GRAMMAR TUTO

Have you **ever** **visited** your mum's country?

présent — *participe passé*

Yes I **have**, but I **haven't been** there **for** 2 years.

= durée

She **has spoken** Hindi **since** she was a kid.

= point de départ

He **has** often **met** people from different countries.

C'est l'expérience vécue qui compte, pas le moment où elle a eu lieu.

* I speak Hindi

On utilise le ***present perfect*** pour établir un **lien entre le passé et le présent** : des choses du passé ont encore un impact sur le présent.

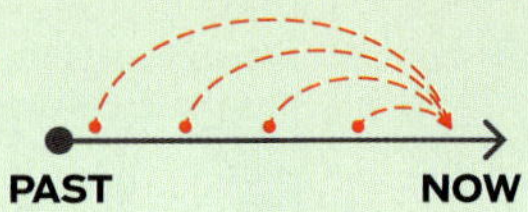

8 — Si l'événement est **rattaché à une date précise**, on utilise le **prétérit.**

1 Choisis la forme verbale qui convient.

a. My parents *left* / *have left* their home country in 1957.

b. Ranja *has studied* / *studied* law for three years now.

c. They *moved* / *have moved* to England recently so their children can succeed.

d. We'*ve lived* / *live* in London for 10 years.

2 Traduis ces phrases en utilisant le *present perfect*.

a. Elle vit à Londres depuis que ses parents y ont immigré.

b. Ils ont réussi parce qu'ils ont pu s'adapter.

c. Je ne les ai pas vus depuis longtemps.

d. Cela fait des années que je rêve de ce moment !

More in *Pump it up!* p. 26

Grammar — Poser des questions

PRÉCIS 28 ET EXERCICES

- En anglais, l'ordre des mots dans les questions est : (auxiliaire) + sujet + verbe (+ complément) + ?
- Il y a deux types de questions :

– **les questions fermées auxquelles on répond par "yes" ou "no" :** *Do/Did you really have to go to Mumbai?*

– **les questions ouvertes commençant par un mot interrogatif :** *How did you guess?*

Who taught you Hindi?

Who est le sujet de *teach* → *teach* est conjugué.

What made you decide to discover India?

What est le sujet de *make* → *make* est conjugué.

Rappel

How peut être suivi d'un adjectif, d'un quantifieur ou d'un adverbe.

How old is your father? → âge – *How far is India?* → distance – *How many languages do you speak?* → quantité dénombrable – *How much* → quantité indénombrable – *How often* → fréquence, etc.

Attention ! ***Be*** est à la fois auxiliaire et verbe et n'a pas besoin d'un autre auxiliaire.
Are you proud of your family's history?

1 Remets les mots dans le bon ordre pour former des questions.

a. what | learn | did | you | ?

b. meet | did | they | who | ?

c. arrive | when | did | they | ?

d. found | who | your ancestors | ?

2 Pose des questions à partir de ces phrases en remplaçant l'élément souligné par un mot interrogatif.

a. They talked about <u>their Indian origins</u> at the gathering.

b. She can speak <u>three</u> languages.

c. <u>My neighbours</u> found out they were of Turkish descent.

d. The big challenge is <u>to fit in</u>.

e. She <u>sometimes</u> visits her cousins in Pakistan.

f. I would like to visit <u>Poland</u>.

More in *Pump it up!* p. 44

Vocabulary — Multiculturalism in the UK

live! MP3 · live! LEXIQUIZ

Language

Plurilingualism
- language barrier
- mother tongue = native tongue
- second language

Level
- bilingual
- fluent
- ill-at-ease
- multilingual
- proficient
- improve
- master

Feelings

Positive feelings
- grateful
- proud
- thankful

Mixed feelings
- confused
- mixed up
- paradoxical

Negative feelings
- embarrassed
- self-conscious
- torn apart

Upbringing

- discipline
- politeness
- work ethic
- demanding
- lenient ≠ strict
- permissive
- blame = reproach
- clash

Double culture

- ancestor
- foreign-born
- immigrant
- of (Indian) descent
- origins
- roots
- second / third generation
- values
- integrate = fit in

1 Réécris ces phrases en remplaçant les mots soulignés par des synonymes.

a. I don't blame them for my upbringing, I <u>blame</u> them for their strictness!

b. My dad is very fluent in Chinese, and he is very <u>fluent</u> in English too.

c. Her mother's mother tongue is Urdu and her father's <u>mother tongue</u> is Bojpuri.

d. My grandmother fit in very well in England, but my grandfather did not <u>fit into</u> this neighbourhood.

2 Trouve les noms correspondant à ces adjectifs, puis classe-les dans la catégorie qui convient. Utilise un dictionnaire si nécessaire.

a. strict b. proud c. kind
d. polite e. thankful f. confused
g. permissive h. fluent i. paradoxical

Noun = adjective + -ness	Others

Phonology — L'intonation des questions

live! MP3 — More in *Pump it up!* p. 44-45

L'intonation est différente selon le type de questions :
– questions **fermées** : l'intonation **monte** ;
– questions **ouvertes** : l'intonation **descend**.

1 Écoute ces questions. Que fait la voix ?

When are you going back to college?

What have you been doing all this time? How often have I told you to get this place ready?

Do you think I am rich?

2 Entraîne-toi à dire les questions ci-dessous, puis écoute et vérifie.

How can I help my child connect with their heritage?

Were you ever embarrassed by your parents?

What are you grateful to your parents for?

FINAL TASK

Take part in a radio show entitled "My Multicultural Family Story".

You have been invited to talk on a radio show: "My Multicultural Family Story". The class is your audience and will ask you questions. Tell an anecdote about your multicultural family and answer the questions.

You are the guest.

1. **Choose** one aspect of multiculturalism that you find interesting.
2. **Relate** an anecdote that is specific to your double identity or multicultural family. **Explain** the dual feelings you had and what you had to do in that situation.
3. **Imagine** and **describe** what feelings you had when the story happened, and what feelings you have now.
4. Get ready to **tell** your story to the audience and to **answer** their questions.

You are a member of the audience.

1. **Listen** to the guest and be ready to **ask** them questions about their family story.

YES YOU CAN! Take part in a radio show

1 INTRODUCTION

Introduis une anecdote à l'aide d'une accroche afin de capter l'attention de ton public.

My parents came here in the Seventies. They probably had more problems than I could ever have. They came here with nothing and they created this amazing world.

2 ANECDOTE

Raconte ton anecdote afin d'illustrer ton propos.

The problem is that they were very strict.

My mum would always try and feed my friends.

When people asked me, "where are you from?", I would always be like, "again?"

3 CONCLUSION

Choisis une formule humoristique ou émouvante pour conclure.

Hey, maybe I should go home and say thank you...

4 REPONSE AUX QUESTIONS

Prépare-toi à répondre aux questions de l'animateur et des auditeurs. Dis par exemple comment tu as réagi à l'époque, d'une manière vivante.

I was like, "Oh, come on! Please!"

Raconte ce que cette expérience t'a appris avec le recul.

But now you realise that it's very important.

It is one of the things I'm most thankful about because...

Later on you become proud...

STRATEGIES Interagir p. 217

TEST YOUR SKILLS

AUTO-ÉVALUATION

WB → p. 23

Compréhension de l'oral

Comprendre une interview radiophonique

Poets Michael Rosen and Dean Atta

live! MP3

Dean Atta's mother

A2 **1. Identify** the main topic of the interview.

A2+ **2. Say** what families are trying to do about this issue.

3. Explain why Dean Atta is a good illustration for the topic.

B1 **4. Give** details about Dean Atta's mother's dual identity.

5. Explain why Dean Atta's mother says her choice of language was bizarre.

Compréhension de l'écrit

Comprendre les détails d'un témoignage de vie

Rita Ora: "I didn't have the answers"

Rita, your parents moved from Kosovo to London in order to give you and your siblings[1] a better life. What does your home country mean to you today?

I feel very close to it, even though I left Kosovo so early in my life. I don't want people to think that I've abandoned where I'm from. I am actually working with UNICEF in order give back for all the love and support I have received from the people there. But I also really admire my mom and dad's brave decision to move.

As a child, were you able to understand what your parents had done for you?

They didn't even speak English and it was a big adjustment, but at the time I just didn't realise how bad it was. The older I got the more I saw what they sacrificed most – their families. It was a pretty dark moment, but my mom and dad always made the best out of a bad situation so they figured it out.

Since your parents gave up their lives to give their kids a better one, how did they react when you told them that you were going to quit school and pursue an uncertain career in music?

I think they were pretty scared when I told them I was going to leave school and see if I can do this. Because honestly – I knew it in my gut[2] – I couldn't do anything else.

the-talks.com, 2014

A2 **1. Give** basic information about Rita (birthplace, where she lives, when she moved).

2. Say why her parents decided to immigrate.

A2+ **3. Find** two reasons why adapting to a new country was difficult for Rita's parents.

4. Find what big decision Rita made.

B1 **5. Explain** how Rita's parents reacted to her big decision.

6. Say how Rita's feelings have evolved.

1. brothers and sisters
2. *au fond de moi*

3 Unexpected happenings

Doc 1

Art sale near Central Park

live! VIDÉO

Doc 2

Surprise at the auction sale

live! VIDÉO

WORDS

- **au**ction: *vente aux enchères*
- b**u**yer
- s**o**cial inj**u**stice

- cheap ≠ exp**e**nsive
- myst**e**rious
- sat**i**rical

- aff**o**rd: *avoir les moyens de*
- attr**a**ct gl**o**bal att**e**ntion
- cr**i**ticise cons**u**merism
- give **o**pen **a**ccess to
- incr**ea**se the v**a**lue of a p**ai**nting
- make pr**o**fit out of

CULTURE SPOT

Sotheby's is a famous auction house in London where works of art are very often put up for sale for huge amounts of money. Collectors go there to buy and add famous paintings to their collections.

Docs 1 and 2. PARCOURS DIFFÉRENCIÉS WB → p. 66

a. **Watch** the first video and **find information** about the event (concept, place, price).

b. **Give** the customers' reasons for buying the canvases.

c. **Guess** why Banksy decided to organise this event.

d. **Watch** the second video and **pick out** information about the event (place, event, price).

e. **Explain** the surprise organised by Banksy.

f. **Comment** on people's reactions.

STEP 3

Take notes about the two events and the questions they raise about art.

BOOST YOUR SKILLS!

Souligner la controverse

- ***even more*** *shocking is what happened seconds later.*
- *that* ***shocking*** *moment at an auction house*
- *the* ***viral*** *prank*
- *an* ***eye-popping*** *1.4 million dollars*
- ***First*** *writing on social media,* ***then*** *revealing...*

4 Making fun of the art world?

Doc 1

An accomplice at the auction?

Nathan live! MP3

WORDS

- buzz (about sth): *battage médiatique*
- headline: *titre dans un journal*
- profit
- subheading: *sous-titre*

- financial
- paradoxical = contradictory

- convey a message
- mock the art world
- play a prank on sb: *jouer un tour à quelqu'un*
- raise money

Doc 2

Why putting £1m through the shredder is Banksy's greatest work

The art world will never be the same again.

For once, an artist has genuinely mocked the system that reduces art to nothing but a commodity[1]. What happened at Sotheby's is Banksy's greatest work. He has said something that needed to be said: art is being choked[2] to death by money. The only real rebellion left is for works of art to destroy themselves the moment they are sold. [...]

When the auctioneer's hammer[3] came down at Sotheby's and a "modern masterpiece" began to eat itself, the stage was set perfectly. Here was the art world's moment of truth – however theatrical and multifaceted it may prove to be. Of course, this revolt will be assimilated. Of course, the market will smile and the cash tills[4] will go on ringing. Yet for once the commodity bit back. Art turned on the hands that feed it.

Abridged from *www.theguardian.com*, 2018

1. *marchandise* 2. *étouffé* 3. *marteau* 4. *caisses*

BOOST YOUR SKILLS!

Faire réfléchir le lecteur d'un article

- *Are we really **supposed to believe** that...*
- *So what **conclusions** can we draw?*
- ***Why** do people **think** this?*

Rapporter des paroles

- *[...] **saying** online: "It appears we just got Banksy-ed."*
- *Experts **say** it might have doubled the worth the painting.*

PRÉCIS 37

Focus on Doc 1 or 2. PARCOURS DIFFÉRENCIÉS WB → p. 67

a. Listen to the audio or **read** the article. What message did Banksy try to convey at Sotheby's?

b. Explain the journalist's theory on the organisation of the event.

c. Comment on the connection between art and money.

STEP 4

In pairs. You have met one of the people at the auction house. **Discuss** and **take notes** about what happened there.

FINAL STEP

Your investigation is over.

Now **write** your article. **Introduce** Banksy, the question of his identity, his artworks and his conception of art.
Comment on this sentence: *"What happened at Sotheby's is Banksy's greatest work."* **Include** a catchy headline and subheading to raise the readers' curiosity.

EXPLORE

2. The adrenaline nation

Into the void

live! VIDÉO

1

Focus on Doc 1 or 2. PARCOURS DIFFÉRENCIÉS WB → p. 25

Doc 1

a. Watch the video and **pick out** elements about tourism in New Zealand (type of activities, attractiveness).

Doc 2

b. Read the blog post from line 1 to line 10. **Explain** how the person feels before jumping.

c. VOCABULARY **Pick out** the words and expressions showing how the person feels before and while jumping.

d. Read the end and **explain** how her state of mind evolves during the fall.

Docs 1 and 2

e. React: Would you like to try these activities in New Zealand? Why or why not?

2

JUUUUMP!

Hands were shaking uncontrollably. My heart was throbbing rapidly. Safety checks performed. Harness snugged around my body. Even the pep talk[1] by the bungy jumping instructor couldn't scare away my fears. With both legs bound together, I started walking toward the edge like a penguin.

I was at the ledge[2] when the jump instructor gave his final set of instructions. The countdown started… "1…2…3…Jump!" I wanted to turn back, but didn't. With arms stretched out, I leaned forward and JUMPED!

My free-fall had taken me to a different world, where nothing was stable or familiar. Wind caressed my tresses at jet speed. My anxieties had vanished into the thin air. I surrendered myself to the surroundings instead of controlling them – and that was the moment when I started to enjoy bungy jumping. I was free falling – head down, feet up! I got the roller-coaster[3] feeling in my stomach. I screamed with excitement. Suddenly, I was pulled up by the bungy. I went to the top again and the free-fall continued.

Alas! All good things must come to an end. Yes, I had done it. I had faced my fears. There's no better feeling than winning over your fear.

If you love an adrenaline rush, are not afraid of free-falling, and want to overcome your fear of heights, you should try bungy jumping.

Archana Singh, *www.mikesroadtrip.com*

1. motivating speech 2. *près du rebord* 3. *montagnes russes*

WORDS

- **e**mptiness
- equ**i**pment = gear
- h**ea**rtbeat
- vertigo /'vɜːtɪgəʊ/ = fear of heights /'haɪts/

- adv**en**turous
- p**e**trified ≠ c**o**nfident
- r**i**sky = h**a**zardous
- safe ≠ **un**safe

- draw /'drɔː/ = attr**a**ct
- have g**oo**sebumps
- overc**o**me one's fears

3

https://www. www.triadventurenz.co.nz

Every year, the IronMan in Taupo draws thousands of tourists and up to 1,200 competitors from over 50 countries. This Ironman is one of the oldest in the world and has a reputation for being the most iconic one.

TriAdventuresNZ offers a range of tours adjusted to your specific needs. From race and accommodation packages to longer guided-tour itineraries. We act as travel agent and guide and can accommodate most requests - from flights and accommodation to adventure activities and race entry.

Jay Lucky
@BondiGoodBoy
Massive congrats! This is so well-deserved! What a great performance! 3 March

Nick Chamberlain
@nckchbl
This is such a stellar achievement! @terenzo1 is our new #IMNZ Champion! #AnythingIsPossible How incredible!

a. **Read** and **find out** what the Taupo IronMan is.

b. **Explain** how this website can help you take part in it.

c. GRAMMAR **Read** the tweets. What kind of sentence is used? What feelings do they express? ► p. 96

d. **React: Imagine** why people come to support the athletes.

YOUR TASK

You have participated in the Taupo IronMan. **Share** your enthusiasm about this unique experience in a couple of tweets.

AT HOME Find a testimony made by a Taupo IronMan competitor and write a tweet about his/her exploits.

WORDS

- challenge
- scenery /'siːnəri/
- triathlon /traɪ'æθlən/ = swimming, biking, running

- demanding: *éprouvant*
- impressed = amazed
- tough /tʌf/ = resistant

- worldwide = international

- attend = take part in
- push one's limits = surpass oneself
- reach/cross the finish line
- ride (a bike)
- support = follow

BOOST YOUR SKILLS!

Partager son enthousiasme

- *There is **no better** feeling **than** surpassing yourself.*
- ***What a great** performance!*
- *The reward is **huge**!*
- *This is **such** a stellar achievement! **How** incredible!*

GRAMMAR ► p. 96

3. Sports for all

Nathan live! VIDÉO

PARCOURS DIFFÉRENCIÉS WB → p. 26

1 The Halberg Disability Sport Foundation

CULTURE SPOT

The **Halberg Disability Sport Foundation** is a charitable organisation founded in 1963 by Olympic legend Sir Murray Halberg. He also created the Halberg Awards to celebrate New Zealand sporting excellence and promote diversity in sports.

a. **Look at** the poster and **read** the Culture spot. **Explain** how the Halberg Foundation contributes to promoting diversity in sports.

b. **Watch** the video and **pick out** information about the competition.

c. PHONOLOGY **Describe** the reporter's tone. ▸ p. 97

d. **Explain** how the kids feel about this competition.

YOUR TASK

DIFFÉRENCIATION

WAY 1 You take part in the organisation of the Halberg Games. **Record** a radio spot to promote the event.

WAY 2 For the opening ceremony of the Halberg Games, **deliver** a short speech highlighting the importance of the event for Kiwi society.

BOOST YOUR SKILLS!

Donner envie, motiver, encourager

- *We are about to find **some amazing** athletes.*
- *You leave with friendships that will **last forever.***
- *Just **push** and **forget** about everything.*
- *Just **keep doing** it!*
- *Just give it a go, just try, you **might even exceed your expectations!***

WORDS

- ach**ie**vement = succ**e**ss
- incl**u**siveness
- tog**e**therness = f**e**llowship
- wh**ee**lchair

- acc**e**ssible
- dis**a**bled = h**a**ndicapped

- be on an **e**qual f**oo**ting
- bond = un**i**te
- bring tog**e**ther
- comp**e**te
- have a chance to = seize the opport**u**nity to
- have **a**ccess to
- be part of = be incl**u**ded in

HOW TO PLAY "MY KIWI ROAD TRIP"

Play in pairs.

You want to organise a tour of New Zealand. Answer the questions to raise funds for your trip: the more money you earn, the more activities you can try.

1. Answer as many questions as you can in three minutes only.
2. After three minutes, check your answers and count how much money you have collected.
3. Depending on the money you have, briefly discuss one activity per day that you would like to do.

GAME ON!

Play for NZ$50

1 What is the name of the traditional Maori dance players do before a rugby match?

2 What is bungy jumping?

3 Which New Zealand competition can you take part in if you are an excellent skier?

4 What is the name of New Zealand's rugby team?

Play for NZ$100

5 What does zorbing consist of?

6 What do you have to do if you want to complete an IronMan? (Give precise distances.)

7 What record does the number 664 refer to?

8 Give two reasons why sheepshearing can be considered to be a real sport.

Play for NZ$200

9 What is the traditional meaning of Haka?

10 How do the Halberg Games influence Kiwi society?

11 How does Ki o Rahi reflect Maori traditions?

12 Explain why New Zealand can be called "the adrenaline nation".

Results

Check your answers to see how much money you collected and decide how long your road trip will be.

- **NZ$00-300:** You will not be able to travel a lot. Your road trip will only last a weekend.
- **NZ$300-600:** Not bad! You can get ready for a 4-day trip.
- **More than NZ$600:** Well done! Get ready for a great journey around New Zealand for a whole week.

BOOST YOUR ENGLISH!

Grammar — Exprimer son admiration et sa surprise

PRÉCIS 27 ET EXERCICES

live! GRAMMAR TUTO

sujet + *be* conjugué + *so* + adj.	sujet + *be* conjugué + *such a/an* + adj. + nom	*what a/an* + adj. + nom + sujet + *be* conjugué	*how* + adj. + sujet + *be* conjugué

1 Complète avec *so*, *such*, *what* ou *how*.

a. New Zealand is ... a beautiful country.
b. Extreme sports are ... stressful!
c. ... a dangerous sport bungy jumping is.
d. ... exciting it is to go to New Zealand!

2 Exprime la surprise en variant les structures.

Ex: Zorbing is very exciting. → Zorbing is **so** exciting!
a. Extreme sports are very popular in New Zealand.
b. Zorbing fans are very enthusiastic.
c. New Zealand landscapes are totally amazing.
d. Haka is a very impressive ritual.

Grammar — Évoquer une action dans le temps et dans la durée

PRÉCIS 15 ET EXERCICES

• Certains marqueurs de temps permettent de **mettre en avant la durée écoulée.**

	Sens	Temps	Exemples
Ago	Laps de temps écoulé depuis la réalisation d'une action	Prétérit	I visited New Zealand five years **ago**. (I visited : action passée ; five years ago : temps écoulé (il y a))
Since	« Depuis quand » une action est en cours	*Present perfect*	I've been in love with NZ **since** my first trip there. (I've been in love : action en cours ; since my first trip there : depuis)
For	Indication de durée d'une action dans le passé ou encore en cours	Prétérit	I played rugby **for** five years. (I played rugby : action révolue ; for five years : durée de l'action (pendant))
		Present perfect	I've been playing rugby **for** five years. (I've been playing rugby : action en cours ; for five years : durée de l'action (depuis))

3 Construis quatre phrases.

a. I tried bungy jumping
b. They have gone kayaking
c. When they were young, they lived in NZ
d. John has shorn sheep

1. since the 1990s.
2. since their trip to NZ.
3. for three years.
4. five years ago.

4 Mets le verbe entre parenthèses au temps qui convient (*present perfect* ou prétérit).

a. Jane (*go*) kayaking in NZ six months ago.
b. They (*organise*) the shearing competition since 1961.
c. John (*live*) in NZ for 4 years now.
d. Ki-o-rahi (*exist*) for centuries.

More in *Pump it up!* p. 30

Vocabulary — Sports in New Zealand

Sports

Competition
- contestant = competitor
- tournament
- athletic
- competitive
- cheer
- compete

Challenge
- adrenaline rush
- fear of heights
- adventurous
- bold = daring = courageous
- careless ≠ careful
- fearless ≠ fearful
- reckless
- risky
- overcome one's fears
- take up a challenge

Tourism

Activities
- bungy jumping (NZ)
- extreme sports
- Haka
- sheepshearing
- zorbing
- eventful

Journey
- capital city
- journey = trip
- road trip
- vlog

Economy
- spending: *dépenses*
- wealth /welθ/
- attract = draw /drɔː/
- contribute to
- enrich

Sense of belonging

Community
- crowd
- inclusiveness
- togetherness
- belong to = be part of
- bond = unite
- stand for = represent

Heritage
- embedded in = rooted in
- everlasting
- find one's roots in
- revitalise

1 ***-ful* ou *-less* ? Crée des adjectifs avec les mots ci-dessous, puis complète les phrases.**
fear – stress – event – care – power

a. I am far too … to practise bungy jumping. I would find it extremely … .
b. New Zealand is a great country for bold people, but if you are … you could get hurt.
c. The Haka is such a … tradition.
d. My road trip around New Zealand has been … and boring.

2 **Associe chaque verbe à la préposition correspondante, puis utilise-les dans des phrases sur la Nouvelle-Zélande.**

a. stand – b. travel – c. root – d. be part – e. belong

1. in – 2. of – 3. to – 4. for – 5. around

3 **Mobilise ton vocabulaire.**
Tu as décidé de t'inscrire dans un club de Ki o Rahi. Explique ce que ce sport représente pour toi.

Phonology — L'intonation des phrases exclamatives

En plus de la structure de la phrase, l'intonation permet de marquer l'exclamation.

1 **Écoute et répète ces phrases exclamatives. Que fait la voix ? Quels sont les mots accentués ?**

a. *What a great country!*
b. *Bungy jumping is such an exciting sport!*
c. *How popular rugby is!*
d. *This is such a wonderful country!*
e. *What a fun activity sheepshearing is!*

2 **Entraîne-toi à prononcer ces phrases avec emphase.**

FINAL TASK

Record a video for your vlog about your sports experiences in New Zealand.

You travel around New Zealand to discover the importance of sports in Kiwi society. Record a vlog to share your experience with your friends and family.

1. **Imagine your programme:** select at least three activities.
2. **Brainstorm ideas and remember to:**
   – Show the importance of sports in New Zealand thanks to numbers and facts (main sports, fans, participants, events);
   – Encourage your viewers to come and live the same adventures.
3. **Record your vlog** during several days of your trip. Make sure you sound enthusiastic and convincing to make people want to discover these activities.

YES YOU CAN! Record a lively video

1 INTRODUCTION

Commence par expliquer où tu te trouves et à quelle activité tu t'apprêtes à participer.

"Now, Rotorua is famous for a few things, and one of them is the zorb."

2 PRÉSENTATION

Montre en quoi certains sports sont spécifiques à la Nouvelle-Zélande.

"All I've heard is that it is a big globe-shaped ball that you step inside and get pushed down a hill. Only in New Zealand!"

"Zorbing was created here in New Zealand. Basically it's an iconic New Zealand creation."

3 ÉTAPES

Explique les différentes étapes de ton activité.

"So what we're going to do now is we're going to sign you up inside, we're going to strap you up to one of our balls and we're going to push you down the hill."

DESTINATAIRES

Adresse-toi directement à la caméra pour mieux partager ton expérience et rendre ton récit accrocheur.

EMOTIONS

Exprime tes émotions grâce à des expressions idiomatiques, mais aussi grâce à ton intonation.

"You can have a lot of fun!"

"Well that was a real experience. It's a must-do here in Rotorua and such a unique experience!"

STRATEGIES Faire une présentation orale p. 215

AUTO-ÉVALUATION
WB → p. 27

Compréhension de l'oral

Comprendre une vidéo promotionnelle

A taste of Kiwi culture

live! VIDÉO

A2 **1. Say** what event is presented.

2. Who are the participants?

B1 **3.** Why do they take part in it?

4. Why is it more than a sports event?

B1+ **5. Explain** what the participants will remember of this event.

Compréhension de l'écrit

Comprendre un témoignage écrit

This secret corner of the Rees Valley feels a world away from the bungy jumping tourist bubble of Queenstown – yet we're only an hour's drive north.

99.9% of people who've been in this valley haven't seen this spot, because you can't get here without a boat.

The aim is to spend the first day hiking (or tramping as Kiwis call it) 13km into the bush[1], set up camp, then use our packrafts to return by river. My backpack holds 20kg of tent, stove[2], food, warm clothes, wetsuit and my secret weapon: folded into a pillow-sized bag and weighing just over 2kg, my packraft.

Soon we're making the first of many river crossings, wading[3] through fast-flowing, knee-high water. Hikers used to view these rivers as a barrier, but with packrafts, rivers and lakes become part of the journey and open up new places.

In a packraft you can lie back and simply feel a place as it drifts by. I see it with fresh eyes. Occasionally we have to carry our boats around fallen wood or shallow sections – but the water quickly gathers momentum[4], and so do we. Panic turns to pleasure as I bounce over splashing rapids, adrenaline racing. And it's all the more thrilling because we're seeing parts of New Zealand most tourists don't get to see.

Adapted from Ellie Ross, *The Guardian*, 2016

A2 **1. Identify** where the scene takes place.

2. In what environment does this activity take place?

B1 **3. Explain** what the activity consists in.

B1+ **4.** Why did the journalist decide to try this uncommon activity?

5. Explain the different steps of the journey and the author's feelings.

6. Imagine the reasons for writing such an article in *The Guardian*.

1. wild, remote areas in Australia
2. *réchaud de camping*
3. walk (through water or long grass)
4. *prendre de la vitesse*

EXPLORE

1. The call of the wild

1 Working in the wilderness in Yosemite

live! VIDÉO

2 Working on the beach in Malibu

live! VIDÉO

PARCOURS DIFFÉRENCIÉS WB → p. 28

Focus on Doc 1 or 2.

a. **Look** at the photograph and **guess** what job is illustrated.

b. **Watch** the video and **check** your hypotheses. **Pick out** more details about the job.

c. **Explain** how the natural environment makes the person feel.

d. **Explain** what this person particularly likes about her job.

e. GRAMMAR **Observe:** "***a few*** *years ago*" (doc 1), "***a lot of*** *times*" (doc 2). What do these words express? ► p. 108

YOUR TASK

You are looking for a summer job. **Write** a short email to a possible employer to **present** your skills and experiences.

WORDS

- landscape
- lifeguard = lifesaver
- park ranger
- security
- wilderness /'wɪldərnəs/: *région sauvage*

- challenging

- magnificent /mæg'nɪfɪsənt/

- drown /draʊn/: *se noyer*
- be in contact with = feel close to
- take care of

BOOST YOUR SKILLS!

Présenter ses compétences

- *I* ***learned about how to*** *teach people the stories of Yosemite National Park.*
- ***It's the best thing I can do to*** *serve the public.*
- *I* ***know how to go through*** *surf in different conditions.*
- *I'm so proud to* ***be able to*** *protect the area.*

3

https://www.aquariumofthebay.org/volunteers

plan a visit | Events | Contribute | Explore | Conservation | Education

Volunteers

Volunteers[1] are vital to the operation of all of our programs. Joining our team through our marine volunteer opportunities can make a meaningful contribution. From helping educate the public to assisting with daily responsibilities, we simply could not do it without volunteers.

1. *bénévoles*

Dear Mr. Fox,

As an engaged, curious student with great organizational skills and a great capacity for work, I am eager to explore volunteer opportunities at the Aquarium of the Bay.

I am studying the diversity of marine microbial communities at the University of Washington, and looking for an opportunity to continue my research in one of the greatest environments our country has to offer. The Aquarium of the Bay is indeed a unique place for anyone passionate about marine wildlife[1] and has some of the world's most beautiful species.

I am ready to meet any of your program's needs and requirements. With my experience and enthusiasm, I am confident that I could make a valuable contribution on the Aquarium staff. Thank you for your consideration.

Yours sincerely,

Jeff Bowman

1. *faune et flore*

Cover letter adapted from *scripps.ucsd.edu*

a. Read the homepage of this website. **Imagine** what may attract people to work at the Aquarium of the Bay.

b. Read the short text and **identify** its nature.

c. Read Jeff's cover letter and **explain** why he applies for that job.

d. Pick out adjectives that characterise Jeff. **Explain** why he would be a good candidate.

WORDS

- applic**a**tion: *candidature*
- c**o**ver(ing) l**e**tter
- sea life

- de**d**icated to
- exp**e**rienced
- sk**i**lled

- app**ly** for
- enr**o**l (UK) / enr**o**ll (US) in: *s'inscrire à*
- give one's time

2. The ultimate dreamland?

1

Emma Stone didn't become one of America's most sought-after actresses overnight[1]. At 15 years old, she moved to Los Angeles to find success. But it took her some time to make any progress. "I went up for every single show on the Disney Channel," she said. "And auditioned to play the daughter on every single sitcom. I got none."

www.cheatsheet.com, 2018

She found that acting wasn't paying the bills. "To make ends meet[2], I took a side job working at a dog-biscuit bakery."

www.cnbc.com, 2017

"I auditioned for (casting director) Allison for three years. She would bring me in for things and they'd never work, but then one Friday evening she called me and said, 'I want to put you on tape for something.' It was *Superbad*." I got the part.

www.rollingstone.com, 2016

After *Superbad*, the offers began pouring in[3]. Finally, she got a lead role with 2010's *Easy A*, and big-time stardom followed.

At the top of her game, Stone left Hollywood. "I started to feel overwhelmed by the energy of Hollywood," she told *The Hollywood Reporter*.

www.people.com, 2017

1. *du jour au lendemain* 2. *joindre les deux bouts* 3. *affluer*

Docs 1 and 2. PARCOURS DIFFÉRENCIÉS WB → p. 29

a. Look at the film poster and **read** the texts. **Pick out** information about Emma Stone (jobs, film, award).

b. GRAMMAR **Focus** on *"She would bring me in for things"*. What does *"would"* express? PRÉCIS 20

c. Listen to the interview. **Pick out** information about her story.

d. Explain how these documents give a contrasting view of "becoming an actress in Hollywood."

WORDS

- American Dream
- fame = stardom
- hard times = hardships
- job opportunity
- challenge

- disillusioned

- famous = well-known
- persevering

- be rewarded with
- cast: *choisir (un acteur)*
- make money
- struggle

A difficult start

live! MP3

2

Nathan live! VIDÉO

3 The most innovative place on Earth

WORDS

- brand: *marque*
- company = firm
- drawback = disadvantage = downside
- headquarters
- IT (information technology) = computer science
- the other side of the coin

- convenient
- fulfilling
- high-tech
- innovative
- rewarding

- be a leader in
- have it all
- make the most of
- seize an opportunity

4 The Silicon Valley: expectations vs reality

	On the surface, Silicon Valley is similar to a lot of other places in the world. To discover what this place truly has to offer, you need to get out of your comfort zone and seek out the opportunities.		Living in an awesome part of the world is a double-edged sword[1]; the more a place has to offer, the higher the demand to live there. I spend 3+ hours a day sitting on a shuttle[2] traveling to and from Mountain View for work. My monthly rent makes me cringe[3] every time I make the payment.
	Working in a start-up, the work culture... Working is fun, it changes and moves all the time.		Most start-ups are very comfortable to work at. You get to wear jeans and a dress shirt, listen to music on your headphones, and the company usually provides a lunch every day or week.

1. *lame à double-tranchant* 2. *navette* 3. *grimacer*

www.medium.com

Docs 3 and 4.

a. Watch the video, **read** the testimonies and **explain** how the natural environment makes Silicon Valley an ideal workplace.

b. Comment on the international dimension of the work done there.

c. Read the comments and **explain** why living in the Silicon Valley is "a *double-edged sword*".

YOUR TASK

DIFFÉRENCIATION

WAY 1 As a student, you have an opportunity to do an internship in a Silicon Valley company. **Explain** to your parents why that is a dream for you.

WAY 2 As a recruiter in a Silicon Valley start-up, you take part in a Youth Employment Forum to attract the best young workers. **Convince** them to join your team.

BOOST YOUR SKILLS!

Parler de ce qui attire et motive

- *Silicon Valley is **richer and more powerful than ever**.*
- ***There's no denying that** Silicon Valley is **one of the most** dynamic places **on Earth.***
- *It is **a leading hub for innovation**.*

BOOST YOUR ENGLISH!

Grammar — Évoquer des quantités

PRÉCIS 6 ET EXERCICES

Nathan live! GRAMMAR TUTO

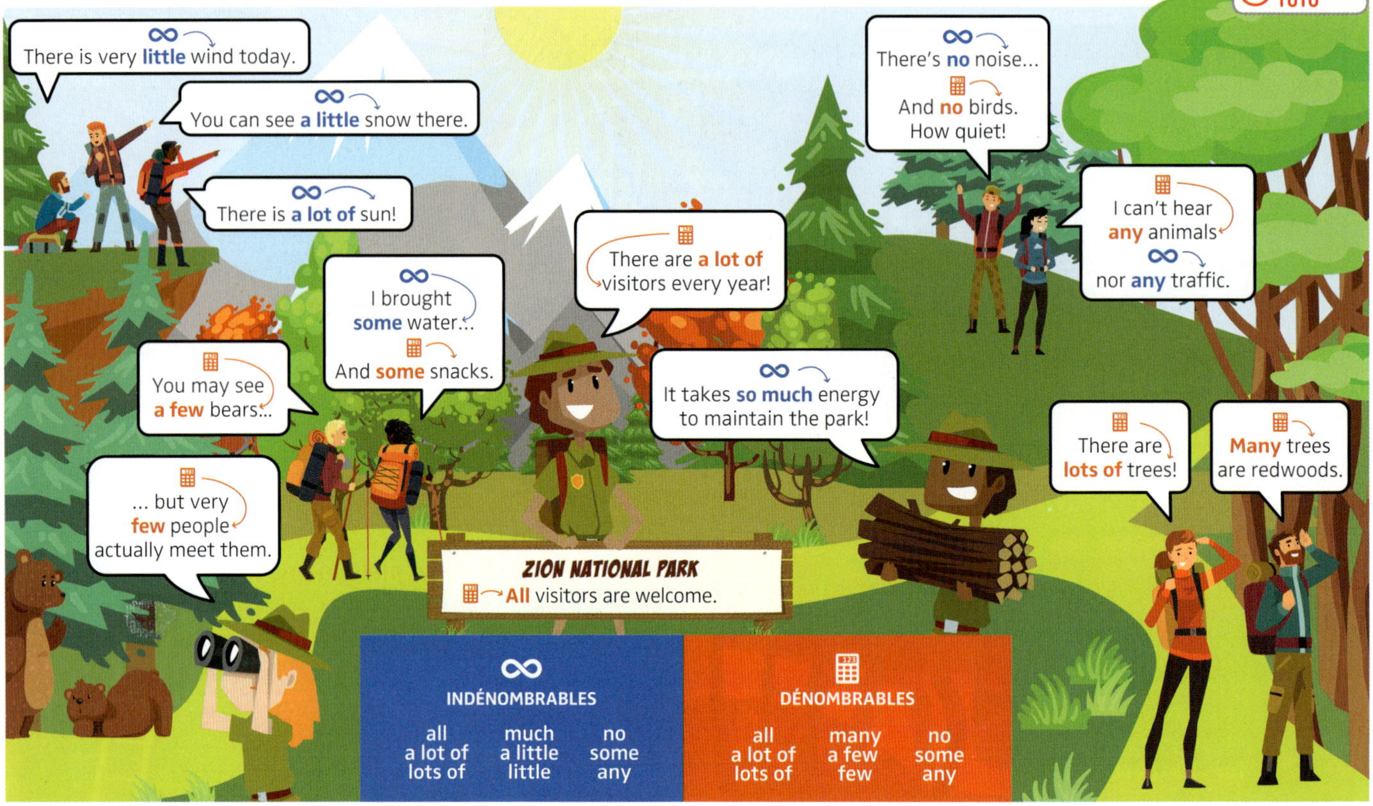

1 Complète les phrases avec un quantifieur. Plusieurs réponses sont parfois possibles. Justifie ton choix.

many – ~~a lot of~~ – little – all – a few – ~~lots of~~ – few – ~~no~~

a. I work in a very busy start-up, I have ... work to do, and ... time to do it!

b. Californian beaches are quiet in the winter because there aren't ... people and only ... tourists.

c. ... stars live in Los Angeles but ... people have seen them.

d. When you work in a start-up, you work ... the time and you have ... holiday, or only ... days.

2 Traduis ces phrases en faisant particulièrement attention aux quantifieurs.

a. Beaucoup de gens ont entendu parler de la Silicon Valley, mais peu de gens la visitent.

b. Quelques ours vivent dans ce parc national.

c. J'ai trouvé peu d'informations sur la faune et la flore de la Californie.

d. J'ai passé quelques jours en Californie et j'y ai rencontré beaucoup de Français, mais aucun Américain !

3 Décris cette image en utilisant des quantifieurs. Tu peux utiliser ces mots :

wind – beach – seagull – sun – swim – people – sand

4 Raconte ton quotidien de jeune acteur à Hollywood. Parle du nombre d'auditions, du temps à passer en répétitions, etc. N'oublie pas d'utiliser des quantifieurs !

More in *Pump it up!* p. 14

Vocabulary — California jobs

live! MP3 · live! LEXIQUIZ

Nature

Places
- beach
- campsite
- hostel
- national park
- nature park
- reservation

People
- ranger
- life guard
- host
- guide

Skills and qualities
- adaptable
- curious
- hospitable
- resilient

Hollywood

Places
- film location
- film set
- film studio
- neighbourhood (UK) / neighborhood (US)

People
- extra
- actor/ actress
- feature role
- film director
- camera operator

Skills
- acting
- artistic
- patient
- talented

Silicon Valley

Places
- headquarters
- office

People
- employee
- executive
- chief executive officer (CEO)
- graduate
- intern

Skills and qualities
- computer savvy
- creative
- organised
- scientific

1 Classe les mots suivants dans leur champ lexical et indique leur catégorie grammaticale. Un mot peut aller dans plusieurs catégories.

set – audition – reservation – headquarters – studio – corporate – executive – park – actor – C.E.O – lifeguard – ranger – start-up – employees – intern

Cinema | Business | Nature

2 Complète cette lettre de motivation.

Dear Sir or Madam,

I would like to ... for the job of ... in Lake Tahoe Nature Park. I think I have the right ... for the job.

I am very ... : I can face challenges and difficulties.

Also, I like contact with people and I am said to be very ... .

I also like to discover and learn new things, so I can easily ... to new situations.

Spelling — L'écriture des nombres

live! MP3

Attention ! Même s'il y a une certaine logique et régularité dans l'orthographe des nombres, il y a quelques petits pièges.

1 Écris ces paires de nombres en lettres. Que remarques-tu pour chacune d'elles ?

14 / 40   15 / 50   16 / 60

2 Écris maintenant ces nombres en toutes lettres.

3,000,000 people   358,970 readers
1,678 visitors   12.8% growth

Comment sont indiqués les milliers ? Les décimales ? Que remarques-tu par rapport au français ?

FINAL TASK

Write a cover letter to apply for a summer job in California.

You are looking for a summer job in California and you see this ad. You find it very interesting and you want to apply. Write the cover letter.

1. **Read** the job ad and **identify** the job, the missions and the skills needed.
2. **List** your skills and your experiences, and **say** why you are interested.
3. **Write** your cover letter. Do not forget about presentation.

TALENT AND CELEBRITY EVENTS INTERN

Nickelodeon's ***Talent and Celebrity Events*** is a Talent Show for Kids.

JOB LOCATION : Anaheim, LA, California *Salary $490/week*

The Talent and Celebrity Events intern will work with both the Talent Relations Team and Events/Celebrity Outreach Team. The intern will assist the team in researching new talents that may be booked for shows for the Nickelodeon channel. This intern will help the team prepare the set for talent shoots and will look after the young talents. He/she will assist the casting manager during the auditions.

The intern must be familiar with Talent Shows and feel comfortable with kids and teenagers. He/she must be very patient, have good organizational and relational skills and be prepared to work long hours.

YES YOU CAN! Write a convincing cover letter

1 SALUTATIONS

Utilise une formule de politesse adaptée.

Dear Mr Fox / Dear Sir or Madam / Dear Mrs...

2 INTRODUCTION

Présente-toi et dis à quel poste tu postules.

As a student in...
I'm looking for an opportunity to...
I would like to apply for...

3 MOTIVATIONS

Exprime tes motivations en fonction de tes compétences et de ce que tu aimes faire.

I am eager to...
I like / love / enjoy...

4 JUSTIFICATION

Explique pourquoi tu as choisi de postuler auprès de cette organisation.

Your organization is indeed a unique place...

5 COMPETENCES

Liste tes compétences et donne des exemples.

I have great organizational skills..
I can... I am able to...
I study...

6 CONCLUSION

Sois convaincant et utilise une formule de politesse adéquate.

I really think we should meet.
Do not hesitate to contact me
Sincerely
(signature)

Dear Mr. Fox,

As an engaged, curious student with great organizational skills and work capacities, I am eager to explore volunteer opportunities at the Aquarium of the Bay.

I study the diversity of marine microbial communities at the University of Washington, and I'm looking for an opportunity to continue my research in one of the greatest environments our country has to offer. The Aquarium of the Bay is indeed a unique place for anyone passionate about marine wildlife and offers some of the most beautiful world species.

I am ready to meet any of your program's needs and requirements. With my experience and enthusiasm, I am confident that I could ...e valuable contribution to the Aquari... ...hank you for your considerat...

...y,

...man

STRATEGIES Développer une idée à l'écrit P. 219

AUTO-ÉVALUATION
WB → p. 31

Compréhension de l'oral

Comprendre une présentation vidéo

live! VIDÉO

Welcome to the start-up

A2 **1. Say** where the host and her guest Luba are (country, state, city, and company).

2. Explain what the host wants to teach people about in her video.

A2+ **3.** What do you learn about the person interviewed (nationality, studies)?

B1 **4. Explain** how Luba was recruited by that company.

Compréhension de l'écrit

Comprendre un témoignage professionnel

MY FAILED ACTING CAREER – AND WHY IT WASN'T A FAILURE AT ALL

My first "performance" was at Yosemite National Park. My sister and I were around nine and 10 years old. We're from Southern California.

The role required that I fall to the ground like a tree that suddenly died. When it was my turn I flailed[1] my arms wildly as if I had been brutally killed. The entire audience laughed.

I was hooked: the thrill, the laughter, the freedom of expression. Acting had me completely—for about 10 years. Besides classes in college, I trained for years at the best acting studios in L.A.

In my 20s I had acting roles in independent films, local theater plays.

My friends on the other hand had more stable careers—ad executive, teacher, lawyer, etc. And they were starting families of their own. But I wasn't concerned. I had the kind of satisfaction that comes with pursuing your dream. I believed that it was just a matter of time before I would get my big break. I didn't like what I was focusing on, but I couldn't stop.

As an actor, you never know when that big opportunity could happen. It's easy to say just one more audition, just one more pilot season, just one more... I was tired of putting my heart and soul[2] on the line. I decided it was time to move on.

Adapted from Roxie SARHANGI, *Huffington Post*, 2013

A2 **1. Say** what job Roxie is speaking about. Is it still her job today?

2. Say when and where she discovered that job.

B1 **3. Explain** why Roxie decided to do this job.

4. Why did she like it?

5. Why was Roxie's life different from her friends'?

B1+ **6.** What decision did she finally make? **Explain** why.

1. *agiter*
2. *âme*

3 A portrait of Nadya Kwandibens

Nadya Kwandibens is Anishinaabe[1] (Ojibwe[2]) from the Animakee Wa Zhing #37 First Nation in northwestern Ontario. She is a self-taught portrait and events photographer and has travelled extensively across Canada for over 10 years.

Vision Statement[3]

We, as Indigenous people, are often portrayed in history books as Nations once great; in museums as Nations frozen stoic; in the media as Nations forever troubled. These images can be despairing; however, my goal seeks to steer[4] *the positive course. If our history is a shadow, let this moment serve as light. We are musicians, lawyers, doctors, mothers and sons. We are activists, scholars, dreamers, fathers and daughters. Let us claim ourselves now and see that we are, and will always be great, thriving*[5]*, balanced civilizations capable of carrying ourselves into that bright new day.*

www.redworks.ca

1. /ænɪʃə'nɑbeɪ/ **2.** /əʊ'dʒɪbweɪː/ **3.** declaration **4.** direct **5.** prosperous

a. Look at the picture of Nadya Kwandibens and **give your impressions** on the artist.

b. Read the article. **Say** how her vision statement relates to her portrait.

c. Explain what Nadya Kwandibens wants to change with photography.

STEP 3 WB → p. 69

Record a presentation of Nadya Kwandibens's experience and project as a photographer.

BOOST YOUR SKILLS!

Parler de ses impressions

- *Nadya Kwandibens* ***looks like****...*
- *She* ***seems / looks****...*
- *She* ***looks as if****...*
- *It* ***gives the impression that****...*

4 "Concrete Indians"

Doc 1

▲ By Nadya Kwandibens, from the series "Concrete Indians", *www.redworks.ca*

Doc 2

▲ By Nadya Kwandibens, from the series "Concrete Indians", *www.redworks.ca*

BOOST YOUR SKILLS!

Comparer et contraster

- *The Native's outfit* ***contrasts with****...*
- *Cars are moving* ***whereas / while*** *the Native woman...*
- ***Although / Though*** *cars are moving, the woman...*
- *The Native character's position* ***is similar to****...*
- *The Native character has* ***the same*** *position* ***as****...*

WORDS

- bear skin
- concrete /'kɒŋkriːt/: *béton*
- crane /kreɪn/: *grue*
- decolonisation /diːkɒlənaɪ'zeɪʃən/
- roots: *racines*
- traffic
- weapon /'wepən/: *arme*

- resilient = strong
- startling = surprising
- traditional
- vibrant /'vaɪbrənt/ (colours) = bright and strong

- empower /ɪm'paʊər/
- push to the forefront
- reclaim = take back

Focus on Doc 1 or 2.

In pairs, each of you **chooses** one of the photographs.

a. Describe what you can see.

b. Pick out elements of contrast between the cityscape and the Native character.

c. Comment on the title of the series "Concrete Indians".

STEP 4 WB → p. 69

Each of you **records** a presentation of one of these two photographs. **Share** your recording with your partner.

FINAL STEP

Now has come the time to **put** all your tracks **together**. Then, **share** your audio guide with the class and give them an audio tour of your exhibition showcasing First Nations photography.

You've completed your mission. Well done!

EXPLORE

1. Bringing people together?

1

How access to more movies and TV shows might improve relationships

When Julie Spira first started seeing her athlete boyfriend, he was confined to bed following a knee replacement, and they were saved by *Breaking Bad*. Spira had never seen the hit series, but her boyfriend was hooked[1]. Given there wasn't much the pair could do together while he spent weeks convalescing, they did what many modern couples do: they binge-watched.

"Some days we'd watch five episodes. It became part of his recovery[2]," Spira said. "We created a new memory together. We still talk about the time we spent watching that show while he was recovering."

Spira isn't alone. A new survey from media company Xfinity found that 66 percent of couples said that they felt watching TV together strengthened their relationship. Just as past generations attended dances or stuck to the old standby[3] of "dinner and a movie," younger couples like to connect over an endless supply of popular shows on services like Netflix.

Chandra JOHNSON, *www.deseretnews.com*, 2016

1. addicted
2. *guérison*
3. *en option*

a. Read the text and **explain** why Julie started watching *Breaking Bad*.
b. Find elements in the text to define the expression "*binge-watching*".
c. Explain how watching series may strengthen relationships.
d. Give your opinion about this couple's story. Do you agree that young people like to connect over series?

AT HOME Go online to *lyceen.nathan.fr/shine-bright2* and watch the video "How Netflix changed TV" to learn more about the origins of Netflix. Share your findings with the class.

2 All for *Star Trek*

WORDS

- convention = congress
- fandom = community of fans
- loneliness, isolation: *isolement*
- tiredness

- (be) alone, (feel) lonely, isolated
- excited / passionate about
- fascinated by / obsessed with / hooked on / addicted to
- tired < exhausted

- can't help + V-ing: *ne pas pouvoir s'empêcher de*
- gather = bring together
- stay on one's own
- waste one's life

a. Look at the photograph and **guess** on what special occasion these people have gathered.
b. Watch the video and **check** your hypotheses. **Pick out** the reasons for this meeting.
c. PHONOLOGY **Listen** to the first sentence carefully and **count** the number of times you hear "*to*". What do you notice? Try to **explain** why.
d. Explain what the video shows about this fan community.

3

live! MP3

PARCOURS DIFFÉRENCIÉS WB → p. 32

Cameron never watched the television anymore. Everything that she wanted to watch was available to stream online on her laptop through sites such as Netflix or Hulu. She became accustomed to[1] watching different episodes on the vast collection of shows on the Netflix database. When she wasn't in the mood for *Orange is the New Black* or *Gossip Girl*, she would top it off with independent, cerebral movies that were recommended to her on Hulu. Cameron decided that the only way she could properly watch a television series nowadays was to binge on an entire season in one afternoon with a hot cup of tea and a jelly donut. Cameron was about to give herself a lazy afternoon in bed with her laptop, mug of Lipton tea, and Krispy Kreme Jelly donut special, sulking[2] in the sad fury of her current unemployed status when Mr de la Cruz called her from the living-room.

"Cameron, look."

Cameron's father was watching WABC[3], as he did every morning.

Kelly Ann GONZALES, *Video Games*, 2014

a. Look at the cartoon and **explain** why it exemplifies binge-watching.

b. Read the text and **explain** the first sentence.

c. Explain what Cameron likes about watching series.

d. Imagine what the consequences of Cameron's binge-watching may be.

1. *habituée à*
2. *bouder*
3. a TV channel

4

a. Identify the goal of the poster.

b. Observe the statistics and **explain** the drawbacks of binge-watching.

c. Do you find this document effective? Why or why not?

d. Imagine other ways binge-watching might impact your daily life.

YOUR TASK

DIFFÉRENCIATION

You take part in a survey about teens and TV series.

WAY 1 **Record** your answer: How often do you watch TV series? How does it impact your life?

WAY 2 **Record** your testimony: Do you binge-watch? What are the pros and cons of this way of watching TV series?

BOOST YOUR SKILLS!

Parler de ses habitudes

- *I **never** watch TV any more, I **always** use my laptop, I **sometimes** watch TV series with friends.*
- *I **am accustomed to** watch**ing** many episodes, I **am used to** watch**ing** series late at night.*
- *I watched a new episode at least **once a day**.*

PRÉCIS 20

EXPLORE

2. How far would you go?

1 GoT tourism

live! VIDÉO

2 The Chinese Friends

live! VIDÉO

BOOST YOUR SKILLS!

Justifier ses choix

- *I love this character* ***so much that*** *I decided to…*
- ***So*** *it has changed my life. /* ***It helped me*** *get through the hard times.*
- *I decided to travel to Ireland* ***because…***
- ***As you can see,*** Friends *is my life.*
- ***Not only*** *does it boost tourism* ***but*** *it creates jobs* ***too.***

Focus on Doc 1 or 2.

PARCOURS DIFFÉRENCIÉS

WB → p. 33

a. Look at the picture and **identify** the series these people are fans of.

b. Watch the video and **describe** what the fans do that proves how much they love this series.

c. Explain what pleasure and benefits the people draw from this experience.

YOUR TASK

DIFFÉRENCIATION

WAY 1 **Discuss** your next trip with your friend. Explain to him/her why you have decided to visit a place which is the shooting location of your favourite TV series.

WAY 2 You want to change your name to your favourite TV series character's. **Discuss** this choice with your parents or your friends.

3 British *Breaking Bad* fan gets Heisenberg arm tattoo in tribute[1]

This Brit is just mad about *Breaking Bad*. So mad, in fact, that he got the image of Walter White's criminal alter-ego Heisenberg tattooed across his entire arm. John Edgerton, from Stockport, central England, said he was "devastated" when the hit show finished last month—and wanted to pay tribute[1] to its "incredible" cast of characters. "It took over my life, I watched the first two seasons in three days," he told the *Daily News*. "It was constant, I was hooked on it and I was addicted. I watched the ending with my partner Danielle, and if she hadn't been there I'd have probably shed a tear[2]," he added. "It was like someone close to me had died."

dailynews.com, 2016

1. homage 2. cry

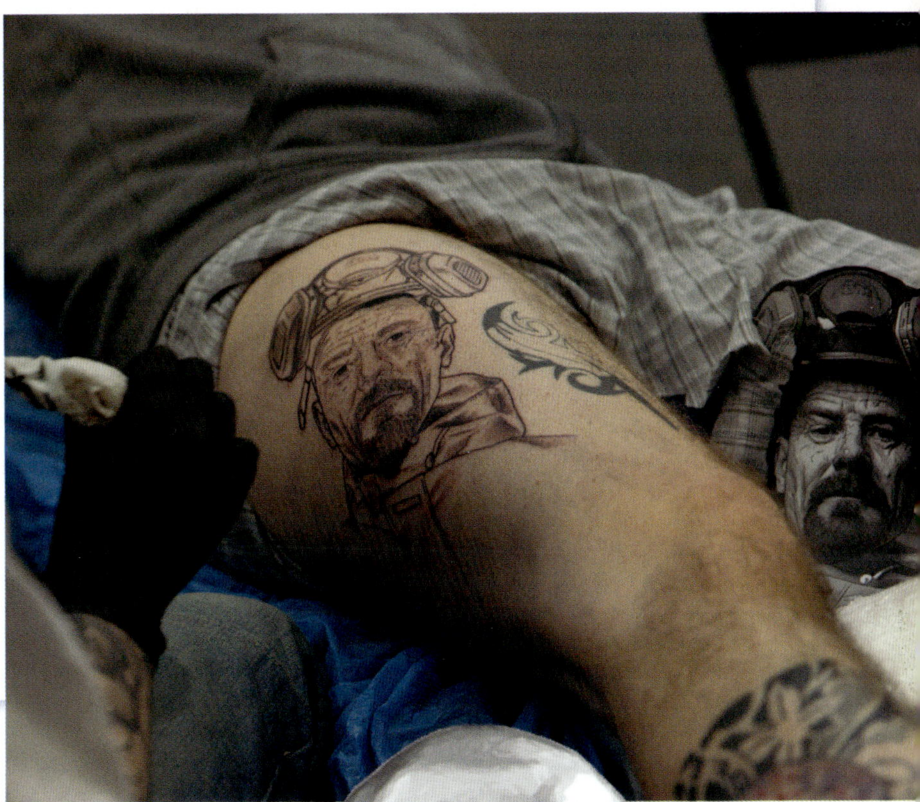

a. **Read** the text and **find** the reasons why John Edgerton had his arm tattooed.

b. **Pick out** elements that show how addicted he was.

c. **Give your opinion** about the way this fan *"pays tribute"* to the series (l.8).

d. VOCABULARY **Identify** the prepositions that go with these words: *mad – tattooed – hooked – close*. **Use** them all to **recap** the document orally.

YOUR TASK

As a series fan, you are interviewed by the *Los Angeles Daily News*. In pairs, **act out** the interview.
State your point of view: How far would *you* go?

WORDS

- freak: *fana*
- icon /'aɪkɒn/
- idol /'aɪdəl/

- excessive = disproportionate
- fictional ≠ real
- unstoppable

- idolise > admire /əd'maɪər/
- blur the lines: *brouiller les frontières*
- dress up as
- experience
- identify with
- imitate
- pay tribute to

3. Beyond the screen

1

PARCOURS DIFFÉRENCIÉS WB → p. 34

The Good Doctor is not the next *Grey's Anatomy*. It's so much better.

The show centers around Dr. Shaun Murphy, an autistic young doctor with savant syndrome. Expertly played by Freddie Highmore, Dr. Murphy is a brilliant physician with an incredible gift to see the hidden detail in every image, the teeny blip of sound in every heartbeat. On paper, any hospital would fight to have him on their surgical team.

But for one thing. That pesky[1] autism diagnosis.

themighty.com, 2018

DAVID SHORE, PRODUCER

"I'm surprised and heartened by its success. This is a character networks would have been afraid to put on the air not that long ago. They would have thought that viewers couldn't empathize with him."

VIEWER

"The show's writers manage to capture key characteristics true of so many with autism. They are often misunderstood and left aside because of their perceived lack of emotion, their poor social skills, and highly concrete way of thinking."

FREDDIE HIGHMORE, MAIN ACTOR

"What we are trying to do is moving away from perhaps the stereotypical versions of people with autism that have been shown on television and in certain movies in the past. The number one misconception about autistic people in previous depictions is that they are somehow devoid of[2] emotion – and of course, that's complete nonsense."

1. annoying 2. without

AT HOME Find another series which deals with a social issue.

WORDS

- dis**ea**se
- p**ur**pose = goal

- **ac**curate = precise
- end**ea**ring
- open-m**i**nded

- true to life

- change one's mind
- conv**ey** a m**e**ssage
- portr**ay**
- raise aw**a**reness ab**ou**t = inf**or**m ab**ou**t

a. Read the article. **Explain** what the series is about and what makes Dr. Murphy exceptional.

b. Read the reviews and **comment** on the impact the series has had on spectators.

c. GRAMMAIRE **Say** what the modal "*could*" expresses in this sentence: "*viewers couldn't empathize with him.*" p. 124

d. Give your opinion: Do you think a good series is one that conveys a message? Why, or why not necessarily?

YOUR TASK

You have just watched a TV series that has made you change your mind about a topic. **Share** your feelings with your friends in posts on your favourite social network.

BOOST YOUR SKILLS!

Exprimer son ressenti et critiquer

- *I'm **surprised** and **heartened**.*
- *The show **captures the key characteristics of** ...*
- *It **manages to** move away from stereotypes.*

HOW TO PLAY "TV SERIES: WHERE IS WALDO"

Play in groups and be the fastest!

1. One student is the quizmaster and scorekeeper. He/she reads one definition.
2. You are the fastest player to raise your hand: point out what part of the picture it corresponds to.
– You are right: you win one point.
– You can also give the corresponding word or expression: you win an additional point.
3. Continue with the next definitions.

The winner is the one with the most points.

GAME ON!

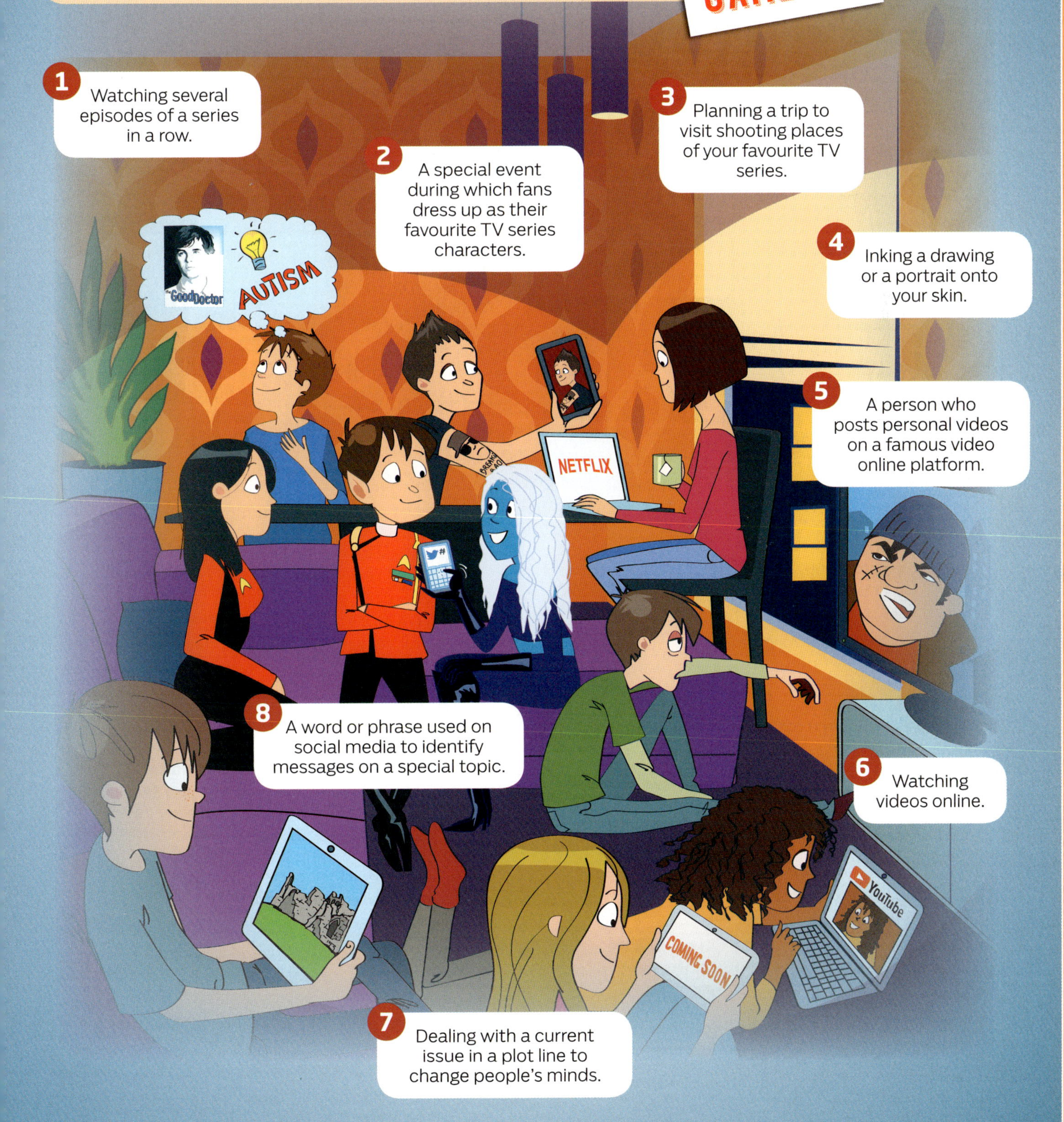

1 Watching several episodes of a series in a row.

2 A special event during which fans dress up as their favourite TV series characters.

3 Planning a trip to visit shooting places of your favourite TV series.

4 Inking a drawing or a portrait onto your skin.

5 A person who posts personal videos on a famous video online platform.

6 Watching videos online.

7 Dealing with a current issue in a plot line to change people's minds.

8 A word or phrase used on social media to identify messages on a special topic.

BOOST YOUR ENGLISH!

PRÉCIS 20 21 ET EXERCICES

Grammar — Exprimer la possibilité, la capacité, l'obligation et l'interdiction

must, may, could, can = modaux — **be forbidden to, be able to, have to** = forme verbale

Nathan live! GRAMMAR TUTO

Recap

MODALITÉ	PASSÉ	PRÉSENT
Obligation	**had to:** Yesterday **I had** to stop watching my favourite series to do my homework.	**must**
Possibilité	**be allowed to:** When I was a kid, I **was allowed to** binge-watch my favourite series!	**may**
Capacité	**be able to:** Last year, I **was able to** watch a GoT season in one sitting; now, I can't, because I'm done with this series.	**can**
Interdiction	**be forbidden to:** Teenagers under 15 **were forbidden to** attend the gathering.	**mustn't**

1 Indique ce que chaque phrase exprime :
possibilité – capacité – obligation – interdiction

a. You have to resist binge-watching.
b. This new series may change my habits.
c. People can identify with the characters.
d. I mustn't miss the next episode.

2 Finis les phrases en exprimant ce qui est précisé entre parenthèses, au présent, puis au passé.

a. (*obligation*) Any GoT fan...
b. (*interdiction*) At school, I...
c. (*possibilité*) After watching the pilot of this new series, I think I...
d. (*capacité*) Josh is so addicted! He...

3 Tu es journaliste pour un magazine médical. Rédige un article sur le comportement à adopter face aux séries télé pour profiter des séries et éviter l'addiction.
Exprime les notions de possibilité, de capacité, d'obligation et d'interdiction et utilise le lexique du chapitre.

4 Traduis les phrases suivantes.

a. Tu dois absolument aller à la convention de *Star Trek*.
b. J'avais le droit de passer des heures à regarder des séries, mais je devais aussi faire mes devoirs.
c. Mes parents disent que je peux être un fan d'un personnage de série, mais je n'ai pas le droit de me le faire tatouer !
d. Tu n'as pas le droit de me raconter la fin car je dois regarder le dernier épisode ce soir avec John.

More in *Pump it up!* p. 38-41

Vocabulary — American series

Beyond series

From emotion to addiction
- addicted to
- glued to the screen
- hooked on
- obsessed = mad about
- be fully into (a show)
- binge-watch

From fiction to reality
- cosplay = the practice of dressing up as a character
- fictional = virtual
- attend an event = participate in
- ink = tattoo
- pay tribute to = honour
- raise awareness

The world of TV shows

Professionals
- cast: actors and actresses
- director
- lead role = main role
- screenwriter

Story
- cliffhanger = ending with suspense
- pilot /'paɪlət/ = test episode
- plot = story
- setting
- teaser
- spoil = reveal the end

Types of shows
- comedy
- crime
- drama
- fantasy
- sitcom
- teen show
- committed: *engagé*
- frightening
- funny < hilarious
- heartbreaking

Watching habits

Technical aspects
- laptop
- network
- screen
- download
- search
- stream = watch online

Social aspects
- geek
- alone ≠ with family or friends
- bond with, connect with
- share with
- strengthen /'strɛŋθən/ relationships

Reception
- audience
- critic
- enthusiastic about
- fascinated by
- rate
- recommend
- review
- share

1 **Classe les séries ci-dessous de celle que ces personnes aiment le moins à celle qu'elles aiment le plus.**

a. They are getting addicted to *Game of Thrones*.
b. They are quite enthusiastic about *Riverdale*.
c. They really enjoy watching *Stranger Things*.
d. They can't get into *Modern Family* at all.
e. They are completely hooked on *Supergirl*.

2 **Retrouve les mots auxquels correspondent ces définitions.**

a. ...: reveal the end of an episode.
b. ...: watch online.
c. ...: an ending which creates suspense.
d. ...: the initial story of a series.
e. ...: someone who is ready to do anything for his/her online hobbies.

Phonology — La prononciation de la graphie <ea>

More in *Pump it up!* p. 76-77

La graphie <ea> peut se prononcer de différentes manières.

/ɪə/ ear	/ɜː/ early	/e/ breakfast	/iː/ peach	/eə/ pear	/eɪ/ steak	/ɑː/ heart

1 **Écoute ces mots et classe-les en fonction de leur prononciation.**

stream – heartbreaking – season – deaf – real – wear – teaser – search

2 **Vérifie tes choix en écoutant les mots et entraîne-toi à les prononcer.**

FINAL TASK

Post a video on your YouTube channel to talk about your life as a series fan.

You own a YouTube channel where you like posting videos about your passion: series. Tell your viewers how they influence your life and what you do as a fan.

1. **Choose** a few series and related elements (convention, online discussion group, places to visit, etc.) you would like to talk about.
2. **Organise** your ideas. Don't forget to:
   – **introduce** yourself,
   – **express** your enthusiasm about your favourite series (quality of the plot and the cast, specific nature of the setting, message of the series),
   – **talk about** your habits as a series fan and the impact being a fan has on your social life.
3. **Record** your video. Make sure you connect with your followers and encourage new viewers to subscribe by making it lively and attractive!

YES YOU CAN! Record a video about yourself as a fan

1 INTRODUCTION

Salue ta communauté et présente le sujet de ta nouvelle vidéo.

Hey guys, what's up? It's Momo! I really like TV so let's talk about my favourite TV shows.

TON

Sois expressif/expressive pour donner envie qu'on t'écoute et qu'on partage ton enthousiasme.

It is a beautiful show; the way it is filmed is just gorgeous.

2 CONTENU

Raconte des anecdotes personnelles pour rendre ton propos vivant.

I like TV so much that I'm always on the hunt for new TV shows to binge.

ORIGINALITÉ

Sois créatif/créative et pense à ajouter des titres, des images, des accessoires (ticket, costume, etc.) lorsque tu filmes.

3 CONCLUSION ET REMERCIEMENTS

Remercie tes fans de leur attention et salue-les.

Thank you guys for watching and I will see you soon for a new video. Bye!

STRATEGIES Faire une présentation orale p. 215

AUTO-ÉVALUATION
WB → p. 35

Compréhension de l'oral

Comprendre une vidéo humoristique

Binge-watching

live! VIDÉO

A2 **1. Watch** the video and **find** information about the speaker (name, age, type of addiction).

2. Explain in what ways his behaviour is addictive. **Give** precise examples.

B1 **3.** How does his addiction affect his life?

B1+ **4.** What is his vision of his addiction? How does it contrast with other people's opinion about it?

5. How would you describe the tone of the document? **Justify.**

Compréhension de l'écrit

Comprendre un article de presse en ligne

Don't watch *Game of Thrones*? Mondays at the office can get pretty annoying

Caroline Malaby works in Reston, Virginia, for an IT company. Many of her co-workers are die-hard[1] Redskins[2] fans and often talk about the team at the office. But that doesn't bother Malaby – she follows the Redskins herself. What she can't stand is the nonstop chatter about a certain fantasy show.

"Every Monday morning they come in and they're like, 'Oh my God, did you see whatever?' 'She's come back.' 'I can't believe he died,'" Malaby says. "I just smile and nod."

Game of Thrones has become the office obsession. Some of her colleagues watch the show when it airs Sunday night and again Monday, to make sure they haven't missed any plot points. During slow meetings, they send emails scheduling watch parties. Some of Malaby's officemates even go to the *Game of Thrones*-themed pop-up bar in Shaw after work. She never goes with them. She has a friend of a friend who once called in sick to catch up on the show.

"I think I watched the opening credits and I saw a dragon and I was like, 'Nope,'" she says.

One advantage the non-watchers might have: more time to get work done.

Adapted from Maia SILBER, *washingtonpost.com*, 2017

A2 **1. Find** information about Caroline Malaby (job, city, interests).

2. Guess what she thinks of *Game of Thrones*.

3. How important is the show to her colleagues?

B1 **4.** How does Caroline feel on Monday morning at work? Why?

B1+ **5. Explain** how the show affects the workplace.

1. very enthusiastic
2. the Washington D.C. football team

2. South Africa's team spirit

1 One victory, one people, one destiny

Nathan live! VIDÉO

▲ Nelson Mandela and Francois Pieenar (captain of the national team) at the Rugby World Cup in 1995

PARCOURS DIFFÉRENCIÉS WB → p. 37

a. Look at the photo and **read** the Culture Spot. **Imagine** the atmosphere in the stadium that day.

b. Listen to Mandela's speech. What does this event represent for him?

c. VOCABULARY **Pick out** words and phrases used by Mandela to express gratitude, pride, and unity.

d. Listen to Francois Pieenar: How did Mandela show his support to the team and how did the spectators react?

CULTURE SPOT

Nelson Mandela (1918-2013) became the first democratically elected president of South Africa in 1994. He put an end to 46 years of **apartheid**, a political regime of white supremacy and racial segregation.

2 Mandela: South Africa's debt to the great South African

Sir Ian McGeechan, former coach of the Scottish rugby team. *The Telegraph*, 2013

The former South Africa president used the game to mend wounds[1] and unite a once-torn[2] country

Nelson Mandela's part in South Africa's Rugby World Cup victory in 1995 was far-ranging[3] and will never be forgotten.

That photograph of him wearing a Springbok No 6 jersey and baseball cap while presenting South African captain Francois Pienaar with the golden trophy is an image that stretched beyond rugby.

The Springbok badge was an emblem of the previous division in the country and of the white supremacy, but Mandela realized that he had to make that Springbok jersey part of the new South Africa.

He knew how important it was to the white South Africans. And so he united the nation in its support of the rugby team. Subsequently, it has had incredible support from all South Africans.

You can talk about sport affecting politics and vice-versa, but what he did on that day was stunning[4]. I think if there was one single action that said a country was different, that this man was special, it was that. To me that was the power of sport at its best. [...]

He changed South Africa, and he used rugby to help that change.

1. *guérir les blessures*
2. that used to be divided
3. very important
4. amazing

a. Read and **find** what symbol Mandela used to reconcile white and black people in the country.

b. Explain the reasons for his choice, and **say** what it represented in 1995.

c. GRAMMAR *"He knew **how important it was** to the white South Africans"*: Does *"how"* introduce an indirect question or an indirect exclamation? **Translate** into French.

d. Explain why the author says *"this man was special"* (l.16).

3 Standing together with the Springboks

Source of the quotes: SuperSport, 2018

a. Listen to and **read** the players' answers to the journalist's question. **Match** the tags with the idea expressed by each player:

NATIONAL SOLIDARITY · TEAM SPIRIT · NATIONAL RECONCILIATION · CULTURAL HERITAGE

b. VOCABULARY **Find** two expressions used to insist on the fact that differences are not important in sport.

c. Explain what rugby represents for these players.

YOUR TASK

Write a "thank you" message to your favourite national sport's team for winning the world championship.

BOOST YOUR SKILLS!

Insister sur l'importance de quelque chose

- *He knew* ***how important it was...*** .
- ***If there was one single action*** [...], *it was that.*
- *You have done us* ***exceedingly*** *proud.*

WORDS

- pride: *fierté*
- solid**a**rity
- tr**o**phy = cup
- vi**c**tory
- proud /praʊd/
- vict**o**rious
- feel proud / h**o**noured
- link up = join tog**e**ther
- r**e**concile
- stand for = repres**e**nt = s**y**mbolise
- stand up for = fight for
- un**i**te /juːˈnaɪt/

EXPLORE

3. Go Nigeria, go girls!

1

WB → p. 38

Nigerian sportswomen represent all Nigerian women

In Nigeria, almost 50% of women will be married before their 18th birthday. Women have less access to education than men (41% are literate, while 61% of men are). However, a greater proportion of Nigeria's sporting success is attributable to women, in terms of both impact and results. In spite of this, there has been an almost systematic neglect of women in sport in Nigeria.

After all the media interviews, it was time for the three women of the Nigerian bobsled team to get on the ice at the Pyeongchang Olympic Games. At first, it did not go so well, as their first trial runs left them in last place. But then, they have attracted interest less because of their medal chances and more for their aim to break barriers and "to help women, the country, the continent," as the team's captain and driver, Seun Adigun, put it.

Despite being all born in the United States, the Nigerian bobsled team have sought[1] to ensure their message resonates in the country and continent they represent.

"Having young girls and women in general be able to see us on the screen and know that we have done this and it's doable" is extremely important, teammember Ngozi Onwumere said. She said she hoped that girls born and raised in the homeland of her parents would realize that even if they come from a country without snow or ice, they could still learn to compete in a winter sport. "This is something that will help the sport, something that will help women, the country, the continent," she said, "and those things do keep me grounded[2] and able to handle[3] it."

Adapted from *www.nytimes.com*, 2018

1. try 2. *les pieds sur terre* 3. deal with

MacDolly @ macdolly

Congratulations to @NGSuper_Falcons for winning the @AWCON2018 Cup. This is a commendable achievement for the country. 🇳🇬 You have done great by sparing no effort in winning this tournament. Words of thanks are not enough to express our appreciation to each of you.

8:21 PM – Dec 1, 2018

a. Read the introduction and **comment** on the place of women in Nigeria.

b. Read the first paragraph of the article and **sum** it **up**.

c. Read the rest of the article. **Explain** why these women's goal goes beyond sport.

d. GRAMMAR **Explain** the role of "do" in the last sentence (l.30). PRÉCIS 26

e. Read the tweet and **discuss** the importance of this victory in football for Nigerian women.

YOUR TASK

As a Nigerian woman, **write** a short post on your blog to say how much these athletes inspire you.

WORDS

- balance: *équilibre*
- gender equality
- purpose = goal
- inspiring
- under represented ≠ over represented
- feel like doing something: *avoir envie de faire qqch*
- raise awareness about = inform about
- reach (equality): *atteindre (l'égalité)*
- struggle = fight

BOOST YOUR SKILLS!

Exprimer des bénéfices

- ***The aim is to*** *help women...*
- *This is* ***something that will help*** *the sport and the country.*
- *This could be* ***a commendable achievement****.*
- ***This message resonates*** *in the country they represent.*

HOW TO PLAY "SPRINTER OR LONG DISTANCE RUNNER"

TEST YOUR CULTURE

Play in groups.

Each of you will run both races. Time how long it takes you to answer all the questions in each challenge.

1. Discover who wins each race in your group.

2. Then compare your rankings with the rest of the group and find out if you are a better long-distance runner or a better sprinter!

GAME ON!

GET READY TO RUN FAST. BOOST YOUR SPRINTING SKILLS!

READY? At home: Revise your lesson.
STEADY? In class: Have your book ready to help yourself.

GO!

1. What activity helped change Joel Kioko's life?
2. What is the name of South Africa's rugby team?
3. Which country do most marathon winners originate from?
4. Which continent has never hosted the Olympic Games so far?
5. What did Faith Kipyegon win on top of her gold medal?
6. Who are the Super Falcons?
7. Who is Francois Pieenaar?
8. What aims at "bringing the benefits of running back to the home of champions"?
9. Give one example of a gender gap in African sports, and one example of gender equality.
10. Imagine why Nelson Mandela is sometimes called "the 16th man of the 1995 match".

GET READY TO RUN A MARATHON. BOOST YOUR ENDURANCE!

READY? Get access to the internet.
STEADY? Find an online dictionary for help.

GO!

11. Which team did the Springboks defeat in the final of the 1995 World Cup?
12. What was the final ranking of the Nigerian bobsled team in PyeongChang?
13. Name the first ever skier to represent Kenya at the Winter Olympics.
14. Wayde Van Nierker is a record-breaking South-African athlete. Which record does he hold? (distance + time)
15. What is a "Springbok", apart from a rugbyplayer?
16. Africa has never hosted the Olympic Games. But which African city was once candidate?
17. Which Kenyan city is nicknamed "the home of champions"?
18. Which sport are Nigerian Paralympic athletes particularly good at?
19. Find two reasons why Kenya is such a good country for runners.
20. Imagine why 2007 was another landmark for South African rugby.

BOOST YOUR ENGLISH!

Grammar — Exprimer le but et la cause

PRÉCIS 35 ET EXERCICES

Nathan live! GRAMMAR TUTO

CAUSE

They couldn't run the race **because** of the power cut.
+ GN

She never gave up **because** she wanted to win!
+ proposition

BUT

She trained hard { **in order to** / **so as to** } take part in the Olympics.
+ BV

She won a gold medal **so that** she could prove women can be champions too.
+ proposition

1 Complète les phrases avec le mot de liaison qui convient selon le sens et la construction de la phrase.

so (that) – because of – in order to – because

a. He wanted to win the race ... represent his country.
b. Her parents supported her ... they knew she would win a gold medal one day.
c. They thought he would never win ... his poor performance.
d. He decided to train a lot ... he could give his best.

2 Finis ces phrases.

a. He wanted to try and run a marathon because...
b. He looked up to a role model so as to...
c. She will never give up because of...
d. Mandela used rugby so that...

3 Rédige des phrases à partir des idées suivantes. Exprime la cause et le but pour chacune.

African children run a lot

It was important for Mandela to unite the country

Many Africans do sports

4 Traduis ces phrases. Attention aux mots soulignés.

a. Les supporters encouragent les joueurs <u>afin qu'</u>ils gagnent le match.
b. Elle était fière sur le podium <u>car</u> elle avait battu un record.
c. Il voulait faire partie de l'équipe <u>pour</u> réaliser un rêve.
d. Il a décidé de quitter son quartier <u>à cause de</u> ses conditions de vie et <u>afin de</u> réussir.

More in ***Pump it up!*** p. 52

Spelling — Les noms et adjectifs de nationalité

- Les **noms et adjectifs de nationalité** prennent toujours une majuscule : *a **K**enyan athlete – a **N**igerian team – a **S**outh **A**frican*
- Les noms se terminant par ***-ese***, ***-ish***, ***-iss*** ou ***-ch*** ne prennent pas de ***-s*** au pluriel : *the British, the Chinese,* mais *the Nigerian**s*** et *the Kenyan**s***.

1 Forme les noms des pays africains suivants en utilisant les terminaisons *-(l)ese*, *-n* ou *-i*. Ajoute un *-s* quand il le faut.

Ex. : *South Africa* → *the South African**s***

Senegal – Ethiopia – Somalia – Togo – Tanzania – Gabon

2 Trouve le pays du continent africain associé à ces adjectifs.

Malawian – Nigerien – Moroccan – Mozambican – Angolan

Vocabulary — Running for Africa

live! MP3 · live! LEXIQUIZ

Atmosphere
- crowd /kraʊd/
- fans = supporters
- breathtaking
- outstanding
- cheer
- encourage
- hold one's breath
- support

Athletes
- competitor = contestant
- coach
- track and field athlete /'æθliːt/
- sportsman / sportswoman
- sprinter
- team
- training session
- practise = train

Pride
- fame
- recognition
- honoured
- proud
- advocate
- hold a flag
- stand for

Sportsmanship — Competition — Development

Places
- bleachers (US): *gradins*
- field
- grandstand: *tribunes*
- stadium = arena /ə'riːnə/
- studio
- track

Results
- medal / trophy
- podium
- world title
- record-breaking
- break a record
- qualify for
- rank
- set a record

Individual
- living conditions
- opportunity
- achieve /ə'tʃiːv/
- aspire /ə'spaɪə/ = hope for
- make one's dream come true

Social and economic aspects
- slums
- contribute to
- improve
- invest in
- promote

Togetherness
- solidarity
- shared
- be part of = belong
- bring together = unite
- reconcile

1 Retrouve les mots correspondant à ces définitions.

a. Piece of clothing covering dancers' legs.
b. Part of an urban area, usually overcrowded and inhabited by very poor people.
c. Possibility to do something.

2 Associe chaque mot de la liste a. avec un verbe de la liste b. pour créer quatre adjectifs. Puis emploie ces adjectifs pour parler de la victoire d'un coureur kenyan.

a. *record – life – breath – out – long*
b. *stand – last – break – take – change*

3 Retrouve les synonymes. Puis complète les phrases avec un des deux termes en le mettant à la bonne forme.

A. enhance	1. applaud
B. achieve	2. improve
C. promote	3. encourage
D. cheer	4. accomplish

a. ... ballet dancing in Nairobi may help children from the slums achieve new dreams.
b. The crowd kept ... them during the match.
c. These women ... something great for their country.
d. It will hopefully ... their image and living conditions.

Phonology — L'accentuation des adjectifs composés

live! MP3

Dans un adjectif composé, chacun des deux éléments a un accent tonique, mais l'accent d'un des deux mots est plus accentué.
Parfois, c'est le premier mot, parfois le second : *open-minded — breathtaking*

Écoute ces adjectifs composés.
record-breaking – close-run – life-changing – well-deserved

a. Quel est le mot le plus accentué, le premier ou le deuxième ?
b. Écoute à nouveau et repère la syllabe accentuée de chaque mot.
c. Répète en reproduisant l'intonation.

FINAL TASK

Write an article to promote an English-speaking African country's bid to host the Olympic Games.

You are a member of an African sports association. Write an article for a sports magazine to explain why your country should host the next Olympic Games.

1. **Choose one of the three countries** you have discovered in this unit.
2. **Collect your ideas, focusing on these issues:** economic development, social progress, national pride, and national unity.
3. **Write your article.** Don't forget to:
   – recall the exploits and achievements of your country,
   – explain what form of progress it would bring,
   – express the feeling of togetherness at stake,
   – present the benefits for the country chosen and for Africa.

YES YOU CAN! Write a convincing article

TITRE

Trouve un titre qui attire l'attention, sous forme de question par exemple.

Guess what country...? Could Nigeria be the next...?

INTRODUCTION

Commence par une anecdote ou un fait marquant pour capter l'attention du lecteur.

Kenya's Faith Kipyegon virtually jogged the opening stages before unleashing a devastating second half of the race...

POINT DE VUE

Introduis le sujet de ton article en donnant directement ton point de vue. N'hésite pas à utiliser la première personne.

That photograph of him wearing a Springbok No 6 jersey and baseball cap [...] is an image that stretched beyond rugby. [...] To me that was the power of sport at its best.

Mandela: South Africa's debt to the great South African

Sir Ian McGeechan, former coach of the UK rugby team. *The Telegraph*, 2013

The former South Africa president used the game to mend wound and unite a once-torn[2] country

Nelson Mandela's part in South Africa's Rugby World Cup victory in 19 was far-ranging[3] and will never be forgotten.
That photograph of him wearing a Springbok No 6 jersey and baseball ca while presenting South African captain Francois Pienaar with the golde trophy is an image that stretched beyond rugby.

The Springbok badge was an emblem of the previous division in the countr and of the white supremacy, but Mandela realized that he had to make th Springbok jersey part of the new South Africa.

CONCLUSION

Récapitule ton message principal en une phrase choc. Sois suffisamment enthousiaste pour emporter l'adhésion des lecteurs.

"The Olympic Games? Yes, we can!"

PREMIÈRE PARTIE

Explique l'une des raisons principales pour laquelle ce pays devrait accueillir les Jeux Olympiques (son esprit sportif, sa nature, ses installations, par exemple).

"Kenya is well known for its tradition of running... "
"In South Africa, we know how important..."

SECONDE PARTIE

Explique en quoi un événement sportif pourrait aider le pays et améliorer la vie des gens. N'hésite pas à fonder tes idées sur des citations vues dans l'unité ou trouvées dans tes recherches.

"This is something that will help the sport, something that will help women, the country, the continent."

STRATEGIES Développer une idée à l'écrit p. 219

AUTO-ÉVALUATION
WB → p. 39

TEST YOUR SKILLS

Compréhension de l'oral

Comprendre un reportage vidéo

Nathan live! VIDÉO

From Kenya to Korea

A2 **1. Watch** the video and **find** information about the men and their dream (origin, sport, competition).

B1 **2.** What makes this dream particularly unexpected?

3. Explain where they are and why. How do they react?

B1+ **4.** What is Alibaba? What is its role?

Compréhension de l'écrit

Comprendre un article de presse

Kenya's slumdog footballers play for pennies and pride

Henry Eshiboko considers himself privileged. The 20-year-old lives with his wife and child in a single, windowless, nine-square-metre room. The tin roof and walls are held firm by wooden beams so there are no leaks[1] when it rains, there is a power socket[2] and, a little way down the alley, a shared water tap.

"This is all thanks to football!" said the local club left-winger and resident of Kibera, a huge slum in the heart of the Kenyan capital Nairobi.

"With the 300 shillings (2.7 euros) I get for training, four times a week, I can feed my family and pay a part of the rent. And with the victory bonuses, we can buy clothes, kitchen stuff and a few extra things. Right now, my wife is at the hairdresser!" said Eshiboko, his face lighting up as it does whenever he speaks of football or family.

In Kibera, a labyrinth of uneven paths crisscrossed by rivers of sewage[3], Eshiboko's life is akin to luxury: 80 percent of the population does not have access to electricity, and many survive on less than a dollar a day.

"Some of our matches are even on television," said Eshiboko.

For the players, football is a way to defy destiny.

"It's not because we come from Kibera that we can't do anything, or that we cannot have ambitions," said Eshiboko.

"When people talk about Kibera, they generally talk about crime, drugs, poverty. We have our issues, we're not denying this, but with football, we prove that Kibera is more than that."

www.dailymail.co.uk

1. *fuite* 2. *prise électrique* 3. *eaux des égoûts*

A2 **1. Read** and **find** information about Henry Eshiboko (age, sport, city).

B1 **2. Describe** the living conditions of most people in Kibera.

3. Explain how Eshiboko's sport has helped him. **Give** concrete examples.

B1+ **4.** How can Henry Eshiboko's story benefit the entire area of Kibera?

3 Write your resume

Doc 1

a. Watch the video and **identify** what qualities and skills the hosts expect from WWOOFers.

b. VOCABULARY **Observe** how the word *"willing"* is formed and **identify** the noun it comes from. **Explain** what the word means.

c. Explain why the hosts are willing to hire WWOOFers.

What it takes to be a WWOOFer — Nathan live! VIDÉO

Doc 2

DAN SMITH

Student

I am a motivated 18-year-old student looking for volunteering experience on an organic farm

Contact

853 Frey Road, New York, NY
212 563 4665
dan.smith@gmail.com
www.dansmith.com

Skills

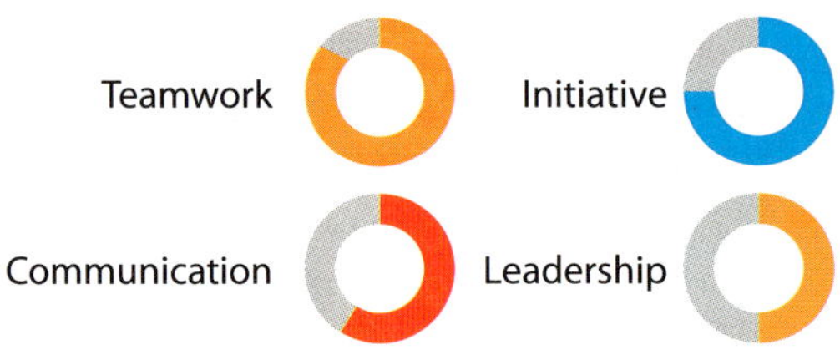

Languages

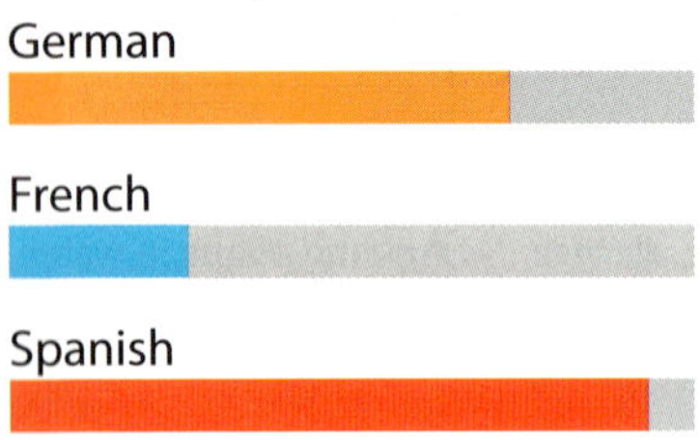

Work experience

2017 – 2019 Pet sitter (New York)
- Scheduling and attending[1] visits
- Walking and feeding dogs

2016 Work placement – Pet Medical Center (NY)
- Assisting with nail trims[2] and calming pets
- Cleaning the facility[3] to meet health standards
- Maintaining[4] the daily laundry

Software

Office, Excel, Word, PP

Hobbies and interests

Sports swimming (3 years), mountain biking
Various reading, guitar (5 years)

Online Info

/dsmith /dsmith

Education

2016-2019 East Bridge High School
- Major subjects: sciences and languages
- Class representative for 3 years
- Tutoring classmates

a. Look at the resume and **select** information about the applicant (country, situation, experience, skills).

b. After reading his resume, do you think Dan Smith would be a good WWOOFer or not? Why?

c. List the categories you found in this resume. **Think** of other categories you could add.

STEP 3

WB → p. 72

Write your own resume. **Practise** using information from your resume to show your future hosts that your profile corresponds to what they are looking for.

WORDS
- easy-going
- hardworking
- respectful
- self-willed /self'wɪld/

- be good at + V-ing
- be proficient in + V-ing
- excel in + V-ing

1. be present at
2. *manucure*
3. place, building
4. keep in good condition

4 Get the most from the WWOOFing experience

BOOST YOUR SKILLS!

Exprimer la permission dans le futur

- ***WWOOFing*** *will* ***enable*** *me to reconnect with nature.*
- ***It*** *will* ***allow*** *me to step out of my comfort zone.*

Enumérer des arguments

- ***First(ly)****, WWOOFing...*
- ***Second(ly)****, it will...*
- ***Third(ly) / Finally****, I will...*

a. **Watch** the video and **explain** what Wes Davies has learnt from his WWOOFing experience.

b. VOCABULARY **Rephrase** the following sentence: "*[WWOOFing is] showing your true colours.*" PRÉCIS 12

STEP 4 WB → p. 73

Explain what you hope to gain from a WWOOFing experience. **Note down** your arguments and **practise** presenting them to your future hosts.

WORDS

- alternative lifestyle
- opportunity
- organic farming
- outdoors /aʊt'dɔːz/
- sightseeing = discovering
- volunteering

- affordable = not expensive
- foreign = from another country
- mature
- rewarding = beneficial
- self-confident

- gain practical experience
- learn new skills
- stay fit and healthy
- travel abroad /ə'brɔːd/

5 How to make a great application video

Watch the video and **identify** what makes a great application video.

STEP 5

Make a list of everything you need to put into your application video.

FINAL STEP

Gather all your notes and your resume. Use them to make an application video for your future hosts. Be creative!

You've completed your mission. Well done!

CONGRATULATIONS

1. Preserving our Welsh wealth

1 What are National Parks?

National Parks are the areas of British countryside which are considered to be the most special and beautiful. They are protected so that people can enjoy them both now and in the future. In the UK there are 15 National Parks, three of which are in Wales:

- Snowdonia National Park
- Brecon Beacons National Park
- Pembrokeshire Coast National Park

The Welsh National Parks contain spectacular and beautiful scenery. […] They are rich in natural and cultural heritage, with a wealth of wildlife, geological, historical and archaeological sites. […] People live and work in the National Parks. The farms, villages and towns are protected along with the landscape and wildlife. National Parks welcome visitors and provide opportunities for everyone to enjoy and learn about their special qualities.

The two purposes of National Park Authorities are laid out[1] by law:

- To conserve and enhance[2] the natural beauty, wildlife and cultural heritage of the National Parks.
- To promote opportunities for the understanding and enjoyment of the special qualities of National Parks by the public.

1. established 2. *renforcer*

www.pembrokeshirecoast.wales

a. Explain what defines a National Park and **name** examples of such parks in Wales.

b. Comment on the Welsh government's interest in creating National Parks.

c. GRAMMAR **Observe** this sentence: "*They are protected so that people can enjoy them*" (l.3-4). What is the function of "*so that*"? What other expressions have the same meaning or function? ► p. 152

d. Give examples of possible activities one can do in a Welsh National Park.

YOUR TASK

Groupwork. You are on a school trip in Wales and have spent the afternoon discovering a National Park. **Exchange** tweets about your experience and **give your opinion** on this natural national site.

BOOST YOUR SKILLS!

Présenter un lieu

- *Three of the National Parks are* ***in*** *Wales.*
- *The Welsh National Parks contain* ***spectacular and beautiful*** *scenery.*
- *The two* ***purposes*** *of National Park Authorities are...*

AT HOME Choose one of the three National Parks mentioned. Search information about it (history, geography, activities you can do there) and present it to the class.

CULTURE SPOT

In 1998, Wales was one of the first nations in the world to have a constitutional duty of **sustainable development.** Since then, Wales has led projects on sustainability with different countries in Africa. In 2015, it was one of the first nations to legislate for Sustainable Development Goals and place them at the heart of the government's policies.

2 Environment (Wales) Act 2016

live! VIDÉO

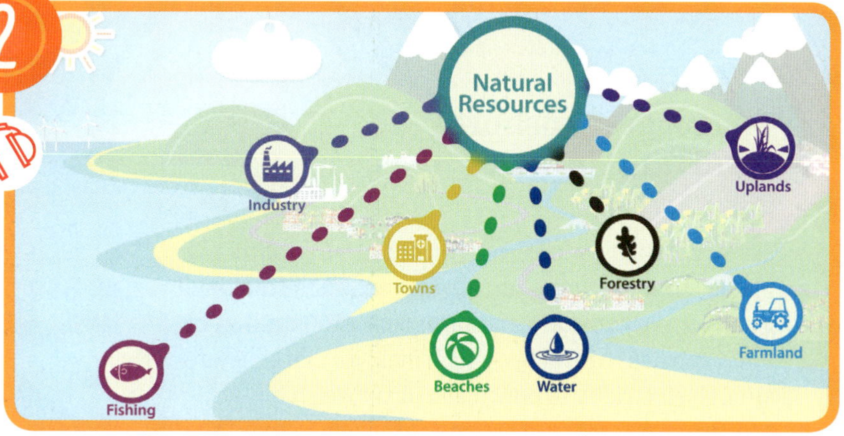

a. Watch the video and **find out** why the Environment Act was passed in Wales.

b. Explain what its aims are and what actions it encourages.

3 Blaenavon mining site turned museum

live! VIDÉO

PARCOURS DIFFÉRENCIÉS WB → p. 40

a. Watch the video and **find out** about Blaenavon (what it used to be and what it has become, why it has been classified as a World Heritage Site by UNESCO).

b. PRONUNCIATION **Pay attention** to the tone used in this sentence: *"This area is important because the town still holds evidence of its status."* What can you conclude about the stress of linking words?

c. Find out what visitors can learn about at Blaenavon.

YOUR TASK

As a member of staff at the Blaenavon Centre, **post** a short **comment** on the centre's website to encourage people to visit it.
Explain why they should come.

CULTURE SPOT

Throughout the nineteenth century, **mining** was key to the economy of Wales as it played a major role in the Industrial Revolution. By the early twentieth century, Wales was home to the two largest coast exporting ports worldwide.

WORDS

- Blaen**a**von /bleɪ'nævən/
- f**a**ctory = **i**ndustry /'ɪndəstri/
- recoll**e**ction = m**e**mory

- educ**a**tional
- hist**o**ric = imp**o**rtant
- hist**o**rical = from the past
- sust**ai**nable: *durable*

- gain kn**o**wledge
- manuf**a**cture /mænjʊ'fæktʃə/ = make in a f**a**ctory
- pres**e**rve = keep al**i**ve
- take a tour = v**i**sit

BOOST YOUR SKILLS!

Coordonner des idées

- *They are protected **so that** people can enjoy them.*
- ***For instance**, the Blaenavon ironworks were essential for developing iron ores.*

GRAMMAR p. 152

EXPLORE

2. Promoting new sources of power

1

The biggest onshore wind farm in Wales

"Wales' biggest onshore[1] wind farm has officially opened in south Wales, after three years in the making. The Pen-y-Cymoedd wind farm cost £365 million to build and has 76 turbines, which means it can generate enough electricity to power one in six Welsh homes.

First Minister Carwyn Jones officially opened the wind farm, built between Neath and Aberdare, on Thursday.

"Wind power is a key part of our efforts to build a sustainable low carbon economy for Wales. I am pleased we were able to support this project, which has shown how the local community, the Welsh economy, and people right across the country can benefit from such a scheme," she said.

The opening came just two days after Environment Secretary Lesley Griffiths said she wants Wales to generate 70% of its electricity from renewable sources by 2030.

The rate[2] is currently at 32%, but Griffiths said it's important for Wales to continue investing in renewable energy. "We know that this is the sort of energy we need to see going forward," said Griffiths, "people know that we need to move away from fossil fuel," she added.

Imogen CALDERWOOD, *www.globalcitizen.org*, 2017

1. on the land (≠ offshore) 2. *taux*

2

Marine energy in Wales

live! VIDÉO

CULTURE SPOT

Since 2016, Wales has supported renewable energies every year by celebrating **Energy Efficiency Day**.

WORDS

- achievement = success
- resource /rɪ'sɔːs/
- Pen-y-Cymoedd /'penɪsiːməʊd/

- advanced /əd'vɑːnst/
- profitable = beneficial

- be at the forefront of = to lead the way in
- enhance
- expand /ɪks'pænd/
- promote = encourage, support, develop

Focus on Doc 1 or 2.

PARCOURS DIFFÉRENCIÉS WB → p. 41

a. Name the type of energy promoted in this document.

b. Explain the reason(s) for the Welsh government to invest in these energies.

c. SPELLING **Observe** this sentence from Doc. 1: "*The Pen-y-Cymoedd wind farm cost £365 million to build.*" Where do you put the currency symbol when you write prices?

YOUR TASK

It is Energy Efficiency Day and your Welsh school has decided to celebrate it. **Write** a short article in the school magazine about the importance of investing in renewable energies in Wales.

BOOST YOUR SKILLS!

Promouvoir un projet

- *We* ***put great hopes*** *in this project.*
- *We* ***believe that it could*** *+ BV*
- *We* ***think the potential*** *is quite big.*

3. Teaching sustainability

1 An eco-school presents the importance of water

live! VIDÉO

a. Watch the video and **explain** who the children are and what the aim of the video is.

b. PRONUNCIATION **Listen** to these words: *reservoir – plants – plastic – toilet – automatically – campaign*. What can you conclude about the pronunciation of "transparent" words? ▸ p. 153

c. Pick out the different ways of saving water. Can you think of any others?

d. Comment on the elements used by the children to sound convincing.

YOUR TASK

You are a student in a Welsh eco-school. **Record** a short video about the importance of saving power.

CULTURE SPOT

Eco-schools are an international environmental education programme run in Wales since 1994. They are student-led and designed to empower and inspire young people to make positive environmental changes at school and within their wider communities.

Eco-Schools Eco-Sgolion

BOOST YOUR SKILLS!

Stimuler la participation chez un auditeur

- ***Did you know*** *that…?*
- ***Join*** *our campaign to… /* ***Let's…***

2 Centre for Alternative Technology#

live! VIDÉO

a. Watch the video and **find out** what type of place the centre is. Who is it aimed at?

b. Explain what you can do and learn about in this centre.

WORDS

- area /ˈeəriə/ = neighbourhood
- city dweller: *citadin*
- device = appliance /əˈplaɪəns/
- power = electricity
- cost-saving = economical
- upgraded /ʌpˈgreɪdɪd/ = improved
- cut down = lower = reduce /rɪˈdjuːs/
- increase = boost
- switch on ≠ switch off

AT HOME Go to *www.keepwalestidy.cymru* and discover the various programmes led by Welsh pupils to protect the environment. Present one of them to your schoolmates.

EXPLORE

4. Youth taking action

1

Canadian Prime Minister Justin Trudeau among world leaders writing to pupils in Blaenau Ffestiniog

The Ysgol y Moelwyn pupils sent Welsh slate[1] to leaders of nearly every country in the world in a bid[2] to secure heritage status for north Wales quarries[3]. So far, the students have received responses from 15 leaders.

Among those was Canadian Prime Minister Justin Trudeau, who said he was wowed[4] by the slate. In the letter he said he "loved to receive letters from young people all over the world."

Other leaders who responded include Prince Albert of Monaco and president of Brazil, Michel Terner.

Geography teacher Gareth Davies, who is coordinating the campaign, said it has instilled a sense of pride in pupils for their local area.

Adapted from *www.itv.com*, 2018

1. *ardoise* 2. attempt 3. *carrières* 4. *impressionner*

▲ Slate mining on the Welsh coast

CULTURE SPOT

The slate industry has played a major role in the economy of the country in the 19th century. Most of the larger quarries finally closed in the 1960s and 1970s.

2

"Plant!" celebrates its 10 years!

In 2008 the Welsh Government made a pledge to plant a native Welsh broadleaf tree for every child born or adopted in Wales. The scheme is called Plant!

Since then, 15 new woodlands[1] have been created across Wales, with more than 380,000 trees planted. [...]

Every month, Natural Resources Wales receives the numbers of babies born and adopted in Wales. It then arranges for a mixture of native broadleaf trees to be planted. Every baby is given the location of the woodland which contains their tree. They also receive a certificate soon after their birth or adoption, stating that a tree has been planted for them.

Kate Thomson, Plant! Coordinator for Natural Resources Wales said: [...] We hope it will encourage young people to think about their environment and the role they have in managing it sustainably.

Adapted from *www.naturalresources.wales*, 2018

1. forest

Focus on Doc 1 or 2.

PARCOURS DIFFÉRENCIÉS WB → p. 42

a. **Read** the text and **present** the project.
b. **Explain** how this project originated and how successful it has become.
c. **Find out** how people are being involved in this project.

DIFFÉRENCIATION

YOUR TASK MÉDIATION

WAY 1 You are a Welsh student. **Write** about the project you discovered on your school blog.

WAY 2 You work for one of these projects. **Write** a letter to tell participants how successful it is.

BOOST YOUR SKILLS!

Donner des indications temporelles

- ***So far***, *the students have received...*
- ***Since then***, *15 new woodlands have been created...*
- ***Every month***, *Natural Resources Wales receives...*

GRAMMAR p. 152

WORDS

- Blaenau Ffestiniog /'blaɪnaɪ fɛs'tɪnjɒg/
- guarantee /gærən'tiː/ = promise
- youth /juːθ/

- celebratory
- invested in = devoted to
- responsible = in charge of

- commemorate an occasion
- grow (a plant) = cultivate

HOW TO PLAY "GO GREEN"

TEST YOUR CULTURE

Play in pairs.

You have decided to apply for a job as an assistant in a Welsh environmental agency. Take the test about sustainable initiatives in Wales to find out if you can be hired.

Play in turns and stop when both players have answered all their questions.

Each correct answer will give you points.

The test is over when one of the two competitors has won 5 points. He/she's hired!

GAME ON!

1. What was originally produced at Blaenavon?
1 pt

2. What is an eco-school? Give at least two characteristics.
2 pts

3. A marathon campaign was organised in Cardiff recently. What was it trying to raise awareness about?
3 pts

4. What was the initiative taken by Blaenau Ffestiniog students to draw attention to Welsh slate?
1 pt

5. Name two National Parks located in Wales.
2 pts

6. Name two types of renewable energy developed in Wales.
1 pt

7. What can you learn at the Centre for Alternative Technology in Wales?
3 pts

8. What animal was reintroduced in Wales in order to protect the ecosystem?
1 pt

9. What is "Plant!"? Give a definition of the scheme.
2 pts

10. What can you do nowadays at Blaenavon Centre?
2 pts

BOOST YOUR ENGLISH!

Grammar — Structurer son discours

PRÉCIS 32 ET EXERCICES

Pour structurer son discours, on utilise des mots de liaison. Ceux-ci permettent d'**ajouter** ou d'**opposer** des idées, de montrer le **paradoxe** ou le lien de **cause à effet** de façon fluide et logique.

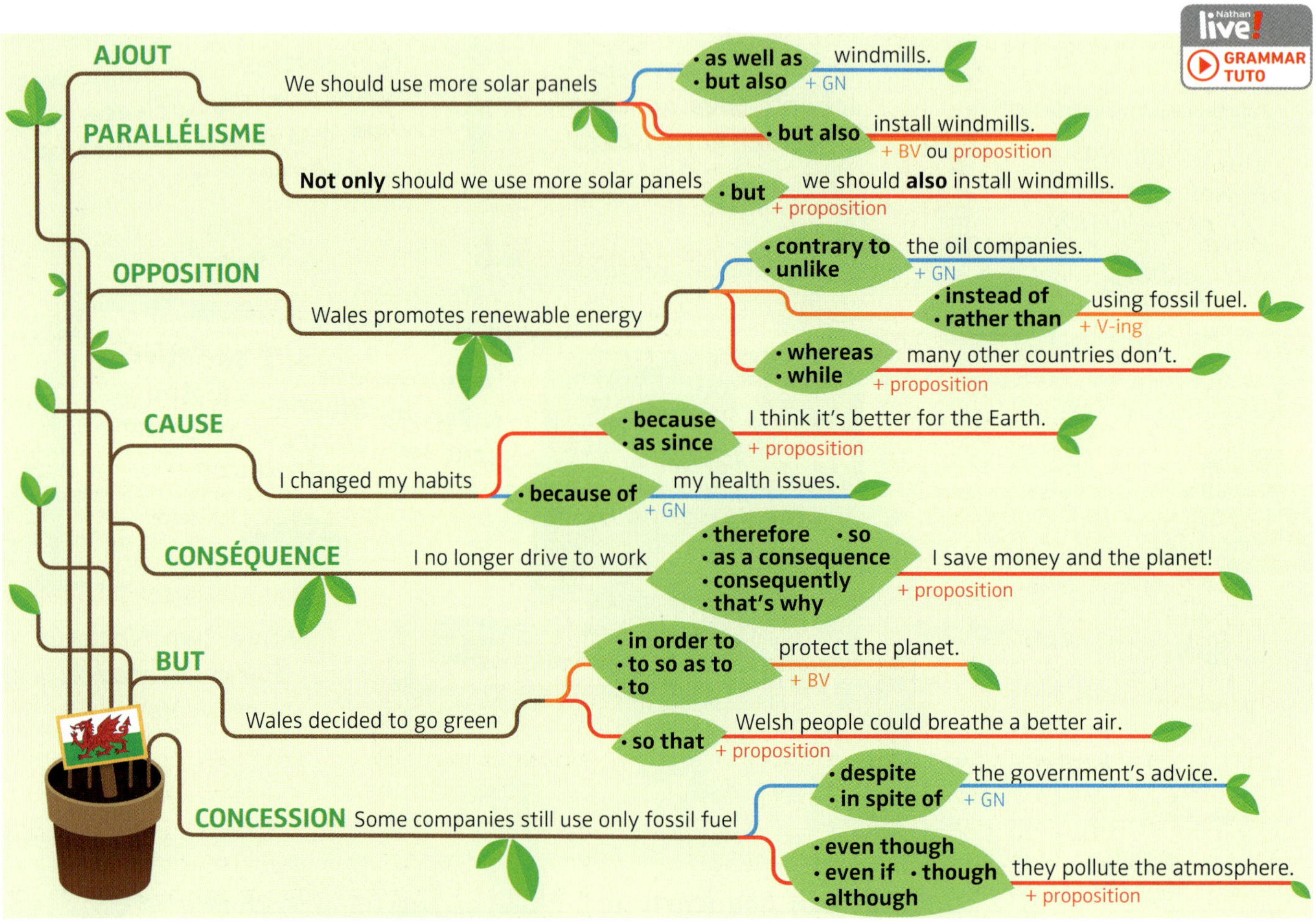

1 Complète ce paragraphe avec les mots de liaison ci-dessous.

instead of – unlike – as well as – First and foremost – In addition – To sum up

..., this Welsh village is working hard on the project. They invested in solar panels ... in windmills. ..., they encourage villagers to recycle. Now, many people ride their bikes to go shopping ... driving. ..., this Welsh village, ... many others, is an example to be followed.

2 Finis les phrases suivantes. Attention au sens du mot de liaison.

a. You should have a shower instead of...

b. To save energy and money, I installed solar panels as well as...

c. Most people are now aware of the issues while...

d. Lowering our water consumption cannot only help us save money but also...

3 Traduis ces phrases en faisant attention aux mots en gras.

a. Nous devons **non seulement** réduire notre consommation d'énergie, **mais aussi** utiliser des énergies vertes.

b. Mener des actions, **tout comme** sensibiliser les gens est un premier pas.

c. **Contrairement** aux énergies fossiles, les énergies renouvelables sont respectueuses de l'environnement.

d. **Pour résumer**, pour gérer les forêts de façon durable, il faut planter des arbres.

4 Rédige un paragraphe pour une campagne de sensibilisation à la réintroduction des castors. Utilise les expressions ci-dessous et des mots de liaison.

be beneficial to the environment – help filter pollutants – naturally regulate the ecosystem – build dams – eco-friendly way to preserve the environment

More in *Pump it up!* p. 46

Vocabulary — Wales goes green

live! MP3 — live! LEXIQUIZ

Environment

Eco-system
- beach /biːʧ/
- coast /kəʊst/
- co**un**tryside
- s**ea**shore
- w**i**ldlife

Practices
- h**e**ritage st**a**tus
- **e**co-friendly /ˈiːkəʊ-ˈfrɛndli/
- exp**a**nd /ɪksˈpænd/
- prom**o**te = supp**o**rt
- raise aw**a**reness ab**ou**t
- sh**o**wcase /ˈʃəʊkeɪs/

Energy

Traditional
- coal
- f**o**ssil fuel

Renewable
- s**o**lar
- t**i**dal /ˈtaɪdl/
- wind

Cost
- c**o**st-saving
- m**o**ney-making
- cut = l**o**wer

Politics

Transmission
- act
- en**a**ct a law = l**e**gislate

Actor
- adv**i**sory comm**i**ttee
- ass**e**mbly m**e**mber
- Env**i**ronment S**e**cretary
- resp**o**nsible for = in charge of

Programme
- **e**co-school
- fund
- lead a pr**o**ject

1 Choisis le verbe approprié pour chaque phrase.

a. When you study in an eco-school, you _enact_ / _lead_ green projects with your schoolmates.

b. The goal of the Cardiff marathon was to _raise_ / _attract_ awareness on the issue of energy.

c. The Welsh government intends to _shut_ / _cut_ carbon emissions by investing in tidal energy.

d. On Energy Efficiency Day, companies and communities are strongly encouraged to _push_ / _promote_ sustainable initiatives.

2 Associe chaque nom à sa définition.

National Park | Blaenavon | eco-school | Plant!

a. An educational programme empowering children and teens in the protection of their environment.

b. A scheme to protect an area as a cultural, natural, or historical asset for the nation.

c. A promise to encourage each Welsh child to take care of the environment by making them responsible for their own tree.

d. A former industrial site now converted into a heritage centre to protect the memory of the Welsh industry.

Phonology and spelling — Les mots transparents

live! MP3 More in *Pump it up!* p. 74-75

Les **mots transparents** sont des mots qui, dans deux langues différentes, **s'écrivent et/ou se prononcent de manière similaire**. Certains mots anglais ressemblent beaucoup à des mots français à l'écrit ; en revanche, à l'oral, il peut être difficile de les reconnaître. Appuie-toi sur cette graphie commune pour les comprendre à l'écrit. À l'oral, entraîne-toi à les reconnaître.

1 Écoute la prononciation des mots transparents suivants et souligne les voyelles accentuées.

future – place – national – beauty – park – manufacture – banana – protection – adventure – encourage

2 Écoute ces mots transparents et classe-les selon leur orthographe.

- Même orthographe dans les deux langues.
- Orthographe spécifique à l'anglais.

FINAL TASK

MÉDIATION

Write and present a report on innovative green practices in Wales.

During a trip in Wales, you have found out how important sustainable development is for this nation. You want your schoolmates to learn about this. Write a report for your school magazine to raise awareness about Welsh innovative green practices.

1. **Introduce** the subject by explaining how important sustainable development is in Wales.
2. **Prepare** your ideas focusing on the various ways Wales innovates on sustainable issues:
   – politics: **mention** the legal decisions taken to encourage green practices, and the projects encouraged by the Welsh government,
   – local projects: **show** how people are involved in new projects to protect the environment,
   – education: **emphasise** the role of education and children on green practices.
3. **Provide** examples: **Give** precise facts, figures and names to support your ideas.

YES YOU CAN! Write a factual report

INTRODUCTION

Présente ton sujet de manière générale avant d'aborder les différents points un à un.

The industrial landscape of Blaenavon is another UNESCO World Heritage Site found in Wales.

SYNTAXE

Opte pour des phrases élaborées (propositions relatives, coordination, subordination) et évite les formes contractées.

For a general overview of the area you can check out the Blaenavon World Heritage Centre, which hosts exhibitions and contains several facilities.

NIVEAU DE VOCABULAIRE

Utilise des termes précis et variés, avec un niveau de langue courant à soutenu.

The World Heritage Sites found in Wales are significant not only to the country's history, but to the history of the entire world.

EXPOSITION DES IDÉES

Présente tes idées dans un ordre logique à l'aide de mots de liaison.

This area is important because the town still holds evidence of its status as a major 19th-century producer of iron and coal.

EXEMPLES

Donne des exemples précis pour soutenir tes idées. Tu peux avoir recours à des noms, des chiffres, des dates, des pourcentages, etc.

For instance, the Blaenavon ironworks, which are now a museum, were essential for developing iron ores around the world.

STRATEGIES Enrichir son vocabulaire p. 218

AUTO-ÉVALUATION
WB → p. 43

TEST YOUR SKILLS

Compréhension de l'oral

Comprendre une vidéo pour une association

Protecting wildlife

Nathan live! MP3

A2 **1. Read** the title and **look** at the picture. **Make hypotheses** about the recording.

A2+ **2. Watch** the video and **find** information about Wildlife Trust for South and Wales (type of project, purpose, places concerned).

B1 **3. Pay attention** to the speaker's request: **explain** what he wants people to do and why.

B1+ **4. Comment** on the words used by the speaker to convince people to support the project.

Compréhension de l'écrit

Comprendre un compte-rendu

Studying in eco-schools

1) Damers First School

Children in the Eco-Committee and Entrepreneur Club at Damers First School worked together to design, make and market an eco-product called Waxtastic No Plastic; the children even designed their own logo!

Waxtastic is a piece of 100% cotton material dipped in Dorset beeswax[1] and dried. It is used as an alternative to cling film[2] to wrap or cover all foods except meat. It is 100% eco-friendly.

The children sold their product outside a local supermarket, at a farmers' market and even at festivals over the summer holidays. They have raised an extraordinary 3,350 pounds so far and are planning to use this money to create a nature area (with a pond)!

2) Penshurst Primary School

At Penshurst we are keen to save water [...]. We placed bottles on display as a visual demonstration of how much water a family in Africa has each day, then throughout the day, we tried to use less water by not flushing[3] as regularly and using hand gel to wash our hands instead of water. The children found the day really interesting!

www.eco-schools.org.uk

1. *cire d'abeille* 2. plastic film 3. *tirer la chasse d'eau*

A2 **1.** What type of document is it? **Justify** your answer.

A2+ **2. Explain** the initiative presented in each situation.

3. Present the authors and the results of each initiative.

B1 **4.** What are the common points between the two stories?

5. Comment on the benefits of such initiatives for both children and society in general.

B1+ **6. Find out** what pronoun is used in each example and **comment** on their effect.

FILE 16

LE PASSÉ DANS LE PRÉSENT

The burger makes history

▶ **How does the burger reflect the evolution of American society?**

More on SPEAKEASY NEWS speakeasy-news.com

FINAL TASK

Take part in an interview to present your new burger food-truck concept.

A

www.cheeseandburger.com

B The Burger Show

live! VIDÉO

CULTURE SPOT

The Burger Show is a famous web series that explores the modern burger culture in America (typical restaurants, new trends, best recipes, etc.).

C WHAT THEY THINK ABOUT EATING BURGERS

MARCUS SAMUELSSON,
WORLD-CLASS CHEF

"When I'm in need of a quick meal, a burger is always my first choice! Burgers are easy, fast, and don't even require utensils to eat, making them the perfect get-together main course, a simple dinner recipe to whip up[1] any night of the week."

....

GIGI HADID,
MODEL

"The first year I lived in New York, I tried a different burger every week to find out my favorite burger in New York."

....

CHARLES KURALT,
JOURNALIST

"You can find your way across this country using burger restaurants the way a navigator uses stars."

....

1. improvise

www.brainyquote.com

WORDS

- course: *plat*
- fast food
- food trend
- patty: *steak haché*

- cheap ≠ expensive
- delicious = tasty
- iconic /aɪ'kɒnɪk/

- be accustomed to + V-ing = be in the habit of + V-ing
- consume
- enjoy

DISCOVER AND SHARE

Join your team and focus on one of the documents.

Doc A Look at the picture and the texte underneath, and **note down** American traditions and symbols. What do they tell you about burgers in the United States?

Doc B Explain what the purpose of this show is and how it contributes to the burger's success in the USA.

Doc C Read the quotes and **find** elements showing how popular burgers are.

NOW SHARE

Present your document, emphasising the elements that show the importance of burgers in American culture.

EXPLORE

1. From barbecue to burger

1 An animated history of the hamburger

Nathan live! VIDÉO

a. Watch the video and **pick out** the names of the countries and cities. **Write down** information about each of them.

b. PHONOLOGY **Listen** to these words from the video: *"hamburger"*, *"fun"*, *"hugely"*. What can you say about the way the <u> is pronounced? ▸ p. 165

c. Associate each major evolution of the burger to a moment in US history.

YOUR TASK

DIFFÉRENCIATION

You have just attended a conference on food history. **Give an interview** to a journalist.

WAY 1 **Tell** the journalist about the origins of the burger and what it originally looked like.

WAY 2 **Explain** the burger's history in details.

CULTURE SPOT

Legend has it that during WWII, hamburgers in the U.S. were renamed **"liberty steaks"** to avoid the German-sounding name.

BOOST YOUR SKILLS!

Raconter l'histoire d'un phénomène

- *The burger* ***used to be*** *a German dish.*
- ***Eventually****, the burger made its way to America.*
- ***It took twenty to thirty years*** *for the first hamburger steak to be served between two slices of bread.*
- ***From that point on****, it became the hamburger.*

2 The Fourth of July barbecue: a Southern tradition

Just after the Revolution, Americans marked Independence Day with public dinners, and in the South those dinners quickly grew into large outdoor barbecues. These massive outdoor barbecues were free to all comers, and since the meat was donated by members of the community, it would be whatever local farmers had on hand. [...]

As settlers moved westward, those from the Southern states took their barbecue tradition with them. Texans were celebrating Independence Day with barbecue by the late 1840s, and in 1858 – just five years after the city's founding – the residents of Kansas City staged[1] their first Fourth of July barbecue, which drew 3,000 attendees[2] and featured a barbecued buffalo.

So if you're dining on barbecue this holiday weekend, you're continuing a long, proud Southern tradition.

Robert Moss, *www.southernliving.com*, 2017

1. organise 2. participants

CULTURE SPOT

Independence Day is the national day of the United States. It commemorates the adoption of the Declaration of Independence on July 4th, 1776, during the American Revolution (1765-1783).

a. Read the first paragraph and **describe** the event.

b. Read the entire article and **explain** the link between the burger and the history of America.

c. Sum up what happened during these barbecue events (people invited, location, food, celebration).

3

The barbecue pits[1] had been slowly burning since last night, with the meats turning on spits above them and the juices trickling down and hissing into the coals. [...] The long picnic tables, covered with the finest of the Wilkeses' linen, always stood under the thickest shade, with backless benches on either side [...]. At a distance great enough to keep the smoke away from the guests were the long pits where the meats cooked and the huge iron wash-pots from which the succulent odors of barbecue sauce floated. [...] The barbecue had reached its peak and the warm air was full of laughter and talk, the click of silver on porcelain and the rich heavy smells of roasting meats and gravies[2].

Adapted from Margaret MITCHELL,
Gone With the Wind, 1936

1. what you cook your barbecue in
2. *jus de viande*

a. Read the text and **make a list** of all the traditional components of a barbecue party.

b. GRAMMAR **Observe** this sentence: *"The barbecue had reached its peak."* **Identify** the grammatical tense used here. What do you use it for? ► p. 164

c. Pick out the expressions showing the atmosphere of this high-quality event.

WORDS

- celebration = social gathering
- cookout = picnic /'pɪknɪk/

- distinguished
- successful

- traditional

- attend
- gather
- roast /rəʊst /

4 The battle of the US political burgers

live! VIDÉO

PARCOURS DIFFÉRENCIÉS WB → p. 44

CULTURE SPOT

The 2012 presidential elections opposed **Barack Obama** (for the Democrats) and **Mitt Romney** (for the Republicans).

a. Watch the video and **identify** the originality of the restaurant.

b. Explain why the chef invented this new menu.

c. Imagine a burger named after an American celebrity and **explain** your choice to your partner.

2. A global empire

1 At the origins of a global empire

Nathan live! VIDÉO

a. Watch the video and **take notes** on the McDonalds (names, family link, job, career evolution).

b. Give an explanation for the changes they made in their new restaurant.

c. PHONOLOGY **Listen** to the pronunciation of the words *"started"*, *"success"* and *"barbecue"*. What can you conclude about the way the <e> is pronounced? ▸ p. 165

AT HOME To learn more about the origins of McDonald's, watch the film *The Founder* (2016) by John Lee Hancock.

2

Why do burgers continue to get more & more popular?

Well, let's see; first of all burgers are typically affordable, and they're becoming more and more imaginative... Oh, yeah, they're also very tasty! America has formed a love affair of sorts with burgers.

Yes, indeed, Americans do love their burgers. In fact, we even have a National Burger Day (May 28th). My guess would be that some Americans celebrate National Burger Day by consuming burgers every day for the entire month of May. Let's face it; I'm sure that a few even celebrate by consuming burgers every single day, all year long.

So here are the warm, soft facts: Americans devour nearly 50 billion burgers each year (that's billion with a b). There are approximately 325,000,000 people in this country, so if my math is indeed correct that means that the average American consumes 154 burgers each year or 3 every week. And that's not taking into consideration that there are many Americans who do not eat burgers at all!

Adapted from *zzzippy.com*

THE FAST-FOOD INDUSTRY

McDONALD'S

235,000 employees in 2017

69 million CUSTOMERS EACH DAY

120 COUNTRIES

37,241 restaurants worldwide in 2017
› **14,027** in the USA,
› **1,458** in Canada,
› **1** in Cuba

Americans Eat Enough **BURGERS** to **CIRCLE** the **EARTH** **32 TIMES** Every Year

US Sales

$36.4 billion	McDonald's	$3.6 billion	Arby's
$9.4 billion	Burger King	$0.8 billion	In-N-Out Burger
$1.4 billion	Five Guys	$2.2 billion	Hardee's
$9 billion	Wendy's	$3.5 billion	Jack in the Box

Sources: *vinepair.com, thoughtco.com*, Statista, YouGov

a. Read the text and **observe** the figures. What can you conclude about the importance of the fast-food industry in the United States?

b. Comment on America's love affair with the burger.

WORDS

- frenzy = excitement
- profit = financial success
- sales

- acclaimed = renowned
- accustomed to = used to
- efficient /ɪ'fɪʃənt/

- global
- passionate about

- be employed by /ɪm'plɔɪd/
- crave for = be extremely fond of
- expand
- serve orders

3. Healthier burgers

1

McDonald's to make the Happy Meal healthier

Your McDonald's Happy Meal is about to look a little different. The fast-food giant announced a series of changes to its Happy Meal menu Thursday, as part of a broader plan to provide healthier options for children. Cheeseburgers will no longer be a menu option, and French fry servings will be downsized. Bottled water will be added as a beverage[1] option, while the chocolate milk will be reformulated to reduce added sugars.

The move comes as the first step in a commitment to limiting calories, sodium, saturated fat, and added sugar in its Happy Meals. By the end of 2022, McDonald's wants at least half of its Happy Meal options to meet the new nutrition criteria: 600 calories or less; no more than 10% of calories from saturated fat; less than 650 mg of sodium; and no more than 10% of calories from added sugar.

Cheeseburger enthusiasts need not fear, however: the Happy Meal cheeseburger will in fact still be available, but by request only. The chain hopes that removing unhealthy items from the menu will nudge[2] diners to change their consumption habits.

Adapted from Nathasha BACH, *www.fortune.com*, 2018

1. drink 2. encourage

www.happymeal.com

a. Pick out three examples of the changes brought to the Happy Meal.

b. Explain how different the Happy Meal will be.

c. Give the reasons why McDonald's wants to implement these changes.

2

Nathan live! VIDÉO

PARCOURS DIFFÉRENCIÉS WB → p. 45

a. Watch the video, **pick out** details on this new burger and **say** what makes it different.

b. Give the reasons why this product is considered better than the original burger.

c. Take notes on the success of this product.

YOUR TASK

You would like to try Impossible Burgers with your American friends, but they think that it is not a good idea. **Convince** them to try these burgers.

WORDS

- calorie
- veganism

- eco-friendly
- healthy /ˈhɛlθi/
- meat-free = vegetarian
- commit to = dedicate oneself to
- downsize = make smaller
- reduce
- serve
- substitute /ˈsʌbstɪtjuːt/

BOOST YOUR SKILLS!

Exposer des raisons

- *It is the **world's only** burger in its category.*
- *It **uses** 75% **less** water.*
- *It is **actually** a **best-selling** burger.*

BOOST YOUR ENGLISH!

Grammar — Évoquer des faits du passé

A Prétérit vs *past perfect*

PRÉCIS 13 16 ET EXERCICES

Nathan live! GRAMMAR TUTO

Le *past perfect* permet d'évoquer un événement antérieur à un autre au prétérit.

They **had** all **gathered** round the barbecue *when* we **arrived**.

- *auxiliaire* **have** *au passé*
- *verbe* **gather** *au participe passé*
- *marqueur de temps*
- *verbe* **arrive** *au prétérit*

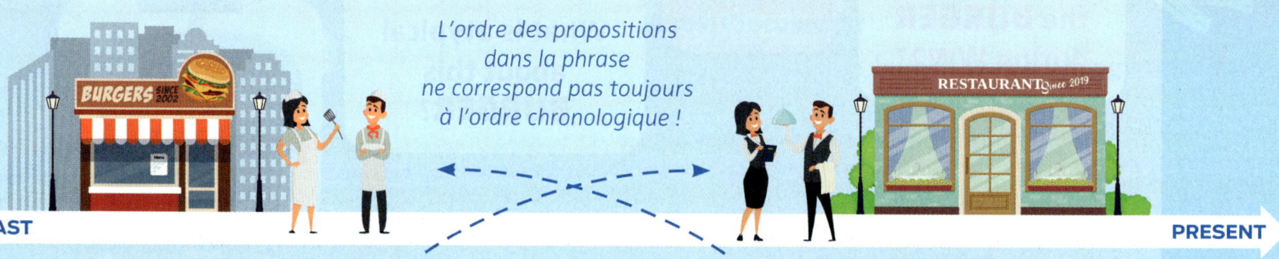

Before they **opened** their restaurant, they **had owned** a burger joint.

1 Mets les verbes entre parenthèses au *past perfect*.

a. They (*open*) their burger joint earlier.
b. He (*eat*) two burgers that same day.
c. Burgers (*be / definitely*) famous in Germany long before.
d. Nobody (*hear / ever*) about burgers before the 1850s.

2 Mets les verbes entre parenthèses au temps qui convient : prétérit ou *past perfect*.

a. They (*try*) many different burgers before they (*find*) their favourite one.
b. I (*cook*) traditional burgers for years when I (*decide*) to try vegan burgers.
c. Before she (*move*) to the USA, she (*taste / never*) a true American burger.

B Situer des évènements du passé

PRÉCIS 34 ET EXERCICES

- On utilise des **marqueurs de temps** (des conjonctions de subordination) tels que *when, before, after, while, as* :
  They were enjoying their burgers ***when*** *they realised it was time to go.*
  Burgers had been famous in the USA long ***before*** *they became fashionable worldwide.*
  They built their burger empire ***while*** *burger venues were opening throughout the USA.*
  They were inventing new meat recipes ***as*** *others were opening vegan burger restaurants.*

Attention !
Le *past perfect* signale l'action la plus ancienne.

3 Complète ces phrases avec un marqueur temporel.

a. Gigi had tried many burgers ... she found the one she liked best.
b. The cook named burgers after politicians ... the elections had taken place, not before.
c. ... I heard of this new place, all my friends had already rushed to taste their burgers.
d. ... she was preparing the BBQ, her husband was preparing the patties.

4 Reconstitue ces phrases.

a. When / vegan burgers / people / delicious / discovered / they realised / they tasted
b. While / all over the world / opened / thousands of burger restaurants / invented/ cooks / fantastic recipes
c. The McDonald brothers / the first McDonald's restaurant / they had opened / in the USA / their first foreign restaurant / 19 years after / opened

More in *Pump it up!* p. 22 et 28

Vocabulary — The American burger

live! MP3 — live! LEXIQUIZ

Food

Ingredients
- bacon
- bun
- cheese
- ketchup
- onions
- patty
- meat-free
- vegan

Taste
- flavour
- enjoy
- relish

Preparation
- French fries
- ground beef
- topping
- grill
- serving

Restaurant

Places
- bar
- burger joint
- drive-through
- venue

Jobs
- chef
- cook
- manager
- waiter, waitress

Actions
- attend to sb = wait on sb = serve sb
- cook
- sell

History

Tradition
- historical dimension
- iconic
- mythical
- embody
- represent
- stand for

Adaptation
- fashionable
- healthy
- innovative
- trendy
- modernise
- reinvent

1 Remplace les mots soulignés par un synonyme.

a. Last year, we opened a new burger restaurant in Los Angeles.

b. A perfectly grilled patty is still the most iconic version of the burger.

c. I would spend the whole day cooking potatoes or attending clients.

d. Meat-free burgers are becoming more and more fashionable.

2 Complète les phrases et termine-les.

the sushi burger – the Impossible Burger – the political burger

a. ... is a brand producing ... .

b. ... is the creation of a Washington chef ... .

c. ... is a modern twist on the regular burger ... .

3 Utilise les mots ci-dessous pour rédiger la brochure d'un nouveau restaurant spécialisé dans les burgers.

innovative – meat-free – fashionable – drive-through – fast food – iconic – toppings – enjoy

Phonology — La prononciation des graphies <e> et <u>

live! MP3 More in *Pump it up!* p. 76-77

Les graphies <e> et <u> ne se prononcent pas toujours de la même manière en anglais.

/e/ red	/ə/ manager	/ɪ/ precede	/iː/ delete	/ɜː/ nerve	/eə/ where	/ɪə/ here

/ʌ/ bus	/juː/ utensil	/jʊə/ pure	/ɪ/ minute	/ɜː/ turn

1 Écoute l'enregistrement tout en observant les voyelles soulignées ci-dessous.

Thousands of burgers are being cooked and served every minute in the United States.
Restaurants open all the time across the country to welcome new clients.

2 Reproduis les tableaux et classe les mots de l'exercice 1 selon la prononciation de la voyelle soulignée.

FINAL TASK

Take part in an interview to present your new burger food-truck concept.

You are the owner of a burger food truck in New York. You serve different types of burgers and have named each of them after a famous American icon. Record a video presentation to attract new customers.

1. **Decide on the concept of your food truck and choose names for your burgers.**
2. **Prepare your arguments, focusing on:**
   – why you chose the burger for an American food truck (personal reasons, history and tradition, customers' food preferences);
   – the types of burgers and the ingredients you first thought about, then what you finally decided on;
   – the different names you listed for your burgers, then those you chose.
3. **Explain** to the journalist why he/she should try your burgers. **Adapt** your level of speech, stress the words correctly, and **express** enthusiasm.

YES YOU CAN!

Take part in an interview to present a concept

1 INTRODUCTION

Présente-toi brièvement, ainsi que ton restaurant.

"All chefs are driven by food culture but I'm motivated by something else, too. Politics. Hardly surprising, the restaurant is one block from the White House."

2 PRÉSENTATION

Présente ton concept. Donne quelques exemples de plats.

"The Romney burger is covered in fry sauce and topped with pastrami and American cheese. It is popular among clients."

3 OPINION PERSONNELLE

Donne ton avis et tes motivations personnelles en tant que gérant d'un food truck. Montre ton intérêt pour l'histoire du burger et celle des États-Unis.

"To me there's nothing more American than a burger."

ATTITUDE

Adopte un ton et une posture professionnels. Donne aux clients l'envie de venir tester ton restaurant.

"Romney is definitely medium-rare. It is delicious."

FLUIDITÉ

Parle sans lire tes notes. Sois aussi naturel que possible.

STRATEGIES Interagir p. 217

AUTO-ÉVALUATION
WB → p. 47

Compréhension de l'oral

Comprendre un extrait de documentaire

live! MP3

Remembering the original burger culture

A1 1. **Listen** to the recording and **say** what this man's passion is.

A2 2. **Listen** again and **take notes** on the speaker's childhood memory.

B1 3. **Find** the name of the city mentioned by the speaker and **say** why this city is important in burger culture.

B1+ 4. **Explain** the link(s) the speaker makes between burgers and cars.

Compréhension de l'écrit

Comprendre un texte de presse

The new generation of veggie burgers

The veggie burger market is starting to look a lot like... meat. How realistic are the meat substitute used? In some stores, they are sold alongside actual meat.

In the interest of research, my husband and I shared a VG Beyond Burger at Veggie Grill, then walked to a brewpub[1] to share a beef burger. To my surprise, the flavor really was similar – although my husband thought the Beyond Burger had a better texture. Both were tasty, but neither was as flavorful as the grass-fed beef we buy from a small local ranch.

Melissa Abbott, a vice-president at The Hartman Group, said health concerns used to be the driver of faux-meat sales. "Now we're in an era where meat analogues are looking a lot different, and they are on the verge of[2] taking over in a way they never had," she said. "It might not be quite the same texture as meat, but it comes closer than it ever has before, and they're in places where you wouldn't expect to see them in years past."

Are Americans ready to give up their meat? Abbott said no – but more and more people want their meat to be sustainable. "They're eating less meat, and it's easier than it ever has been before," she said.

Adapted from Carrie DENNETT, *www.seattletimes.com*, 2018

1. *brasserie* 2. they will soon be

A2 1. What type of burger is presented in the document?

A2+ 2. **Comment** on the differences between these burgers and regular burgers.

B1 3. **Rephrase** the personal anecdote told by the author. What conclusion does she reach about burgers?

B1+ 4. Why did people originally eat these burgers?

5. **Explain** why more and more Americans eat them nowadays.

EXPLORE

2. Towards local empowerment

PARCOURS DIFFÉRENCIÉS WB → p. 49

1 Maasai warriors in Kenya now protect African wildlife

A little kid is hunched over his school book in a dusty classroom of a village school in Kenya, drawing a lion. Probably no more than seven, he beams with pride: "This lion is my friend!"

A gradually unfolding revolution in Kenya is seeking to reconnect Africans to their wildlife. For as they start to share in the income from a booming sustainable tourism industry, so they become eager to help protect and preserve the lion, leopard, rhino, buffalo and elephant that bring many of these tourists to their lands.

Once Maasai warriors would kill a lion on their coming of age[1] to prove their strength and courage: now they are being persuaded that to be a guardian of lions carries much more prestige and honour. Rhinos used to be so often targeted by poachers[2] for their valuable horns. Now locals are much keener to report any newcomer they suspect may be a poacher.

Adapted from *www.traveller.com.au*, 2017

1. when they become adults 2. illegal hunter

a. Read the text and **describe** the Maasai tradition.

b. Explain the meaning of the *"revolution"* (l.5).

c. VOCABULARY **Pick out** the words used to contrast the situation in the past and the situation today. PRÉCIS 20

d. Explain the impact of this evolution on the Maasai community.

CULTURE SPOT

The Maasai are well-known for their unique culture and tribal dress. They represent 20% of the Kenyan population.

AT HOME Watch the video entitled "Maasai life through a child's eyes" on *lyceen.nathan.fr/shine-bright2* and pick out more information about the Maasai community.

2 Kenya conservancy and tourism

Nathan live! MP3

a. Listen to the recording. **Find** information about the new role given to the Maasai.

b. Explain how much it benefits the community.

c. PHONOLOGY **Listen** to these words from the video: *migrating, visiting, rapidly, firstly, increased, employed*. **Find** the root words and the suffixes: does the suffix modify the stress?

BOOST YOUR SKILLS!

Décrire une évolution

- ***Now*** *with the increasing population... /* ***A few years ago*** *a school opened /* ***Nowadays*** *the Maasai participate in tourism /* ***In recent years****, global efforts have been made.*
- *Once Maasai warriors* ***would*** *kill a lion...*
- *The Maasai population* ***used to*** *own the land.* PRÉCIS 20

YOUR TASK

DIFFÉRENCIATION

Interview a Maasai chief.

WAY 1 **Focus on** the evolution of the tribe's way of life.

WAY 2 **Describe** the changes within the Maasai community and **explain** how they empower the people.

HOW TO PLAY "HOW GR

Work in pairs.

You have decided to take part in ar
environmental organisation. Test y
and find the best solutions for Keny

1. Discuss the best solution for each
2. Count your ■ ● ♦ and add up y
3. Read your profile and see how gr

1 You need
to develop the country's economy:

- ■ Develop huge flower farms thanks to chemical pesticides.
- ♦ Use natural pesticides to grow flowers.
- ● Stop growing flowers near lakes to prevent their pollution.

6 You want
to empower the Maasai community:

- ♦ Give them responsibility in the safari tourism industry.
- ● Give them advice to protect wildlife.
- ■ Allow poaching.

5 You want
to expand

- ● Make sure hotels on th strong lights.
- ♦ Inform tourists about t
- ■ Develop low-cost safar

Results

From 9 to 12
Congratulations! You are making a
really good effort to save our country.
Keep up the good work!

■ = 0 pt ● = 1 pt ♦ = 2 pts

3

https://sautikuufoundation.org

AUMA OBAMA FOUNDATION
Powerful voices for our future generation
Sauti Kuu

DE | EN DONATE HERE

WHAT WE DO WHO WE ARE PROJECTS JOIN US LOCATIONS NEWS

THE GREENHOUSE PROJECT

The greenhouse[1] was built as a pilot project in 2012 using low-cost materials. It is used to produce non-native crops[2] that are sold to generate an income. The objective is to show community members that they, too, can produce plants for sale and not just for their own subsistence.

GROW TO EAT AND LEARN TO EARN

The project was launched in March 2014. The first step consisted of teaching participants how to create kitchen gardens at home. Families were introduced to the basics of composting and organic farming.

The 'Grow to Eat' project has changed the lives of the families involved and improved their chances of feeding themselves and setting money aside in the process. Although most meeting attendees are women, men are taking an increasingly active role in the work of the kitchen gardens.

1. *serre* 2. agricultural produce

a. Look at the document and **identify** the basic elements: type of document, name and type of organisation.

b. Read about the projects and **explain** what they consist in.

c. VOCABULARY **Compare** the way these compound words are written: *greenhouse, kitchen garden, low-cost, non-native*. **Rephrase** them to give a definition.

d. Discuss: How do you think these projects may help the local populations?

WORDS

- cha**r**ity = foundation
- chief /tʃiːf/
- ha**r**vest: *récolte*
- tour guide /ˈtʊə gaɪd/
- tribe = comm**u**nity

- educ**a**tional = instr**u**ctive
- h**e**lpful
- r**u**ral /ˈrʊərəl/
- sust**ai**nable

- trad**i**tional

- emp**o**wer = stre**n**gthen
- g**a**ther = ass**e**mble
- inv**o**lve sb in sth = make sb part**i**cipate in sth
- pick: *cueillir*
- reass**e**rt
- rehab**i**litate
- sust**ai**n = (*ici*) feed

EXPLORE

3.

1 Make plastic beaut

a. Look at the photos and **imagi**
might be made of.

b. Watch the video, **check** your h
out more information about th

c. Explain how this project may i
of Kenya.

YOUR TASK

You are a client of that compar
Write a review on their website
other buyers to support this ini

AT HOME Watch the video ent
a second life" on *lyceen.natha*
bright2 and discover another

BOOST YOUR SKILLS!

Convaincre

- *The sculpture **that** I received is **so***
- *The workers **who** make this project*
*are **so** creative.*
- *This is **such** an amazing initiative. It*
experience to see the final outcome

BOOST YOUR ENGLISH!

Grammar — Les relatives

PRÉCIS 33 ET EXERCICES

live! GRAMMAR TUTO

Animals bring tourists to Kenya. + Many animals in Kenya are endangered species.
sujet — *sujet*

→ Many animals **which** / **that** bring tourists to Kenya are endangered species.
antécédent — *sujet*

The Maasai live in tribes. + The Maasai traditionally were warriors.
sujet — *sujet*

→ The Maasai, **who** live in tribes, traditionally were warriors.
antécédent — *sujet*

Kenya is a country. + **Only in Kenya** can you meet caracals.
sujet — *complément de lieu*

→ Kenya is the only country **where** you can meet caracals.
antécédent — *complément de lieu de can meet*

Spring is a season. + Elephants migrate in spring.

→ Spring is the season **when** elephants migrate.
antécédent — *complément de temps de migrate*

Le pronom relatif peut être :

- sujet de la relative
(donc suivi directement d'un verbe à conjuguer à la bonne personne) :

I chose a safari
that respects wildlife.
sujet

- complément de la relative
(donc suivi d'un S + V) :

The first wild animal
that I saw was a giraffe.
COD

Le pronom relatif *who* ne s'utilise qu'avec des êtres humains.

1 Pour chaque proposition principale, trouve la bonne proposition relative.

a. I hate tourists ...
b. There are so many places ...
c. Holiday resorts ... are becoming more and more popular.
d. I met a Maasai warrior ...

1. where I'd like to go
2. who told me about his everyday life
3. who don't respect wildlife
4. that are eco-friendly

2 Complète avec le relatif qui convient.

a. The turtles ... I saw yesterday were impressive.
b. I met producers ... love their jobs.
c. That was the moment ... I realised how fragile the Earth is.
d. Kenya is a country ... I would love to discover.

More in *Pump it up!* p. 50

Grammar — Le gérondif

PRÉCIS 10 ET EXERCICES

Nature
Le gérondif est une **forme en V-*ing*** que l'on appelle parfois nom verbal.
Il est utilisé comme un nom.
Il peut avoir des compléments :
***Banning** bright lights can help...*

Fonction
Il peut être **sujet** :
***Diving** is forbidden in nature reserves.*
ou **complément** :
*They tried organic **farming** and **composting**.*

Emploi
Il peut être induit par certaines prépositions :
*It improved their chances of **feeding**...*
*Before **leaving**...*
Ou par certains verbes :
*They enjoy **diving**.*

*The main problem is **preserving** the environment.*
Dans cette phrase, *preserving* n'est pas le verbe *preserve* conjugué au présent *be* + V-*ing* : le sujet du verbe est *problem* et il ne fait pas l'action décrite par *preserving*. Pour être sûr(e) de toi, tu peux remplacer le gérondif par un autre nom : *The main problem is **the preservation** of the environment.*

3 Repère les gérondifs et donne leur fonction (sujet, complément).

Sightseeing is a great activity but many tourists are now realising that the Earth is in danger and needs preserving.

The big challenge we are facing today is changing our habits. Kenya has been trying to preserve its wildlife for a few years and we must continue acting in an eco-friendly way.

4 Mets le verbe à la bonne forme : gérondif ou base verbale.

a. Before *(visit)* Kenya, I didn't know it was so beautiful.
b. The resort stopped *(use)* pesticides in order to *(preserve)* the planet.
c. *(protect)* the environment is our new challenge and we must *(succeed)*.
d. Instead of *(wait)*, we should all *(react)* and *(act)*.

Vocabulary — Preserving Kenya

live! MP3 — live! LEXIQUIZ

People

Maasai
- chief
- community
- tradition
- tribe
- ancestral

Activists
- campaign
- protest (n)
- denounce
- fight for ≠ fight against
- get involved in
- protest (v)
- raise awareness

Tourists
- ATV (all-terrain vehicle)
- binoculars
- safari
- tour guide
- book a tour

Sustainability

Recycling
- waste = trash = litter
- collect
- reduce
- sort: *trier*
- transform

Agriculture
- compost
- crop
- greenhouse: *serre*
- locally-grown
- organic
- import ≠ export

Tourism
- eco-tourism ≠ mass tourism
- resort = holiday centre
- damage
- respect

Preservation

Wildlife
- elephant
- fish
- giraffe
- jungle
- leopard
- ocean
- rhino
- species /'spi:ʃiz/
- turtle
- zebra
- endangered
- threatened

Protecting
- guard /ga:d/
- (natural) habitat
- ivory /'aɪvəri/
- horn
- shore = coastline
- anti-poaching
- poach: *braconner*
- preserve
- respect
- track = follow

1 Classe ces mots selon leur catégorie grammaticale : nom, verbe ou adjectif.

pollutant – polluting – polluted – pollution – pollute

Ensuite, utilise-les dans des phrases pour décrire la situation actuelle au Kenya.

2 Classe ces mots selon les catégories suivantes : *issues / solutions*.

litter – compost – damage – poach – organic – endangered

3 Décris des impacts écologiques en trouvant le verbe approprié ; mets les verbes à la bonne forme.

contaminate – threaten – damage

a. Chemicals from the flower industry are ... the lake.

b. There are so many safaris that they ... Kenyan wildlife.

c. The ATVs bringing tourists to Maasai villages are ... the landscape.

4 Explique ce qu'il faudrait faire pour résoudre les problèmes ci-dessus. Utilise ces verbes :

protect – save – limit – denounce – should – could

Phonology — La prononciation de la graphie <o>

live! MP3 — More in *Pump it up!* p. 76-77

En anglais, le <o> peut se prononcer /ɒ/ (*hot*), /əʊ/ (*note*) ou /ɔ:/ (*short*). Il se prononce /ə/ (*memory*) quand il n'est pas accentué.

1 Observe ces mots et classe-les selon la prononciation de la lettre <o>.

crops – ocean – protest – compost – rhinos – hotel – resort – ivory

2 Vérifie tes choix en écoutant les mots et entraîne-toi à les prononcer.

FINAL TASK

Create a webpage for a Kenyan environmental organisation.

You work for an environmental organisation involved in the preservation of Kenya. Write the homepage for your website.

1. **Choose the type of environmental organisation** you want to represent (eco-tourism, wildlife protection, sustainable agriculture, etc.).
2. **Choose the name of your organisation, design your logo, and find a slogan.**
3. **Write the website homepage.** Don't forget to:
   – describe the situation in your country,
   – present your work and some examples of your actions,
   – convince readers to join in.

YES YOU CAN! Create a great website homepage

NOM ET LOGO
Pense à un nom d'association qui évoque ses actions et fasse clairement référence au Kenya.

ONGLETS
Donne aux lecteurs envie d'aller lire d'autres pages. Utilise des titres d'onglets courts et clairs.

SLOGAN
Résume le but de l'association en une phrase percutante qui donne envie d'en apprendre plus sur ses actions.

PHOTO
Choisis une photo qui illustre clairement la problématique environnementale.

TEXTE D'ACCUEIL
Donne plusieurs exemples concrets pour montrer le sérieux de ton association. Adresse-toi directement au lecteur pour le convaincre de l'importance des enjeux.

AUTO-ÉVALUATION
WB → p. 51

Compréhension de l'oral — Comprendre un documentaire

Kenyan wildlife

live! VIDÉO

A2 1. What problem does wildlife face today?

B1 2. **Give** information about the living conditions of the animal mentioned.

3. What do the men use a GPS for?

4. Is the animal affected by this device?

B1+ 5. **Explain** the purpose of the association's action.

Compréhension de l'écrit — Comprendre un article de presse en ligne

From Nairobi to Mombasa

Cries of "save our park", "save our animals" were heard echoing through Nairobi's National Park in Kenya earlier this month, as protesters thronged[1] to challenge the construction of a six and a half kilometre railway bridge. If it all goes ahead, the bridge will stretch through the protected parkland, running above giraffes, black rhinos, lions and leopards.

The railway is a scheme[2] to reduce travel time between the capital Nairobi and Mombasa, Kenya's second largest city. Supporters of the railway claim that it will boost exports, create jobs, and create a far greater ease of movement for Kenyans and tourists alike.

But, in 2017, a petition from wildlife campaigners demanded the completion of an environmental impact study. Construction was stopped and a legal tussle[3] ensued.

Kenya Railways insist that the railway has been designed with animal welfare[4] in mind. In the stretch of railway through the national park, the train will be elevated above the ground, allowing animals to pass freely underneath the tracks. It will also be camouflaged, soundproofed and vibration-proofed.

Adapted from *www.theworldweekly.com*, 2018

1. gather (many people) 2. plan 3. fight 4. well-being

A2 1. **Say** what project is mentioned in the article.

2. How did the people react to this project?

B1 3. **Explain** the pros and cons of this project.

4. How advanced is the project today?

B1+ 5. **Focus** on the last paragraph and draw the project.

ESCAPE

Ce

▶ How have

YOUR MISSION

PLAY IN GROUPS.

- You are a gr research in the in Ireland.
- You are stud mysterious st Suddenly a thi You are trappe

The roo contai Solve the a clue

1. Towards freedom

The scene takes place in Mississippi in 1840. Huckleberry Finn, a young boy, has decided to escape from his violent father and run away from civilisation. On his journey he meets Jim, a slave.

a. Read this extract from the graphic novel and **explain** why both Huck and Jim have decided to run away.

b. Why is Jim nervous about meeting Huck?

c. Comment on Huck's mixed feelings.

d. Explain the goal of this modern version and **comment** on the speech bubble *"Here's a problem to think on."*

YOUR TASK

DIFFÉRENCIATION

WAY 1 You are working on this graphic novel. **Create** a storyboard for the next three vignettes of the story: Huck and Jim are now on the raft sailing down the Mississippi River.

WAY 2 You are working on a new adaptation of *Huckleberry Finn*. **Write** a short script with dialogues to adapt this page on screen.

BOOST YOUR SKILLS!

Décrire des émotions

- *I **finally feel like**...*
- *He was **afraid**.*
- *That **worried** me **some**.*
- *At the same time, **I didn't want** Jim **to** get caught.*

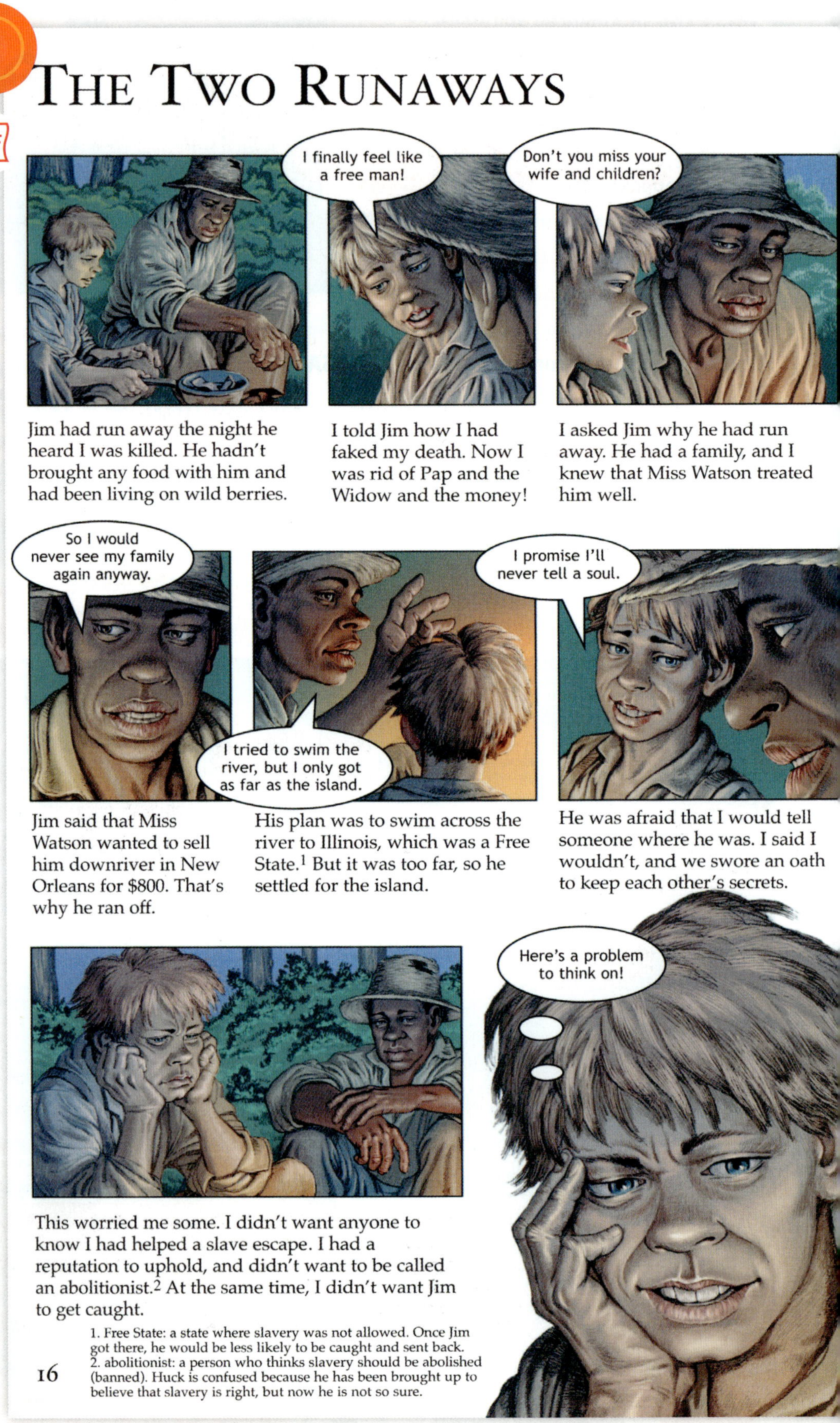

▲ Mark Twain, *The Adventures of Huckleberry Finn*, retold by Tom Ratliff, illustrated by Penko Gelev, 2008

2 My New Plan

Huckleberry Finn feels he should tell Jim's owner, Miss Watson, where Jim is. He writes her a note.

So I tore up the note and decided to continue my wicked ways and steal Jim out of slavery.

a. Read these other extracts and **guess** what happened to Jim.

b. Identify Huck's new plan and **comment** on his emotions in the passage.

WORDS

- **b**ubble
- **c**aption
- disc**o**very
- fr**ie**ndship
- inj**u**stice
- plant**a**tion
- t**u**rning point
- ast**o**nished
- comm**i**tted
- d**ou**btful /'daʊtfəl/
- h**e**lpful
- h**o**peful
- keen on
- moved
- p**u**zzled: *perplexe*
- betr**ay**
- den**ou**nce
- fight r**a**cism
- prom**o**te equ**a**lity
- prot**e**ct

3 Why read *Huckleberry Finn* today?

Nathan live! MP3

PARCOURS DIFFÉRENCIÉS WB → p. 52

a. Listen to this BookTuber and **pick out** the reasons for reading Huck and Jim's story today.

b. Recap Mark Twain's message and **comment** on the BookTuber's tone in her review.

YOUR TASK

Post a comment on your BookTube channel to **explain** your views on *Huckleberry Finn* and **say** why you want to read the novel.

BOOST YOUR SKILLS!

Émettre un point de vue

- *I **absolutely / truly** love that book.*
- ***I think** it's **essential**.*
- ***I'm going to tell you why I feel that way**.*

AT HOME Go to *lyceen.nathan.fr/shine-bright2* to learn more about Mark Twain.

EXPLORE

2. The Underground Railroad

1 A kid explains history

Nathan live! VIDÉO

a. Watch the video and **take notes** about Harriet Tubman (identity and actions).

b. Pick out elements to explain what the Underground Railroad was about.

c. GRAMMAR **Focus on** this expression: "*they were called abolitionists.*" **Comment** on the verbal form used and **explain** this choice. ▸ p. 194

d. Comment on the choice of a child YouTuber to talk about the past.

2

▲ This cartoon was inspired by a banknote project paying tribute to Harriet Tubman.

◀ Bronze sculpture by Jane DeDecker, 2006

A tribute to Women's History Month: Harriet Tubman Underground Railroad State Park opens

Hardy visitors who braved the cold to attend the grand opening weekend of the Harriet Tubman Underground Railroad State Park and Visitor Center got a taste of the bleak[1] winds and open country[2] that Tubman maneuvered when she led family and friends from slavery to freedom more than 150 years ago.

The atmosphere inside was anything but bleak. The state park that will now anchor[3] Tubman's contribution to American history was alive and brimming[4] with energy, curiosity and reverence for the abolitionist, Union Army spy, and women's rights advocate who continues to inspire people around the world, almost 200 years after her birth in Dorchester County.

Marvin Winans, keynote speaker at a breakfast in honor of Tubman, said, "We cannot hide ourselves in our own comfort and not recognize and tell the stories of how we got here."

"What I noticed about Harriet Tubman is that once she was free, she could have kicked back and said, 'I made it'," Winans said, recalling Tubman's repeated trips back into the South to rescue more than 70 persons and give instructions to more than 100 others.

"How free do you think you are when someone who looks like you is not free?" Winans asked the audience.

Deborah BAILEY, *The Baltimore Times*, 2017

1. cold 2. *paysage dégagé* 3. *ancrer* 4. *débordant*

a. Observe the cartoon and **explain** the message it conveys.

b. Read the article and **find** information about the event (place, atmosphere, goal).

c. Pick out Harriet Tubman's multiple qualities and missions, and their impact on visitors.

d. According to Marvin Winans, what aspect of Harriet Tubman's personality is important to remember?

WORDS

- **i**con /'aɪkɒn/
- **r**unaway

- deter**m**ined
- **g**enerous

- uni**q**ue

- pay tri**b**ute to /'trɪbju:t/ sb: *rendre hommage à*
- praise sb for

3

PARCOURS DIFFÉRENCIÉS

WB → p. 53 Nathan live! MP3

The scene takes place in Georgia. Cora and Caesar are two slaves who have decided to run away from their plantation to go north on the Underground Railroad. They are soon joined by an unexpected traveler.

They had made it only a small ways when they heard the voice and stopped. Cora looked at Caesar for a cue[1]. He held his hands out and listened. It was not an angry voice. Or a man's voice.

Caesar shook his head when he realized the identity of the culprit. "Lovey – shush!"

Lovey had enough sense to be quiet once she saw them. "I knew you were up to something[2]," she whispered when she caught up. [...]

"You get on back before you ruin us," Caesar said.

"I'm going where you going," Lovey said.

Cora frowned. If they sent Lovey back, the girl might be caught sneaking[3] into her cabin. Lovey was not one to keep her tongue still. She didn't want to be responsible for the girl.

"He's not going to take the three of us," Caesar said.

"He knows I'm coming?" Cora asked.

He shook his head.

"Then two surprises as good as one," she said. She lifted her sack. "We got enough food, anyway."

He had all night to get used to the idea. It would be a long time before they slept. Eventually, Lovey stopped crying out at every sudden noise from the night creatures, or when she stepped too deep in the water, but she did not recognize the other side of her friend, whatever had overtaken the girl and made her run. But every slave thinks about it. In the morning and in the afternoon and in the night. Dreaming of it. Every dream a dream of escape even when it didn't look like it. When it was a dream of new shoes. The opportunity stepped up and Lovey availed herself, heedless of the whip[4].

The three of them wended[5] west, tromping through the black water. Cora couldn't have led them. She didn't know how Caesar did it. But he was ever surprising her. Of course he had a map in his head and could read stars as well as letters.

Colson WHITEHEAD, *The Underground Railroad*, 2016

1. *signal* 2. *quelque chose se tramait* 3. *se faufiler* 4. *sans de soucier du fouet* 5. *se diriger vers*

▲ Colson Whitehead, multi-awarded writer

a. **Identify** the character joining Cora and Caesar and **explain** why they were afraid in the first place.

b. **Pick out** elements in the text showing that their journey was difficult.

c. GRAMMAR **Read** the first sentence (*"They had made it [...] and stopped"*). **Give the reason** for using two different verb forms. PRÉCIS 13 16

d. **Explain** and **comment** on the characters' dream to go north.

YOUR TASK

MÉDIATION

DIFFÉRENCIATION

WAY 1 You are Cora's great granddaughter: **tell** your ancestor's story to a friend.

WAY 2 You are a member of a book club. **Present** the passage and **insist** on the importance of remembering through books.

WORDS

- flight /flaɪt/ = escape
- quest /kwɛst/
- role model

- frightened

- perilous

- flee sth
- go on a journey /ˈdʒɜːrni/

- overcome obstacles
- put one's life in danger
- rely on sth/sb /rɪˈlaɪ/
- seek refuge

BOOST YOUR SKILLS!

Parler de faits passés

- *They **had made** it only a small ways **when they heard**...*
- *She **didn't** want to be responsible...*
- *But he **was** ever **surprising** her.*

PRÉCIS 13 16

EXPLORE

3. The importance of remembering

Confronting the painful history of slavery

live! VIDÉO

PARCOURS DIFFÉRENCIÉS WB → p. 54

1

a. Watch the video and **find** basic information about the museum (name, place, founder).

b. Explain what visitors can see there and why the founder decided to create it.

CULTURE SPOT

Slave-owners would buy slaves to work on **the plantations** to grow and pick cotton or cane, or do farm jobs.

2

Black celebrities share the importance of Juneteenth

By **Christina Santi** – On June 19, 2018

Juneteenth is a holiday celebrated by Black Americans on June 19, commemorating the abolition of slavery in the United States. Many African-Americans view the day as their rightful Independence Day over the national holiday on July 4, throwing parades and events. Many Black politicians and entertainers flocked to their social media platforms to spread awareness of the day and to honor how far we have come since the days of slavery.

www.ebony.com

Shonda Rhimes
@shondarhimes

"We need to advocate for an accurate history."
#Juneteenth2018

460 6:11 PM Jun 19, 2018

Ms. Opal Lee's Juneteenth Dream
At 92 years young this activist is as determined as ever to see Juneteenth recognized as a national holiday.
shondaland.com

Barack Obama
@BarackObamar

It's #Juneteenth! Let's celebrate the great people in our past that have made contributions to society, no matter what party they are with. pic.twitter.com/2hGhiSul8K
— Barack Obama (@BarackObama) June 16, 2018

Bernice King
The King Center

#FreedomDay
#Juneteenth
[Not familiar with the day? Do some research today. Let's be educated and empowered!]

1.890 1:26 PM Jun 19, 2018

www.ebony.com

a. Read the article and **recap** the goal of Juneteenth.

b. Focus on the celebrities' tweets and **explain** why this day is important for them.

YOUR TASK

Exchange tweets to react to Shonda Rhimes' one on "Let's advocate for an accurate history."

HOW TO PLAY "BLACK HISTORY MONTH HALL OF FAME"

Play in pairs.

Are you ready to pay tribute to figures who contributed to break the chains for Black History Month?

Roll the dice and answer the questions. Win one point for each right answer.

When you land on a "star", you must state three facts about the person or thing to get the point. If you do not do so, wait until the next round to try again and move forward.

The first team to reach the finish line is ready to celebrate Black History Month.

GAME ON!

1 ***Revelations* is ... describing the journey of African-Americans from freedom to slavery.**
a. a song
b. a choreography
c. a book

2

3 **Give the dates of the American Civil War and the main reason for the conflict.**

4

5 **On the Underground Railroad, who were the "conductors" and the "passengers"?**

6

7 **Give one of Mark Twain's messages in *The Adventures of Huckleberry Finn*.**

8

9 **Name two ways of making sure past events are remembered.**

10

11 **Give two reasons to create memorials.**

12

FINISH LINE

EXPLORE

1. Everlasting tales

1

live! MP3

"Your Silver Shoes will carry you over the desert," replied Glinda. "If you had known their power you could have gone back to your Aunt Em the very first day you came to this country."

"But then I should not have had my wonderful brains!" cried the Scarecrow[1]. "I might have passed my whole life in the farmer's cornfield."

"And I should not have had my lovely heart," said the Tin Woodman. "I might have stood and rusted[2] in the forest till the end of the world." [...]

"This is all true," said Dorothy, "and I'm glad I was of use to these good friends. But now that each of them has had what he most desired, and each is happy in having a kingdom to rule beside, I think I should like to go back to Kansas."

"The Silver Shoes," said the Good Witch, "have wonderful powers. And one of the most curious things about them is that they can carry you to any place in the world in three steps, and each step will be made in the wink of an eye. All you have to do is to knock the heels[3] together three times and command the shoes to carry you wherever you wish to go."

"If that is so," said the child joyfully, "I will ask them to carry me back to Kansas at once."

She threw her arms around the Lion's neck and kissed him, patting[4] his big head tenderly. Then she kissed the Tin Woodman, who was weeping in a way most dangerous to his joints. But she hugged the soft, stuffed body of the Scarecrow in her arms instead of kissing his painted face, and found she was crying herself at this sorrowful[5] parting from her loving comrades. [...]

Dorothy now took Toto[6] up solemnly in her arms, and having said one last good-bye she clapped the heels of her shoes together three times, saying:

"Take me home to Aunt Em!"

L. Frank BAUM, *The Wonderful Wizard of Oz*, 1900

1. *épouvantail* 2. *rouiller* 3. *talons* 4. *caresser* 5. very sad 6. Dorothy's dog

CULTURE SPOT

The Wonderful Wizard of Oz is a famous American children's novel, which was written by L. Frank Baum in 1900 and adapted for the cinema in 1939. Readers follow Dorothy on her quest from Oz back to Kansas.

▲ *The Wizard of Oz*, musical directed by Victor Fleming, starring Judy Garland, 1939

a. Read the text and **identify** the characters. Then **say** how the Scarecrow and the Tin Woodman have changed.

b. Explain the role of the silver shoes. What does Dorothy wish now?

c. Explain what makes Dorothy happy.

d. GRAMMAR **Observe** the last sentence. Why do you think the writer used direct speech? ▸ p. 206

2 Emma Watson plays Belle

live! Nathan MP3

PARCOURS DIFFÉRENCIÉS WB → p. 56

a. Listen to the interview and **list** the main character's qualities.

b. Explain how Emma Watson feels about the story.

c. PHONOLOGY **Listen** carefully to the sentence, *"As a child you love Disney, but as an adult, you still love Disney,"* and **say** how the rhythm helps Emma share her emotions about the story.

d. Explain why some adults still like fairy tales.

YOUR TASK

You are the journalist who interviewed Emma Watson. **Write** an email to your editor-in-chief to **report** the main things Emma Watson said during the interview.

BOOST YOUR SKILLS!

Partager son ressenti

- *And* ***that to me just seemed like such an*** *interesting kind of relationship.*
- *I had* ***never seen before****...*
- ***There was just something so*** *beautiful.*
- ***You know... is just*** *amazing.*

WORDS

- hope
- quest /kwɛst/

- dr**ea**my
- ench**a**nting
- f**ee**l-good
- insp**i**ring
- m**a**rvellous

- f**o**llow one's dreams
- make a dr**ea**m come true
- wish for s**o**mething

3 Why Disneyland is just as magical for adults

So I'm here at a matinee performance of the live musical *Frozen* in Disney California Park. The auditorium is packed with primary school-aged children; a woman asks if the empty seat beside me is reserved. I ask what she's doing watching *Frozen* alone. Turns out she's the chief executive of a women's refuge charity in Australia, and has just presented a paper at the United Nations in New York. But she's added four days, at her own expense, for "me-time".

"Really? Disney? Why?" I ask.

"It's a release from the real world, a chance to bathe in the innocence of youth, to escape the shackles of adult conformity."

Suddenly it doesn't seem so weird being an adult without kids at a Disney resort.

So what's the attraction? When Walt Disney opened Disneyland in 1955, there was nothing like it. Legend has it that Disney was bored sitting on park benches while his children had all the fun. So he imagined an amusement park that would entertain the entire family.

Once the park was open, he greeted visitors, reminding employees they were all members of "a cast" and should never appear "out-of-character".

Steve MEACHAM,
www.traveller.com.au, 2018

a. Read the article and **identify** the age range of people present in the auditorium. **Comment** on the journalist's reaction.

b. Explain what the Australian woman is looking for at Disneyland.

c. Sum up Walt Disney's goal with the creation of his theme park.

d. Comment on Walt Disney's instruction to his staff to *"never appear out-of-character"* (l.27).

EXPLORE

2. Twists and turns

1

The Ugly Duckling still felt gross compared with everyone else. But then she got Instagram, and there's this one filter that makes her look awesome.

Pinocchio e-mailed his professor and said, "I've had a family emergency and need one more day to work on my final paper."

Rapunzel chopped off all her hair, and everyone was loving her new profile picture.
But then she was like, *Wait, did everyone hate my long hair and they just weren't telling me?*

Tim Manley, *Alice in Tumblr-Land and Other Fairy Tales for a New Generation*, 2013

Docs 1 and 2.

a. Observe the illustrations first and **guess** what the stories could be about.

b. Now **choose** one of the texts. **Identify** the twisted elements and **explain** how this story is modern.

c. Comment on the tone and the message of these stories.

d. Listen to Tim Manley's interview and **recap** the goal of his project.

YOUR TASK

You are Tim Manley working on the next volume of *Alice in Tumblr-Land and Other Fairy Tales for a New Generation*.
Choose a famous fairy tale, **write** a short twisted version of it and **illustrate** it.

BOOST YOUR SKILLS!

Parodier et détourner

- *The **overly picky prince** determined to find a **true princess**.*
- *"I fear I shall never find a true princess that is **truly true**, and now **it's beginning to rain**."*
- *"So, the moral of the story: always be nice to people and **don't hide your vegetables under the bed**."*

live! MP3

Tim Manley on writing *Tumblr*

2

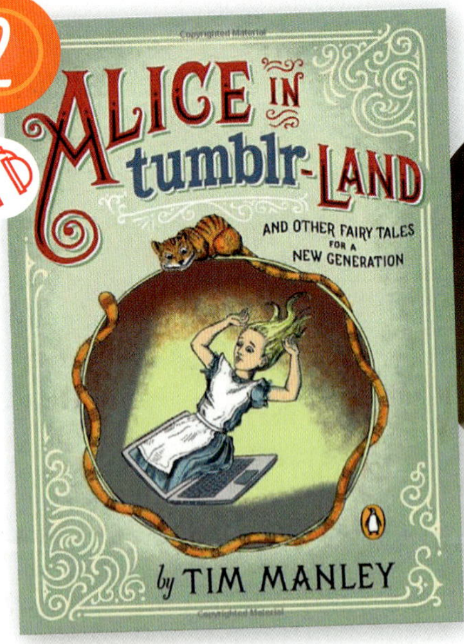

WORDS

- anachronism
- discrepancy /dɪˈskrɛpənsi/: *divergence*
- twist: *rebondissement*

- classic
- disrespectful

- humorous
- ironic

- make fun of
- play with the genre
- rewrite

3 The Princess and the Pea

live! VIDÉO

PARCOURS DIFFÉRENCIÉS WB → p. 57

a. Watch the video and **compare** the prince's attitude with the princess's at the beginning of the story.

b. Explain the prince's mother's plan.

c. Describe the princess's reaction when she finds out about it.

d. Explain the ending of this modern version of the story.

4

live! MP3

Cinderella and I are on all fours washing her stepsisters'[1] clothes in the tub[2] in the basement. At least they have running water in Floom, otherwise we'd be standing on a riverbank.

I'm soaping. Cinderella is rinsing, and Jonah is hanging. We have a whole production line going on. Next we're ironing wrinkled[3] dresses. [...]

"I don't understand what Farrah wants from me," Cinderella says. "How can I rescue myself?"

"Let's think about it," I say. "You said you were stuck here, right?"

"I am stuck here. I have nowhere else to go."

"But you're not chained to the house," I say. You can leave if you want to."

"Where's your dad?" Jonah asks. "Is he dead?" [...]

"He's a sailor," Cinderella says. "And he sailed away. I doubt I'll ever see him again. And he left me there. Stranded[4]. I have no money and nowhere to go. That's why I need the prince to rescue me."

"Why don't you get a job?" I say, rinsing a pair of striped socks. "Then you'll have your own money and you can get your own house."

Sarah MLYNOWSKI, *Whatever After: If the Shoe Fits, Book 2*, 2015

1. *demi-soeurs*
2. *bassine*
3. *froissées*
4. *coincée*

WORDS

- c**a**ricature
- (perfect) h**ou**sewife
- st**e**reotype /'stɛriətaɪp/

- det**er**mined
- gr**u**mpy
- h**o**peless
- id**y**llic = w**o**nderful
- indep**e**ndent

- bec**o**me em**a**ncipated
- conv**ey** a m**e**ssage
- take one's life in one's hands
- whine /waɪn/: *se plaindre*

a. Read the text and **identify** the characters and their activities.

b. Explain the main character's problem.

c. Rephrase and **comment** on the suggestion made by her friend.

d. What message do you think the author wanted to convey?

BOOST YOUR ENGLISH!

Grammar — Rapporter des paroles

PRÉCIS 37 ET EXERCICES

Nathan live! GRAMMAR TUTO

DISCOURS DIRECT
Les propos entendus sont répétés à l'identique par celui qui les rapporte.

On décrit ce qui se passe, au présent.

Dorothy **says**,
"I **want** to go home."

Les propos ont été dits dans le passé.

The Big Bad Wolf **said**,
"I'**m** hungry."

→ *Le loup avait faim à ce moment-là.*

On rapporte la question telle quelle.

The Princess **asked**,
"Where **is** Prince Charming?"

DISCOURS INDIRECT
Les paroles entendues sont reformulées par celui qui les rapporte, sans guillemets.

Dorothy **tells** them
(that) **she wants** to go home.

The Big Bad Wolf **said**
(that) **he was** hungry that day.

→ *Au moment où l'on parle, le loup n'a plus faim.*

The Princess **asked**
where Prince Charming **was**.
She **wondered if** he **loved her**.

⚠ Attention aux **pronoms,** à l'**accord des verbes** et à la **concordance des temps.**

⚠ ***where*** et ***if***
Attention à l'ordre des mots : **S + V**.

1 **Rapporte les propos ci-dessous au style indirect. Utilise des verbes introducteurs au passé.**

"Is Grandma home?"
(Little Red Riding Hood)

"I've loved fairy tales since my childhood."
(Emma Watson)

"When will I find the enchanted forest?"
(Prince Charming)

"I hate the Wicked Witch of the West."
(Dorothy)

2 **Réécris ces phrases au style direct.**

a. The princess asked if the witch had cast a spell.
b. She said she was still in love with Disney characters.
c. He asked me if I wanted to read this Tumblr version.
d. Prince Charming wondered where he could find his princess.
e. The stepmother said that she would have her revenge.

3 **Rapporte ce dialogue entre Blanche-Neige (*Snow White*) et la sorcière (*the Witch*) au style direct, puis au style indirect.**

"Can you open the door please?"
"Who are you? Do I know you?"
"Please, I'm a poor woman and I have something for you."
"You're very nice, this apple looks tasty and juicy."
"Of course, my dear, help yourself!"

More in ***Pump it up!*** p. 54

Vocabulary — Once upon a time

Nathan live! MP3 — Nathan live! LEXIQUIZ

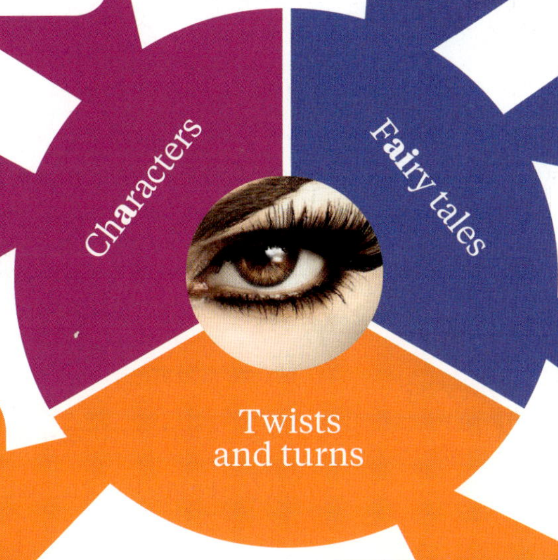

Good guys and villains
- beast
- big bad wolf
- dwarf / dwarves
- fairy godmother
- prince charming
- princess
- wicked witch
- wizard

Personalities
- quality ≠ flaw
- brave
- fearful
- narrow-minded
- rebellious
- supportive

Settings
- castle
- enchanted forest
- far-away kingdom
- remote village

Actions
- good deed ≠ mischief
- go on a quest/journey
- live happily ever after
- look forward to a happy ending
- seek revenge

Ingredients
- true love's kiss
- cast a spell
- curse
- Once upon a time
- overcome obstacles

Adaptation
- new moral
- new plot
- new setting and location
- rewriting
- screenwriter
- create a story
- relate to/identify with a character

Parody
- humour
- irony
- distort = twist
- play with the genre

1 Complète chaque phrase avec l'expression qui convient.

Prince Charming – happily ever after – overcome obstacles – seek revenge – cast a spell – far-away

a. A fairy tale character usually has to ... before the end of the story.

b. In a fairy tale, a kind, brave young man usually goes to a ... kingdom where an endangered princess awaits ... . He saves her, then they live ... .

c. A wicked witch who ... will sometimes ... on an entire village.

2 Complète chaque phrase avec le mot entre parenthèses qui convient.

a. In *The Princess and the Pea*, the prince is *(charming / sexist)*.

b. Pinocchio finally becomes a real boy because of his *(mischief / good deeds)*.

c. Emma Watson admires Belle because she is *(narrow-minded / open-minded)*.

d. In the twisted version of *Sleeping Beauty*, Maleficent is *(an / a / evil / kind)* character.

Phonology — Les liaisons

Nathan live! MP3

Lorsque l'on parle, les mots s'enchaînent de façon fluide, sans pause. Aussi, lorsqu'un mot finissant par un son consonne est suivi d'un mot commençant par un son voyelle, on fait la liaison.

1 Écoute ces exemples et concentre-toi sur les passages en rouge :

Since I was about four years old...

As a child you love Disney, but as an adult...

2 Observe les extraits suivants et anticipe les liaisons que tu vas entendre. Écoute et vérifie.

They really disliked each other at the beginning, and they didn't get on.

The movie came out the year I was born, in 1990.

3 Entraîne-toi à prononcer les phrases ci-dessus en respectant les liaisons.

FINAL TASK

Write your own version of a fairy tale for an American production.

You are members of the screenwriters' team of the series *Once Upon a Time*. Write a new, very short version of a traditional tale you know.

Writing a fairy tale

1. **Choose** the fairy tale you would like to adapt.
2. **List** and **describe** the characters (qualities and flaws, roles, etc.).
3. **Think about** the twists and turns you would like to include (new location, new setting, new characters, new conflict, humour).
4. **Decide** on a new moral: what message would you like to send to your readers?
5. **Start writing and enjoy!**

Collaborative writing

1. **Brainstorm** ideas and **choose** a fairy tale.
2. **Decide** on everybody's tasks: sharing is caring!
   – One of you (the producer) will **moderate** the discussions and help the writers **negotiate**. He also makes the final decision in case of hesitations.
   – The writers are each in charge of a key element: the setting, one special character, one special moment (a funny moment and a tense situation).
3. **Start writing**, using an online tool like *Framapad*.
4. **Enjoy** this collaborative experience!

YES YOU CAN!

Write a modern fairy tale

Nathan live! MP3

TITRE

Choisis un titre court et percutant qui donnera un indice sur le conte adapté.

Si tu es producteur/productrice, explique et justifie ton choix à tes scénaristes.

The Girl and the Wolf

CADRE GÉNÉRAL

Commence par décrire le lieu et le ou les personnages principaux.

Si tu es le/la scénariste en charge du décor, ajoute des détails avec l'outil d'écriture en ligne.

One afternoon a big wolf waited in a dark forest for a little girl to come along.

DIALOGUES

Utilise des dialogues pour rendre ton conte dynamique et vivant (tu peux utiliser du discours direct et indirect).

N'hésite pas à relancer tes co-auteurs pour trouver la meilleure idée.

"Are you carrying that basket to your grandmother?" asked the wolf. The little girl said yes, she was. So, the wolf asked her where her grandmother lived and the little girl told him and he disappeared into the wood.

Extracts from James Thurber, *Fables for Our Time and Famous Poems Illustrated*

NOUVEL ÉLÉMENT

Ajoute une touche d'humour et un élément nouveau à cette intrigue connue. Utilise des mots de liaison pour souligner les différentes étapes.

Chacun peut ajouter sa petite touche personnelle d'humour dans le nouvel élément de votre histoire.

She had approached no nearer than twenty-five feet from the bed when she saw that it was not her grandmother but the wolf [...]. So the little girl took an automatic out of her basket and shot the wolf dead.

STRATEGIES Développer une idée à l'écrit p. 219

AUTO-ÉVALUATION
WB → p. 59

Compréhension de l'oral — Comprendre une interview

Disney directors create new characters

live! MP3

A2 1. **Listen** to the document and **identify** the different speakers.

2. **Pick out** the names of the famous Disney characters mentioned.

A2+ 3. **Explain** the new character's quest.

B1 4. **Give the reason** why the directors chose not to include any romance in the film.

5. **Rephrase** and **comment** on the message they try to convey.

Compréhension de l'écrit — Comprendre un extrait de conte de fées

For the baby Aurora's naming ceremony[1] the king and queen invited everyone they knew, as well as three evil fairies. [...]

And all the guests gave gifts to the beautiful little baby. [...] And then it was the three evil fairies' turn. [...]

The first fairy laughed wickedly,[2] "Hmmm. How about beauty? She may as well be pleasant to look upon while she slaves for us eternally."

The second fairy said, "I'll give her the gift of song and dance. Perhaps she can entertain us."

The third fairy said, "I give her parents the power they wish and supernatural help they need to attain their hearts' desire. And on her sixteenth birthday, we will claim the princess as ours."

The three wicked fairies laughed.

"*No!*"

Hidden among the guests was one of the last remaining good fairies in the kingdom. [...]

"My lord and lady," Maleficent said, coming forward. "You cannot do this. You cannot *sell* your child to the likes of these."

"I thought we had done with[3] the last of you," the king growled. [...]

"Poor child," she murmured. "My powers are not strong enough to prevent this wicked transaction. But I swear on my own life I will be back and set everything to rights. On your sixteenth birthday, goodness and nobility will be restored to this wretched[4] kingdom."

And she vanished in a puff of green smoke.

Adapted from Liz BRAZWELL,
Once Upon A Dream: A Twisted Tale, 2016

1. *baptême* 2. evilly 3. *en avoir fini avec* 4. *maudit, misérable*

A2+ 1. **Read** the text and **identify** the different characters.

2. **Rephrase** the story in a few words.

B1 3. **Compare** and **contrast** Maleficent to the other fairies.

4. **React** to the parents' decision.

B1+ 5. **Comment** on the tone and **explain** why the tale is modern.

STRATEGIES

Comprendre un document audio

Step 1
ANTICIPER AVANT L'ÉCOUTE

Avant d'écouter le document, **anticipe à partir du titre, de l'image** (lorsqu'il y en a une) et des autres documents que tu as étudiés dans la séquence.

TIPS
Fais des hypothèses sur le contenu du document.

live! Nathan MP3

2 **An investigation of Pluckley**

• Lis le titre et mets-le en relation avec l'image : *Maybe there was a crime in Pluckley.*

• Concentre-toi sur la photo : *The scene might take place in a countryside pub. We can imagine that something evil happened there.*

Step 2
IDENTIFIER LA SITUATION ET SAISIR LES INFORMATIONS ESSENTIELLES

• Lors de la première écoute, concentre-toi sur le repérage des éléments suivants :
– **le nombre de locuteurs** et leurs caractéristiques : *A woman interviewed by a man, Sarah: landlady, grew up in the village* ;
– **les mots qui sont répétés** afin de dégager le thème central : *horses, village* ;
– **les dates ou lieux** si l'information est donnée : *Pluckley* ;
– **les mots accentués** : *ghost, legend, swear, misty*.

• Utilise tous **les indices sonores** : pars du connu pour deviner ou compenser l'inconnu. Repère **les bruits de fond, les accents, les intonations** (colère, surprise, excitation, etc.) et plus largement tout ce que l'oreille peut saisir : *sound* → *galloping horses in the background*.

TIPS
Prête attention à l'intonation des phrases : elle peut être **montante**, **descendante** ou **descendante-montante**.
– **L'intonation montante** indique souvent une **question fermée** (réponse par oui ou non), ou des énoncés avec une **intention de rassurer, d'exprimer sa sympathie ou son désaccord** :
"And you are living in a reputedly haunted village?"
– **L'intonation descendante** indique des **informations neutres**, une **question ouverte**, ou encore l'**exclamation** :
"My name is Sarah."
– l'**intonation descendante montante** (*fall rise*) : dans ce cas, le locuteur **apporte une précision** ou **réagit** à ce qui vient d'être dit :
So, it seems!

Step 3
FAIRE DES LIENS ET CONTINUER À ANTICIPER

• Pendant les écoutes suivantes, prends des notes sous forme de **mots clés** et d'**expressions courtes** (STRATEGIES p. 211).

• Après chaque écoute, complète tes notes et prends le temps de **faire des liens** avec ce que tu as repéré lors des écoutes précédentes.

TIP
Attention, on ne te demande pas d'écrire le script du document audio, le but est bien d'en extraire des informations utiles.

Step 4
RASSEMBLER ET ORGANISER

• Au terme des écoutes, **réorganise tes notes** afin de **préparer la restitution orale ou écrite**.

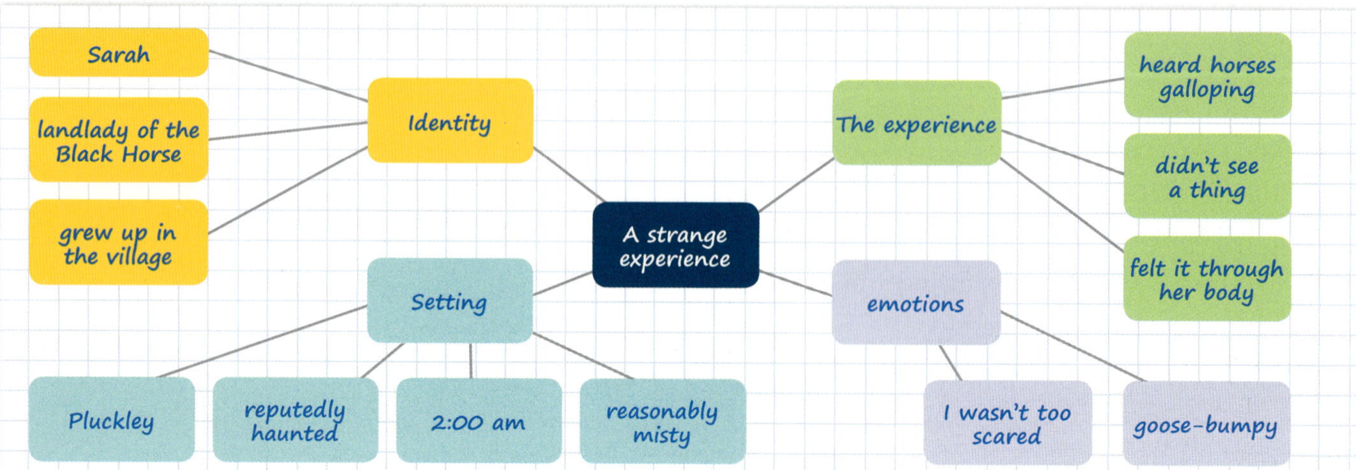

Prendre des notes

STRATEGIES

Tu peux être amené(e) à prendre des notes dans beaucoup de circonstances :
- *en écoutant un document (audio ou vidéo) ;*
- *en écoutant des camarades ou ton professeur (lors d'un exposé, d'une restitution de document) ;*
- *lorsque tu lis un texte.*

Step 1

IDENTIFIER L'OBJECTIF

Lorsque tu prends des notes, interroge-toi sur **leur finalité**, demande-toi à quoi elles vont te servir :

Outil de mémorisation ?
Support pour te souvenir de ce que tu as lu ou entendu

OU

Outil de restitution ?
Point d'appui pour partager des informations que tu as recueillies

TIP

Dans le cas d'une restitution, garde bien en tête que tes interlocuteurs n'ont pas toujours connaissance du support que tu as découvert. Prends bien en notes toutes les informations qui pourront les aider à découvrir le document.

Step 2

SÉLECTIONNER LES INFORMATIONS PERTINENTES

Lorsque tu prends des notes, **tu ne peux pas tout écrire**. L'objectif est de **trier les informations** pour **repérer l'essentiel**.

- **Prépare-toi en amont :** assure-toi que tu sais quel type d'information tu recherches. Cela t'aidera à orienter ta prise de notes.
- **Écoute ou lis attentivement :** repère les mots accentués, les répétitions. Si tu prends des notes à partir d'une vidéo, pense à observer aussi les images.

TIP

Relis les questions posées par ton professeur et appuie-toi sur les hypothèses que tu as émises.
STRATEGIES p. 210

Step 3

ÉCRIRE EFFICACEMENT

- Constitue-toi **un stock d'abréviations** qui te serviront dans plusieurs situations (compréhension orale ou écrite, écoute de camarades, etc.).
- **Écris clairement et aère ta prise de notes.** Tu pourras la compléter en relisant ou en réécoutant le document, si tes camarades donnent des précisions ou en autonomie, à la fin de l'exercice.

TIPS

- Certaines abréviations ne sont pas spécifiques à l'anglais : pense à ce que tu utilises dans les autres matières. Pense aussi à abréger les noms de pays (UK, NZ).
- Écris lisiblement pour être sûr(e) de parvenir à te relire, même à la fin du chapitre.

Step 4

ORGANISER SES NOTES

- Appuie-toi sur **la structure du document** et/ou **sa présentation**.
- **Repère les connecteurs logiques** et utilise des symboles pour montrer comment les idées s'enchaînent : + / ↗ / ≠ ...
- Il n'y a pas de méthode idéale pour prendre des notes. Il faut donc t'entraîner pour trouver celle qui te convient. Tu peux par exemple **prendre des notes de façon linéaire** (exemple 1), ou **utiliser un système de carte mentale** (exemple 2).

TIPS

- Si tu prends des notes à partir d'un document audio ou vidéo, pense à tirer un trait après chaque locuteur.
- Profite des pauses pour organiser les informations.
- Dessine une carte mentale sur ton brouillon avant même de commencer à écouter ou à lire. N'hésite pas à noter **?** quand il y a des informations que tu n'as pas réussi à noter. Tu complèteras plus tard.

2.5 million people
→ NZ: adventure act.
Man jumps
= big opportunity
→ challenge / life is a challge
Tourism > bungy-jumping:
24 years ago
Queenstown
Kiwi tourism: $18 billion

Exemple 1 : notes à partir du doc 1 p. 92 *Into the void*

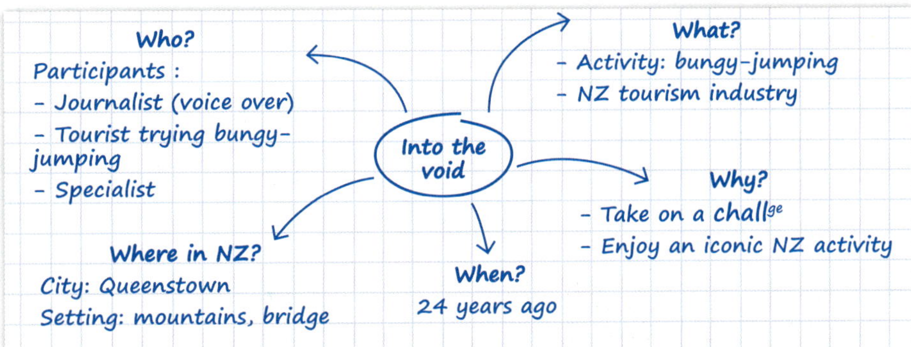

Exemple 2 : carte mentale à partir du doc 1 p. 92 *Into the void*

STRATEGIES

Lire et comprendre un texte

Step 1

CHERCHER DES INDICES ET ANTICIPER

- Commence par **repérer le paratexte** pour déterminer le type de texte que tu vas lire (titre, auteur, source, date de publication, illustration ou photographie, etc.) et **faire des hypothèses** sur le contenu.
- Utilise ces informations pour déterminer **la nature du document** (texte de fiction ? texte de presse ?, etc.), puis fais une première lecture globale pour dégager le thème.
- Les repérages à effectuer diffèrent selon la nature du texte. ▶

Nature du texte ?

Texte de fiction	Texte de presse
• **Qui :** les différents personnages, le narrateur • **Quoi :** les éléments principaux de l'intrigue • **Quand et où :** le lieu et le moment de l'action, la date de publication, le contexte d'écriture	• **Qui :** l'auteur de l'article (journaliste ? auteur ?, etc.) • **Quand et où :** la source, la date de publication, le contexte d'écriture • **Quoi :** le sujet abordé, la thèse défendue, le point de vue du journaliste

Step 2

FAIRE DES REPÉRAGES EFFICACES

- Appuie-toi ensuite sur les éléments suivants pour approfondir ta compréhension du texte.

1. Les possessifs et les pronoms : repère à qui ou à quoi ils se rapportent afin de comprendre les liens entre les différents éléments du texte.

2. Les mots transparents : aide-toi des ressemblances fréquentes entre les mots anglais et français, mais prends garde aux faux-amis !

3. Les mots de liaison : utilise les mots de liaison pour cerner le lien entre les différentes informations de la phrase (liens temporels, de cause, d'opposition, etc.).

Step 3

RÉSOUDRE LES DIFFICULTÉS

1. Les mots inconnus

– appuie-toi sur le contexte. Demande-toi si le mot a un sens positif ou négatif ;

– cherche les mots dont a été dérivé le mot inconnu :
- *healthier ➔ healthi + -er* (forme comparative) *= better for the health*
- *downsized ➔ down + size + -ed* (prétérit) *= to reduce the size of something*

2. Le culturel

Appuie-toi sur tes connaissances culturelles, historiques, géographiques pour **situer le contexte du document**. Cela peut t'aider à percevoir le point de vue de l'auteur, à comprendre certains mots inconnus et te donner des pistes de réponse aux questions qui te seront posées.

Step 4

RECONSTRUIRE LE SENS

Fais des liens entre les mots clés que tu repères. Appuie-toi sur les pronoms, les mots de liaison, les adverbes de temps, la ponctuation. Il te faut mettre en lien tous les éléments que tu as repérés pour en déduire le sens du texte.

- *Happy Meal ➔ different ➔ healthier options*
- *nutrition criteria ➔ calories ➔ reduced*

TIP

Fais le va-et-vient entre les questions et le document : **entoure**, **surligne**, **souligne** les différents éléments de réponse afin de les **repérer** rapidement.

MacDonald's to make the Happy Meal healthier

Your McDonald's Happy Meal is about to look a little different. The fast-food giant announced a series of changes to its Happy Meal menu Thursday, as part of a broader plan to provide healthier options for children. Cheeseburgers will no longer be a menu option, and French fry servings will be downsized. Bottled water will be added as a beverage option, while the chocolate milk will be reformulated to reduce added sugars. The move comes as the first step in a commitment to limiting calories, sodium, saturated fat, and added sugar in its Happy Meals. By the end of 2022, McDonald's wants at least half of its Happy Meal options to meet the new nutrition criteria: 600 calories or less; no more than 10% of calories from saturated fat; less than 650 mg of sodium; and no more than 10% of calories from added sugar.

Adapted from Nathasha BACH, *www.fortune.com*, 2018

BOOST YOUR VOCABULARY!

Le vocabulaire des consignes

- *pick out / find (out)* = cherche des mots ou des expressions qui expriment l'idée donnée dans la question
- *comment on* = commente un extrait du texte
- *sum up / explain with your own words* = résume / explique les éléments du texte
- *quote / give a quotation on* = trouve une citation pertinente pour illustrer ton propos
- *justify* : donne des arguments pour justifier ton point de vue
- *rephrase* : reformule
- *account for* : explique

Comprendre un document iconographique

Step 1

IDENTIFIER ET RÉAGIR

- **Relève les informations relatives à l'image** : son titre, sa nature, le nom de l'auteur et sa date de publication ou de création.
- **Exprime ton ressenti :** quelle émotion cette image suscite-t-elle ? **Appuie-toi sur cette émotion** pour comprendre le document.

__This document is__ a poster of the series Stranger Things. __It was released__ in 2017.

This document __arouses/conveys feelings of__ danger and terror.

cartoon painting
advertisement
map photograph portrait poster
comic strip work of art

Step 2

OBSERVER ET ANALYSER

- **Concentre-toi sur ce que tu vois** et note des **mots clés** pour décrire l'image.
- **Identifie sa structure** en situant les différents éléments dans l'espace.
- **Explique** ce que l'on peut apprendre des **personnages** (personnalité, histoire, situation, etc.) en décrivant leurs gestes, leur attitude, leur regard, leur expression.
- **Prête une attention particulière aux lignes et aux couleurs** qui composent le document et identifie les éléments de contraste et/ou de similitude qui s'en dégagent.

__The picture can be divided into__ two symmetrical parts.

__In the middle__, we can see three boys who __are riding__ their bikes.

The scene __may take__ place in the 1980s. __Obviously__, the main character has supernatural powers.

The monster-like figure __at the top__ is mimicking the young boy's attitude __as if__ it were controlling him.

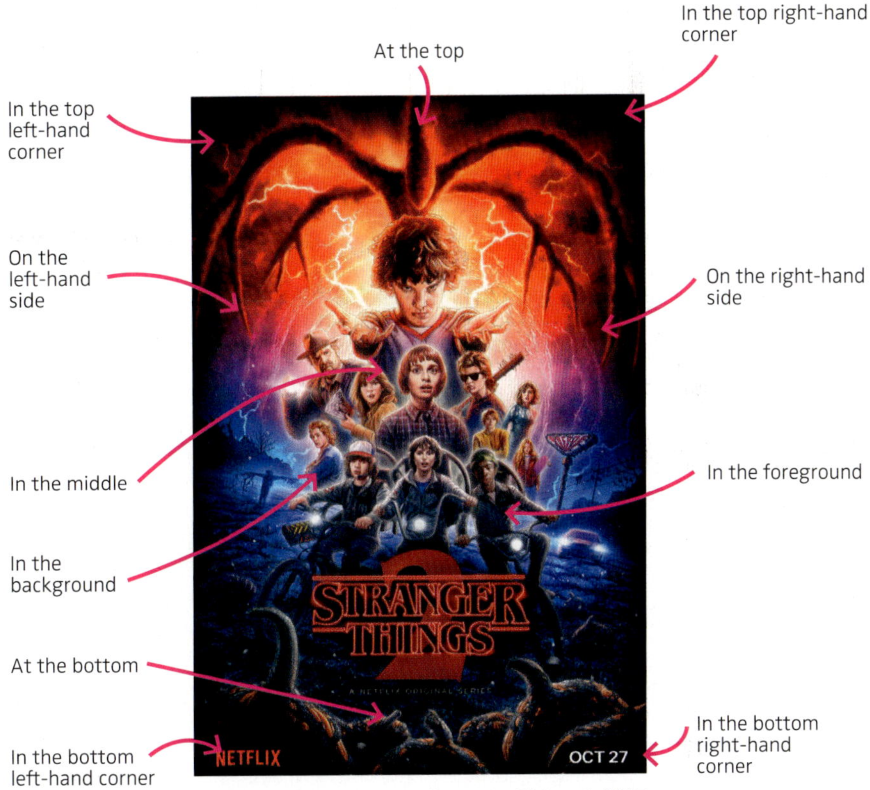

Stranger Things 2, 2017

Step 3

INTERPRÉTER

- **Place le document dans son contexte** culturel, historique ou artistique et détermine l'intention de l'auteur. **Explicite le titre** si nécessaire.
- **Partage ton opinion** sur le message de l'auteur, l'efficacité des techniques utilisées ou encore la valeur du document aujourd'hui.

__By using / Through the use of__ supernatural elements..., the author __wants to / intends to__ encourage sci-fi fans to watch the series.

I'm afraid I don't like it __because__...

It is a very __effective way to__ convey terror because...

BOOST YOUR VOCABULARY!

- Exprimer son ressenti : ***What I find (the) most** striking in this picture is (that)...* • ***What strikes me the most** about this picture is (that)...* • ***It arouses a feeling of** joy ≠ sadness • empathy ≠ disgust* • *It makes me **want to** laugh ≠ cry, etc.*
- Parler de ses impressions : *The young boy **looks** strange* • *The picture **reminds me of**...* • *We are **under the impression that**...*
- La prise de vue : *a close-up ≠ a wide-angle view* • ***The subject is seen from** above / below.*
- Le regard : ***stare at*** (regarder fixement) • ***gaze at*** (contempler) • ***glance at*** (regarder furtivement) • ***glare at*** (lancer un regard furieux)
- Mettre en relief : *The author wants to **highlight** / **emphasise** / **draw the viewer's attention to** / **point out** something.*
- L'atmosphère : *The author **manages to convey** / **create** a light-hearted ≠ oppressive • peaceful ≠ threatening • warm ≠ cold • idyllic ≠ nightmarish • pleasant ≠ desolate atmosphere*
- Le but recherché: ***The author intends to** show/demonstrate/prove/denounce/suggest/encourage/motivate...*

STRATEGIES

Comprendre une vidéo

Step 1

ANTICIPER

Avant de regarder la vidéo, appuie-toi sur le titre et sur le visuel lorsqu'il y en a un. Lors de cette anticipation, interroge-toi sur ce que tu as fait en cours et sur tes connaissances personnelles sur le sujet.

TIP

Tu peux aussi faire une liste de mots que tu t'attends à entendre ou de questions que tu te poses : *sheep, shear, farmer, shave, animal, win, etc.*

Sheepshearers — Nathan live! VIDÉO

1

- Lis le titre et pose-toi des questions : *Who are the shearers? What sport do they practise? Why does this image illustrate NZ traditions?*
- Observe le visuel :
  – émets des hypothèses : *l'homme est sûrement un shearer* ; *shearing* doit donc signifier...
  – soulève d'autres questions : *How are sheep involved in this sport? Can other animals be concerned?*

Step 2

LE PREMIER VISIONNAGE

- Regarde la vidéo une première fois **sans prendre de notes** : aborde le document de manière globale pour essayer d'**identifier le contexte** (qui sont les participants, à quelle occasion et dans quel but se rencontrent-ils ?) et de répondre aux questions que tu t'es posées lors de l'anticipation.
- Appuie-toi sur **les images** pour obtenir **des informations sur le lieu et l'évènement**.

TIP

Pour mieux te concentrer sur les images, tu peux couper le son.

0'15 ➔ What type of landscape?

2'43 ➔ What type of event?

4'58 ➔ How is it organised?

- Appuie-toi sur **le travail de montage** pour repérer **comment on passe d'une présentation générale à un exemple particulier**.

0'145 ➔ Présentation générale

0'205 ➔ Exemple particulier

Step 3

LE DEUXIÈME VISIONNAGE

- Regarde la vidéo une deuxième fois et, cette fois-ci, **prends des notes en même temps** (STRATEGIES p. 211). Concentre-toi sur les prises de parole :

– essaye d'**identifier plus précisément les participants** : focalise-toi sur leur rôle plutôt que sur leur nom (journaliste ? spécialiste ? participant ?) ;

– appuie-toi sur **les mots accentués** pour repérer les idées principales ;

– observe **l'atmosphère du document** (festive ? sérieuse ? conflictuelle ?) en t'appuyant sur la présence de la voix off, de la musique d'introduction, les bruits de fond du public. Tu peux aussi interpréter les intonations de voix des participants.

- Au terme de ton visionnage, essaie de **relier ces nouvelles informations à tes premiers repérages**.

Step 4

LES VISIONNAGES SUIVANTS

- Avant de regarder à nouveau la vidéo, relis tes notes pour cibler ton attention sur certains passages qui t'ont posé problème.
- Essaye de repérer **les connecteurs logiques et la chronologie des faits** pour dégager **la structure du document** : *It was in 2009, every year, since 1986, before long...*

TIP

Dans un document comme celui-ci, avec beaucoup de nombres, tu n'es pas obligé(e) de tout repérer. Concentre ton attention sur ce qu'ils mettent en évidence : une augmentation ? une évolution rapide ? un très petit nombre ?

Faire une présentation orale

STRATEGIES

Step 1

ORGANISER SES IDÉES

Introduction → Idée 1 + exemple → Transition → Idée 2 + exemple → Transition → Idée 3 + exemple → Conclusion

TIPS

- **Fais un schéma** de ta présentation pour mieux te souvenir des différentes étapes.
- **Mémorise** les transitions pour gagner en fluidité.

Step 2

PARLER À PARTIR DE NOTES : QUEL EST MON PROFIL ?

Je prépare ma présentation

J'arrive à parler à partir de mots isolés

Prévois des synonymes ou des expressions proches de tes mots clés essentiels pour pouvoir expliciter une idée : *leader* • *role model* • *set an example for* • *look up to*

J'ai besoin d'écrire des phrases complètes

Écris tes phrases, puis surligne tes idées clés. Entraîne-toi à lire à haute voix, puis supprime progressivement les mots outils.

Je m'entraîne à faire ma présentation

Je sais enchaîner mes idées naturellement

Indique clairement le passage d'une idée à l'autre : *this leads me to another idea...* • *and my next part will be about...* • *and last but not least...*

Je perds le fil quand je passe d'une idée à l'autre

Retrouve le fil de ta présentation en reprenant tes idées. Pour te donner le temps de réfléchir, utilise des expressions comme : *so you see...* • *so my point is...*

En prononciation...

Je m'en sors plutôt bien !

Je dois m'améliorer sur certains sons

Identifie les sons récurrents qu'il te faut travailler. Entraîne-toi à bien les prononcer en répétant des mots qui les contiennent : **em/en** → *September, envious, member, genuine* • **h-** → *have, hot, heart, how, humans* • **-er** → *river, teacher, faster, remember*

Je fais ma présentation

- **Installe-toi confortablement et correctement** face à ton auditoire.
- **Parle haut et fort** pour que tout le monde puisse t'entendre.
- **Adapte ton débit. Énonce les idées principales lentement**, les exemples **plus vivement** et **fais des pauses** quand tu passes d'une partie à l'autre.

TIP

Fais ou refais les activités de phonologie de la séquence concernée et utilise live! LEXIQUIZ pour écouter et répéter les mots.

TIPS

- Pose tes notes sur une table ou un bureau pour avoir les mains libres.
- Éloigne-toi des murs ou du dossier de ta chaise pour ne pas te relâcher.
- Si tu vois qu'un interlocuteur perd le fil ou ne comprend pas, reformule ou explique ton idée à l'aide de synonymes, de périphrases ou d'exemples.

STRATEGIES

Donner son opinion

Lorsqu'on te demande de donner ton opinion, tu dois expliquer pourquoi en développant tes idées. Avant de donner ton avis, reprends les différents documents étudiés auparavant qui te donneront des idées, puis décide quel point de vue adopter et développe tes arguments.

Step 1

IDENTIFIER LE POINT DE VUE À EXPRIMER

Le sujet t'inspire un avis...

Très positif ?

Tu es absolument d'accord ? Favorable ? Convaincu(e) ?

I definitely agree! • I think you're right. • That's absolutely true.

Très négatif ?

Tu n'es absolument pas convaincu(e) ? Pas d'accord ? Tu es défavorable ? choqué(e) ?

I disagree with... because... • I don't agree. • I think you're wrong. • I'm shocked by...

Nuancé ?

Il y a du pour et du contre ? Certains points sont positifs et d'autres moins acceptables ?

Lis le texte suivant et relève les expressions qui permettent de donner son opinion.

Henry Louis Gates Jr: You think he deserved it?
Anderson Cooper: Yeah! I have no doubt.
Henry Louis Gates Jr: It's a horrible way to die, Anderson.
Anderson Cooper: He had twelve slaves, I don't feel bad for him.
Henry Louis Gates Jr: Okay.
Anderson Cooper: Honestly, part of me thinks that's awesome. [...] I wish I knew more. I wish I knew the name of the slave. You know, when you think about how many people's names history just never remembers, and people whose stories are never told.
Henry Louis Gates Jr: Absolutely.
Anderson Cooper: It's, it's shameful. And I feel a sense of shame over it. And at the same time, it's the history of this country.

« Finding your roots », *PBS*, 2014

- Utilise des expressions pour nuancer ton propos :
On the one hand / on the other hand... • First... yet / however / but • More or less • Even if it's true that... • At the same time...
- Donne ton avis à l'aide d'expressions qui t'engagent :
I consider... • I'm convinced that... • I guess / I suppose / Yes, I think so • To my mind / Let me put it this way / What I'm trying to say is... / Honestly...
- Utilise la concession :
despite / in spite of + N • although / though it is... • Even if / even though there is...

Step 2

AFFIRMER SON OPINION ET ÊTRE CONVAINCANT

- **Exprime ton avis** et **renforce-le** par **des arguments**. Donne du poids à tes idées en les développant et en utilisant des mots de liaison, adverbes, adjectifs, etc. : *Personally • I think • No, I don't think so • I couldn't agree more • Actually / In fact • You see... • I totally disagree with you on that point*
- Pense à utiliser des **synonymes** :
good → amazing • great • fantastic • positive • surprising
bad → terrible • negative • horrible • shocking • shameful
- Accentue les **mots clés** et adopte un **ton** convaincant pour donner ton opinion.

Interagir, débattre à l'oral ou à l'écrit

Step 1

LIRE LE SUJET ET REPÉRER

- **le contexte** (conseil municipal, débat parlementaire, émission de radio ou télévision, forum de discussion, fil Twitter) ;
- **l'enjeu de cette interaction** (vote d'une loi, décision pour la communauté, sujet de société, débat d'idées...).

Choisir ta place dans le débat

- Tu dois **mener** le débat.
- Tu es **en faveur** du thème abordé.
- Tu es **neutre** et modérateur.
- Tu es **opposé(e)** au thème abordé.

Step 2

SE PRÉPARER

- Analyse ton rôle pour le jouer pleinement.
- Assure-toi d'adapter ton registre de langage à ton rôle.
- Sois prêt(e) à présenter le sujet et les différents intervenants dans le débat.

- Liste le plus d'arguments possibles pour appuyer ton point de vue.
- Utilise des exemples précis pour illustrer tes arguments.
- Anticipe les arguments des autres participants et réfléchis à la manière dont tu pourras les renforcer ou contrer.

Step 3

À TOI DE JOUER !

À l'oral. Utilise des expressions qui rendent **l'interaction naturelle**, comme des *gap fillers* (sans en abuser !).

Well... • Actually... • So... • You know... • I mean...

À l'écrit. Utilise des émoticônes, des gifs ou des abréviations qui montrent la connivence : *LOL • BTY • FYI • IMO...*

- Exprime ton **accord** :

I agree with you... • You're right when you say... • It is true that...

- Ou ton **désaccord** :

I don't think so • I (totally) disagree with what you're saying • I don't share your viewpoint

⚠ Si tu n'es pas d'accord, attaque les idées, jamais la personne.

Exprime clairement ton **point de vue** pour commencer.

I personally believe that... • In my opinion... • I think that... • I guess... • I believe... • I'm convinced that... • To my mind... • From my point of view... • To me...

- **À l'oral**. Fais attention à ton **intonation** : tu seras le plus convaincant si tu montres que tu crois en tes arguments. Accentue les mots importants, fais des pauses, accélère ou ralentis le rythme.
- Travaille aussi ta **posture** : regarde ton interlocuteur et adresse-toi directement à lui en l'impliquant.

Don't you think... ? • We all know that.... • You can't deny... • Right?

- Souligne tes propos par des **gestes**.

- **Écoute** ou **lis attentivement** les autres interlocuteurs et reformule leurs arguments pour mieux rebondir :

What did you mean when you said/wrote/posted that... • May I ask you why you said/claimed... • Did you really mean... • I would like to come back to what you said/wrote...

- N'hésite pas à **dire à ton (tes) interlocuteur(s) que tu n'as pas compris** : *Could you repeat please? • Do you mean that...? • I'm not sure I understand what you mean...*
- En **concédant** certains arguments, tu seras encore plus convaincant.

Although it seems... • Yes, I suppose so, however... • Admittedly..., but... • Sure, but still... • And yet...

TIP

Si tu veux intégrer une présentation orale dans ton interaction, tu peux utiliser les conseils de la fiche ***Faire une présentation orale***, p. 222.

STRATEGIES

Enrichir son vocabulaire

On entend souvent les gens dire : « Je n'ai pas assez de vocabulaire pour parler ou comprendre l'anglais... » Voici quelques conseils pour remédier à cela !

Step 1

SAVOIR DÉRIVER DES MOTS

- De nombreux mots anglais sont formés à partir d'une **racine** commune à laquelle on a ajouté un **préfixe** et/ou un **suffixe**. On dit qu'ils sont « **dérivés** ».
- En ajoutant un préfixe ou un suffixe à un mot, on crée un mot nouveau qui change souvent de catégorie grammaticale.

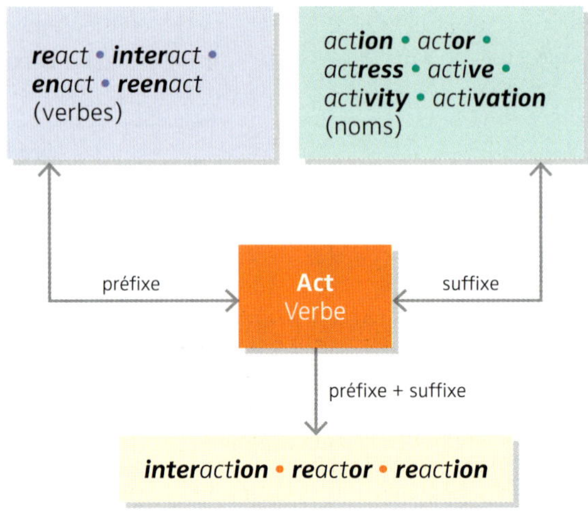

BOOST YOUR VOCABULARY!

Les principaux préfixes et suffixes en anglais

Préfixe	Valeur	Suffixe	Valeur
un-, dis-, in-, non-, il-, im-, ir-	opposés = préfixes à valeur négative	*-ness, -dom, -able*	état
re-	retour, répétition	*-er, -or, -ee, -ent, -eer, -ist*	celui qui fait ou subit l'action
mis-	mauvais(e), présence d'une erreur	*-less / -ful*	idée de manque, d'absence / idée de plein
pre- / post-	avant / après	*-ly*	manière

Step 2

APPRENDRE PAR THÈME

- Apprendre du vocabulaire est tout de suite plus facile lorsqu'il est **placé dans un contexte**. Par exemple, si tu pars du mot *Harlem*, tu peux créer une **carte mentale** autour pour créer **son champ lexical**. Ton cerveau fonctionnant par association, tu auras moins de mal à retenir ces groupes de mots que des mots pris isolément.

► Carte mentale complète p. 25

TIPS

- **Champ lexical** = groupe de mots reliés par leur sens, par opposition à un mot isolé associé à sa définition.
Pense à utiliser live! LEXIQUIZ pour apprendre ton vocabulaire !
- **Ménage ton cerveau !** La capacité de mémorisation est très variable selon les individus. Le mieux est donc de se fixer un objectif réalisable mais régulier (10 mots par jour, par exemple).

Step 3

MOBILISER SON VOCABULAIRE

Pour enrichir ton expression, pense à utiliser :

- des adjectifs, des adverbes et des subordonnées pour être précis et donner des détails :

The Harlem Renaissance was a cultural movement → In the 1920's, the Harlem Renaissance was a huge cultural movement which was expressed through African-American arts, especially literature, music and dance.

- des pronoms, des groupes nominaux de substitution ou des synonymes pour éviter les répétitions :

The Harlem Renaissance made African-American artists famous all over the world.
The Harlem Renaissance helped to change the perception of African-Americans all over the world. → It helped to change the perception of African-Americans on an international level.

- des **mots de liaison** pour structurer ton propos.

PRÉCIS 32

TIPS

Crée des fiches pour chaque nature de mots (adjectifs, adverbes...) et organise-les par catégories pour mieux les mémoriser :

- **Adverbes :** temporels, spatiaux, de fréquence, d'ajout, de degré, de liaison, de manière...
- **Adjectifs :** portrait physique, portrait moral, sentiments, atmosphère...

Développer une idée à l'écrit

STRATEGIES

Step 1

IDENTIFIER L'OBJECTIF

Avant d'écrire, commence par **bien lire le sujet** et **repérer** :

- le **contexte** ;
- la **nature du texte à rédiger** (article de presse, récit, dialogue, email, lettre, etc.) ;
- l'**objectif de cette production** (raconter ? décrire ? convaincre ? prendre position ?) ;
- le **destinataire** (un lecteur non identifié ? un proche ? un personnage rencontré dans un texte lu ?, etc.).

You are part of the screenwriters' team of the series Once Upon a Time. Write your own version of a fairy tale for an American production.

Step 2

TROUVER DES IDÉES

L'angoisse de la page blanche est bien connue des écrivains. Pour la contrer, tu peux **créer une carte mentale ou un tableau pour organiser tes idées**.

Pars des termes du sujet et note autour **toutes les idées qui te viennent à l'esprit**, en t'appuyant sur ce que tu as étudié précédemment.

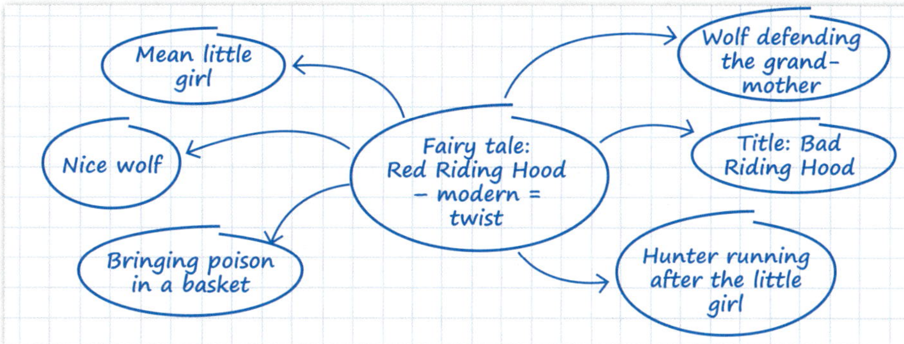

TIPS

- Tu peux partir des questions récurrentes ***Who? Where? When? What? Why?***

Step 3

FAIRE UN PLAN

Cette étape est très importante car sans plan, on ne sait pas où on va. Ton plan dépendra beaucoup du type d'écrit qu'on te demande.

Récit fictionnel	Écrit argumentatif	Article de presse	Lettre, courriel
Plan chronologique Le point de départ Le rebondissement/ l'événement nouveau Le point d'arrivée	Plan par opposition ou comparaison Pour / Contre Avantages / Inconvénients Ici / Ailleurs…	Plan logique ou thématique Situation > causes/problèmes > conséquences/solutions Problématique générale > sous-thème 1 > sous-thème 2 > … > conclusion	Plan thématique Rappel du sujet ou des questions du destinataire. Développement du sujet ou réponse aux question. Ouverture (i.e. questions pour le destinataire en retour)

Step 4

RÉDIGER

Pour passer des notes à la rédaction de phrases, prends garde à :

- **La structure et la longueur de tes phrases**. Par exemple, tu pourrais écrire : *I was looking for my car. I saw a porter. He knew the station very well.* Préfère : ***While** I was looking for my car, I saw a porter **that** knew the station very well.*
- Utilise **des propositions relatives** pour développer tes idées : *The man **who** helped me find my car was a tourist from Germany.*
- Veille à utiliser **des substituts du nom** (pronoms, synonymes, etc.) pour ne pas te répéter : *The car was huge and **it** was crowded, there were many people, we were crammed in…*
- Choisis **les mots de liaison appropriés** pour relier tes idées : ***When** I arrived, I did not know where my train was. **Then,** fortunately someone helped me.*

Par ailleurs, un texte écrit n'est pas juste une juxtaposition de phrases : il faut **structurer ton texte** en **paragraphes identifiés**. Pour ce faire, reviens toujours à ton plan et ne perds pas de vue l'objectif de ton écrit.

TIP

Généralement, on dit **un paragraphe = une idée.**

Step 5

CONTRÔLER SA PRODUCTION

Avant de recopier ton texte au propre, fais une relecture attentive :

- Vérifie l'**orthographe**, la **ponctuation**, la **concordance des temps** employés et la **conjugaison** ;
- Contrôle la **logique interne** de ton texte ;
- Assure-toi que la **mise en page** correspond au type de texte que tu dois rédiger.

Sommaire

Le groupe nominal

Le groupe verbal

De la phrase simple à la phrase complexe

Le groupe nominal

Fiche 1 Les noms

A Dénombrables et indénombrables

Les noms peuvent être dénombrables ou indénombrables.

- Les noms **dénombrables** désignent des éléments que l'on **peut compter** :
a chair • *a cat* • *a town* → *two chairs* • *three cats* • *four towns*
- Les noms **indénombrables** désignent des éléments que l'on ne peut **pas compter**, comme les noms d'aliments ou de matière :
bread • *butter* • *water* • *plastic* • *silk*, etc.
ou les mots qui renvoient à une notion indéfinie :
joy la joie • *health* la santé • *soccer* le football, etc.

Attention ! Certains mots dénombrables en français sont indénombrables en anglais :
advice les conseils • *furniture* les meubles • *information* les informations • *luggage* les bagages • *news* les nouvelles • *toast* les toasts, etc.

- Pour dire qu'il y a un seul élément en anglais, on utilise parfois ***a piece of*** :
I bought ***a piece*** *of furniture.* J'ai acheté **un** meuble.
He took ***two pieces of*** *toast.* Il a pris **deux** toasts.
On utilisera aussi souvent le nom sans article :
That is good news! C'est **une** bonne nouvelle !
He ate bacon and toast. Il a mangé **du** bacon et **des** toasts.

B Singulier et pluriel

Pour former le pluriel d'un nom en anglais, on ajoute un **-s** à la fin du mot : *a horse* → *horses* • *a month* → *months*

- Pour les mots qui se terminent au singulier par -**s**, -**x**, -**z**, -**ch** ou -**sh** et pour certains mots qui se terminent au singulier par -**o**, on ajoute un -**e** avant le -**s** du pluriel :
a bus → *buses* • *a match* → *matches* • *a hero* → *heroes*
- Pour les mots qui se terminent au singulier par une consonne + -**y**, la terminaison au pluriel est -***ies*** :
a party → *parties*
- Pour les mots qui se terminent en -***f(e)***, la terminaison est -***ves*** : *a wolf* → *wolves* • *a wife* → *wives*
- Certains noms d'animaux sont invariables :
a sheep → *sheep* • *a fish* → *fish*

MIND THE TRICK!

- Certains pluriels sont irréguliers :
a man → *men* • *a child* → *children* • *a mouse* → *mice* • *a foot* → *feet* • *a tooth* → *teeth* • *a phenomenon* → *phenomena* • *a hypothesis* → *hypotheses*, etc.

La prononciation du pluriel

- si le **nom** se termine par une consonne sonore, le ***s*** se prononce /z/ : *bags* • *cars*
- si le **nom** se termine par une consonne sourde, il se prononce /s/ : *cats* • *cups*
- si le **nom** se termine par les sons /s/, /ʃ/, /dʒ/ ou /z/, le pluriel se prononce /ɪz/ : *buses* • *brushes* • *cages* • *phrases*

La prononciation des pluriels irréguliers

Attention, les mots suivants se prononcent différemment au singulier et au pluriel :
a woman → *women* • *a child* → *children*
/ʊ//ə/ /ɪ/ /ɪ/ /aɪ/ /ɪ/

MIND THE TRICK!

- Certains mots singuliers en français sont au pluriel en anglais et inversement :
My luggage ***is*** *heavy.* Mes bagages **sont** lourds.
The news ***is*** *good!* Les nouvelles **sont** bonnes !
- Les pays constitués de plusieurs États sont suivis d'un verbe au singulier :
The USA ***is*** *a country I would like to visit.* Les États-Unis **sont** un pays que j'aimerais visiter.
- Les noms qui se réfèrent à un ensemble appellent généralement le pluriel : *The police* ***are*** *arriving!* La police arrive.

1 Pour chaque phrase, dis si le mot en gras est dénombrable ou indénombrable.

a. It is the first **time** I have been in London.
b. We need **time** to make a real difference.
c. I followed your **advice** and went to the MoMA to see "Humans of New York".
d. The **information** about the trip was clear.

2 Mets les noms suivants au pluriel.

a. buffalo
b. box
c. tooth
d. path
e. child
f. leaf
g. sheep
h. glass
i. wife
j. phenomenon

3 Traduis les phrases suivantes.

a. I would like some information about the trip.
b. What means of transport will you take?
c. They will study politics.
d. We had to face a series of events.

4 Traduis les phrases suivantes.

a. Les femmes ont obtenu le droit de vote en Grande-Bretagne en 1918.
b. Il a fait des progrès spectaculaires.
c. J'ai vu des loups, des chevaux et des poissons au zoo.
d. Alice ne pouvait pas voir ses pieds.

Fiche 2 Les noms composés

Les noms composés sont construits à partir de deux mots distincts. Ils peuvent être constitués, par exemple :
- de deux noms : *a raincoat* un imperméable
- d'un nom et d'un verbe : *sightseeing* du tourisme
- d'un verbe et d'un nom : *a swimming-pool* une piscine
- d'un adjectif et d'un nom : *a greenhouse* une serre
- d'une préposition et d'un nom : *an onlooker* un badaud
- d'un adverbe et d'un adjectif : *an evergreen* un conifère
- d'un nom et d'une préposition : *a passer-by* un passant
- d'un verbe et d'une préposition : *a take-off* un décollage
- d'un participe passé et d'une préposition : *a grown-up* un adulte

Attention ! En français, le nom principal porteur de sens est placé en premier alors qu'en anglais, il est en deuxième position. Pour traduire un nom composé de l'anglais au français, commence par la fin !
Exemple : *an aircraft carrier* un porte-avions

1 Trouve le mot composé qui correspond aux définitions suivantes.
a. A person who has grown up.
b. You get a new one when the hairdresser cuts your hair.
c. A tank for fish.
d. Somewhere where the bus has to stop.

2 À partir des mots ci-dessous, forme des noms composés, et trouve leur sens dans le dictionnaire.

SUN
glasses bathe
light set

OUT
cut black
time burn

3 Complète les phrases à l'aide des mots suivants : *mother-to-be – stepmother – mother-in-law – grandmother*, puis traduis-les.
a. Cinderella's ... was mean to her.
b. Red Riding Hood visited her ... .
c. The princess met her ... only one week before the wedding.
d. The ... painted a unicorn in the future baby's bedroom.

4 Traduis les éléments de cette liste de matériel de bureau.
a. a desk lamp
b. a keyboard
c. an office chair
d. a footrest
e. a desktop computer
f. a pencil sharpener
g. notebooks
h. a fountain pen

Fiche 3 Les démonstratifs (*this/these – that/those*)

Les démonstratifs peuvent être **adjectifs ou pronoms**.
- En tant qu'**adjectifs**, ils correspondent à « ce, cet(te), ces » en français.
- En anglais, il y a deux adjectifs démonstratifs ***this*** (***these*** au pluriel) et ***that*** (***those*** au pluriel).
- Leur emploi diffère en fonction de la proximité (***this***) ou de l'éloignement (***that***) avec celui qui parle.
  ***This** is my house!* (proximité géographique)
  *In **those** days...* (éloignement temporel)
  ***That** was your idea!* (éloignement affectif)
- En tant que **pronoms**, ils correspondent à « celui-ci, celle-ci, ceux-ci / celui-là, celle-là, ceux-là ».
  *I don't want **these** shoes. I want **those**.* Je ne veux pas ces chaussures. Je veux celles-là.

NB : Le choix de *this* ou *that* peut aussi avoir une **valeur de commentaire**.
What's this? (surprise, découverte d'une nouveauté)
What's that? (expression d'un jugement, positif ou négatif)

1 Complète ces phrases avec *this*, *that*, *these* ou *those*.
a. I can't bear ... polluting industry!
b. Take ... stickers, they are free.
c. When did you hear ... information?
d. At ... time, lions were hunted.
e. I hope I will not meet ... poachers!

2 Traduis les phrases suivantes.
a. Ces fleurs sont si jolies !
b. Cette voiture n'est pas la mienne : ma voiture est là-bas.
c. Je ne fais pas confiance à cet homme.
d. En ce temps-là, il y avait des cassettes.
e. J'aime bien cette idée !

3 Traduis les phrases suivantes.
a. I did not expect that!
b. This luggage is not mine.
c. Don't take that dish. Take this one.
d. I am well aware of that!

4 Dis si le mot souligné est un adjectif ou un pronom démonstratif.
a. I learnt that yesterday.
b. That witch is frightening.
c. What's this?
d. I want those ones which are behind them.

Fiche 4 Les articles

Les articles et les adjectifs démonstratifs sont des déterminants. Ils précèdent les noms pour apporter une information supplémentaire.

A L'article indéfini *a/an*

L'article *a/an* sert à désigner un élément isolé, par rapport à un ensemble, une classe.
*We saw **a** cat in the garden.* Nous avons vu un chat dans le jardin.

- On utilise ***a*** si le mot qui suit commence par une consonne ou par le son /j/ : *a uniform*
- On utilise ***an*** si le mot qui suit commence par une voyelle ou par un <h> muet : *heir • honest • honour • hour*

Ainsi, on dira : ***an** apple* → ***a** big apple*
***a** story* → ***an** unbelievable story*

Attention !

- On utilise ***a*** devant des noms de métier : *His mother is **an** accountant.* Sa mère est comptable.
- On utilise ***a*** après certaines prépositions : *without a friend* sans ami
- On utilise également ***a*** pour exprimer un rapport : *once a month* une fois par mois • *80 miles an hour* environ 130 km/h
- ***A*** ne s'utilise pas avec les indénombrables : *She gave me advice.* Elle m'a donné un conseil. *You shouldn't add sugar.* Tu ne devrais pas ajouter de sucre.
- Au pluriel, si l'on veut déterminer quelque chose d'indéfini, on ne met **pas d'article**. *We saw **a cat** in the garden.* → *We saw **cats** in the garden.*

B Absence d'article ou article zéro (Ø)

Lorsque l'on veut désigner plusieurs éléments d'une manière indéfinie, on n'utilise pas d'article :
*I have **Ø** friends in Toronto. = I have friends in Toronto.*
J'ai **des** amis à Toronto.

Attention ! En grammaire, le symbole Ø est une façon de symbolisez l'absence d'article, mais il ne s'écrit jamais le reste du temps.

Pour désigner une généralité, on n'utilise pas d'article :
Photography is her passion.
Her pictures reveal freedom and happiness.

Attention ! En anglais, on ne met pas d'article devant les noms de pays : ***Ø** Canada* • ***Ø** France* • ***Ø** South Korea*,
sauf devant les noms composés d'États : ***the** United States* • ***the** United Kingdom*.
On ne met pas d'article devant les noms propres : ***Ø** Queen Elizabeth* la Reine Elisabeth • ***Ø** President Trump* le président Trump.
Mais on dira *the Queen* ou *the Prime Minister* quand le nom n'est pas précisé.

C L'article défini *the*

The sert à désigner :

- un ou plusieurs éléments dont on a déjà parlé ou qui sont connus de ceux qui parlent :
  *Will you go to **the** exhibition?* (celle dont on a déjà parlé)
  ***the** earth, **the** sun, **the** stars, **the** internet*
- un ou plusieurs éléments qui sont caractérisés par ce qui suit :
  ***The** city I like most is Toronto.*
- un groupe dans sa totalité (en utilisant un adjectif) :
  the homeless les sans-abri • *the elderly* les personnes âgées

On l'utilise aussi dans certaines expressions figées :
*She plays **the** oboe and **the** piano.* Elle joue du hautbois et du piano.

MIND THE TRICK!

- On dira :
  ***Ø** homeless people* (pluriel de *a homeless person*)
  ***Ø** elderly people* (pluriel de *an elderly man/woman*)

La prononciation de *the*

- Si le mot qui suit commence par une **consonne** ou un **<h> aspiré**, ***the*** se prononce **/ðə/** :
  the photo • the city • the hero
- Si le mot qui suit commence par une **voyelle** ou un **<h> non aspiré**, ***the*** se prononce **/ði/** :
  the image • the hour

Ainsi, on prononcera différemment :
***the** man* /ðə/ → ***the** old man* /ði/ •
***the** image* /ði/ → ***the** splendid image* /ðə/

---

1 Complète ces phrases avec *a* ou *an*.

a. He is ... honest man.
b. To be a guardian of lions is ... honour!
c. Hands up! This is ... hold-up!
d. I think it's going to be ... hot day!

2 Complète les phrases suivantes avec *a/an*, *the* ou rien.

a. ... Kenya is ... country where ... innovation is everywhere.
b. ... Maasai are ... tribe that protects ... African wildlife.
c. ... flower industry may be ... danger for ... environment.
d. ... Prince Harry likes helping ... humanitarian associations.

3 Ajoute l'article *the* quand c'est nécessaire.

... Netherlands – ... Italy – ... United Kingdom – ... Great Britain – ... South Africa – ... India

4 Traduis les phrases suivantes.

a. Elle est venue sans valise.
b. L'homme qui a sauvé la tortue est vétérinaire.
c. Ils vont au Kenya une fois par an.
d. Elle n'a pas utilisé Internet là-bas.
e. Il joue du lungo, un instrument traditionnel kenyan.

Fiche 5 Le génitif et la possession

A Le génitif

Le génitif est un déterminant du nom qui exprime une relation entre deux éléments ou personnes. Il correspond au complément du nom en français. Comme tout déterminant, il se place devant le nom qu'il détermine et pourrait être remplacé par un article ou un adjectif possessif. Il se forme avec **'s** ou seulement avec **'** si le nom qui précède est au pluriel (pluriel régulier) *the doctor* → *the doctor's...* *doctors* → *doctors'...*

Le génitif peut exprimer :

- la possession : *the doctor's car* la voiture du docteur • *my parents' house* la maison de mes parents • *my children's cat* le chat de mes enfants
- un lien entre deux personnes : *Andrew's sister* la sœur d'Andrew • *my neighbours' friend* l'ami de mes voisins
- un repère temporel : *today's menu* le menu du jour
- un repère géographique : *London's museums* les musées de Londres
- une durée : *a year's work* un travail d'un an
- une catégorie : *a girls' school* une école pour filles, *a kids' menu* un menu enfant

Attention ! Utilise le génitif pour dire « chez » :
I went to the hairdresser's. Je suis allé chez le coiffeur.
I had lunch at Susan's. J'ai déjeuné chez Susan.

B Les adjectifs possessifs

Ils marquent un lien de possession (mon, ma, mes, nos, etc.). Ils se placent avant le nom ou groupe nominal.

I → *my*	*it* → *its*
you → *your*	*we* → *our*
he → *his*	*you* → *your*
she → *her*	*they* → *their*

Attention ! Contrairement au français, les adjectifs possessifs s'accordent en genre et en nombre avec le **possesseur** et non avec le nom qu'ils déterminent :
*John lives with **his** mother and **his** grandfather, while Martha doesn't see **her** parents a lot.*
Pour parler des parties du corps en anglais, on utilisera l'**adjectif possessif** alors qu'en français, on utilise l'article simple et un verbe pronominal réfléchi :
*He washed **his** hands.* Il s'est lavé les mains.
*She hurt **her** leg.* Elle s'est blessée à la jambe.

C Les pronoms possessifs

I → *mine*	*we* → *ours*
you → *yours*	*you* → *yours*
he/she/it → *his/hers/its*	*they* → *theirs*

Ils renvoient à l'objet possédé en évitant la répétition.
This notebook is mine. = my notebook

Attention ! Utilise le pronom possessif pour dire « un de mes » :
He's a friend of mine. C'est l'un de mes amis.

La prononciation du pronom possessif
Il est accentué pour insister sur la possession.
It's not your book, it's mine!

1 Reformule les passages soulignés à l'aide d'un génitif.

a. The new neighbours of my grandma made too much noise last night.
b. The young people that live today love old pop music.
c. The guitar that belongs to Anna is a replica of the one that belonged to Eric Clapton.
d. The songs that were performed by the brothers were all hits.

2 Complète ces phrases avec un adjectif ou un pronom possessif.

a. We took ... rucksacks and travelled the world.
b. I have forgotten ... pen. Can you lend me ...?
c. The artist offered ... latest painting to the charity.
d. Those children are looking for ... parents.

3 Traduis les phrases suivantes.

a. Il lui a serré la main.
b. Elle s'est brossé les dents.
c. Il s'est fait mal au genou.
d. Elle brosse les cheveux de sa fille.

4 Termine ces énoncés en remplaçant l'information entre parenthèses par un pronom.

a. It's not my car, it is (*Paul*).
b. I did not take my keys, I took (*her keys*).
c. I do not live in my flat, I live in (*their flat*).
d. He did not need to buy a washing-machine, we have given (*Andrew*) (*our washing-machine*).

Fiche 6 Les quantifieurs

Les quantifieurs permettent de préciser une **quantité**. Le choix du quantifieur dépend de la quantité, mais aussi de la nature du nom (**dénombrable ou indénombrable**).

A La quantité

Quantité	Indénombrables	Dénombrables
Une quantité nulle : pas de, aucun(e)	***no*** – *There is **no** water in Death Valley.* ***not... any*** – *She did **not** have **any** water in her flask.*	***no*** – *There were **no** signs of life / There was **no** sign of life.* (aucun signe de vie) ***not a*** – *There was **not a** drop of water in her flask.* (pas une goutte) ***none of them*** – ***None of them** drank it.* (aucun d'eux) ***no one*** – ***No one** drank it.* (personne)
Une petite quantité : peu, un peu de, quelques	***little*** – *There was **little** water in his flask.* (peu d'eau) ***a little*** – *There was **a little** water in his flask.* (un peu d'eau)	***few*** – *There were **few** animals in the desert.* (peu d'animaux) ***a few*** – *There were **a few** animals in the desert.* (quelques animaux)
Une certaine quantité (non précisée) : du, de la, des	***some*** – *There was **some** water in their flasks.* (de l'eau) ***some*** – *Did he bring **some** salt?* (on s'attend à une réponse positive) ***any*** – *Did he bring **any** salt?* (à tout hasard)	***some*** – *There were **some** animals in the desert.* (des animaux) ***some*** – *Did she bring **some** chocolate bars?* (on s'attend à une réponse positive) ***any*** – *Did she bring **any** chocolate bars?* (à tout hasard)
Une grande quantité : beaucoup de	***much*** – *It took **much** courage to fight the poachers.* ***a lot of*** – *It takes **a lot of** courage to live in the desert.*	***many*** – ***Many** people spoke about their courage.* ***a lot of*** – ***A lot of** people spoke about their courage.*
Une quantité à déterminer : combien de	***How much*** – ***How much** water do you have in your flask?* *He never said **how much** he suffered.*	***How many*** – ***How many** people travelled with you?* *He just told me **how many** cats he had! Eight!*

MIND THE TRICK!

- Dans les questions, tu emploies ***some*** lorsque tu attends une réponse positive. *Would you like some tea?* (demande polie)
- Tu emploies ***any*** lorsque tu ne sais pas quelle réponse va être faite. *Is there any tea in the pot?*
- Attention ! Avec ***no*** et ***never***, on n'ajoute pas ***not*** pour former la phrase négative. *There is no water here.*

La prononciation de *some* et *any*

Some et *any* sont généralement **non accentués** lorsqu'ils expriment une **quantité non définie**.
Any est **accentué** lorsqu'il signifie « **n'importe lequel** ».
Any traveller can go there!

B De l'unité à la totalité

one – un seul, une seule	***One** guide accepted to go there.*
both – les deux	***Both** guides accepted.*
each + singulier – chaque	*We checked that **each** participant had already been in the desert.*
every + singulier – tous les, chaque	***Every** day they walked for miles.*
most – la plupart de	***Most** people knew it would be difficult.*
(the) whole – tout/toute (entier/entière)	***The whole** country would be impressed.* *His **whole** family supported him.*
all – tout, toute	*They would walk **all** week with **all** their bags.*
either... or... – soit..., soit...	***Either** he travels with this guide **or** he does not come.*
neither... nor... – ni... ni...	***Neither** Henry **nor** his brother came with us.*

1 Complète les énoncés avec *some* ou *any*.

a. For this cake you need ... flour but you don't need ... butter.
b. Would you like ... orange juice?
c. Did you bring ... water? If you like, I have ... .
d. You showed ... courage during the race. I don't think ... man or woman can do it.

2 Complète les phrases avec *little, a little, few* ou *a few*.

a. I was disappointed. He gave me ... advice.
b. If you want, I can give you ... money.
c. He had taken ... bottles to refresh the participants.
d. ... participants will be able to finish the race. It is too tiring!

3 Complète les phrases avec *every, each* ou *all*. Deux solutions sont parfois possibles.

a. They used to go to the cinema ... Monday.
b. I read ... the novels by John Steinbeck, and I remember ... of them in detail.
c. ... student will have the right to do sport.
d. I have already seen ... of them.

4 Complète les phrases avec *much, many, few, a few* ou *little*.

a. He spent ... hours working on this project to win the contract.
b. Contrary to what he had promised, he spent ... time helping him.
c. You are not late. The flat is ... blocks from there.
d. They couldn't finish the meal. There was too ... food.
e. ... workers are disappointed by the company. The working conditions are great!

5 Complète les phrases avec *all* ou *the whole*.

a. The festival is well-known in ... country.
b. I waited for you ... day.
c. ... festival was interesting.
d. ... the bands played well.

6 Traduis les énoncés suivants.

a. Soit il déménagera dans la Silicon Valley, soit il partira à San Francisco.
b. Ni Jenny ni Amber ne veulent devenir actrices.
c. La plupart des voyageurs s'arrêtent à Palm Springs.
d. Il a consacré sa vie entière aux sports extrêmes.

Fiche 7 Les adjectifs

A La place et l'ordre des adjectifs

En anglais, les adjectifs sont **invariables**.

- Lorsqu'ils sont épithètes, les adjectifs se placent **avant** le nom : *a prosperous city* une ville prospère
- Certains adjectifs ne peuvent pas être épithètes et se placent toujours après le verbe : *alive • asleep • afraid • awake • ill • glad. She is asleep. He looks ill.*
- Lorsqu'il y a plusieurs adjectifs devant un nom, ils sont classés du **plus subjectif au plus objectif**. Voici une formule pour t'aider :
  QOTAFCOM : Quantité, Opinion, Taille, Âge, Forme, Couleur, Origine, Matière

B Les adjectifs composés

- Les adjectifs composés peuvent être formés à partir d'un **adjectif** :
  adj + adj : *a **light-blue** dress* une robe bleu clair
  nom + adj : *a **navy-blue** suit* un costume bleu marine
- Il y a deux formations possibles à partir d'un **verbe** :
  – on ajoute ***-ing*** à la base verbale s'ils ont un sens actif :
  a story that breaks the heart → *a **heart-breaking** story* (nom + V-*ing*)
  a city that grows quickly → *a **quickly growing** city* (adv + V-*ing*)
  a child that looks good → *a **good-looking** child* (adj + V-*ing*)
  – on utilise le **participe passé** s'ils ont un sens passif :
  a cake made at home → *a **home-made** cake*
  a mountain covered with snow → *a **snow-covered** mountain*
- S'ils sont formés à partir d'un **nom** (parties du corps, vêtements, traits de caractère, éléments distinctifs), on ajoute ***-ed*** à la fin du nom :
  *a **white-striped** shirt* une chemise aux rayures blanches
  *a **bad-tempered** man* un homme de mauvaise humeur

La prononciation des adjectifs composés

L'accent porte généralement sur la 2e partie : *red-haired • heartbreaking*

1 Forme ces groupes nominaux en plaçant les adjectifs dans le bon ordre.

a. a / sea / fabulous / activity
b. a / red / old / tiny / car
c. a / blue / traditional / woollen / skirt
d. a / 15-year-old / cheerful / brown-haired / roommate

2 Transforme ces groupes nominaux en remplaçant les mots soulignés par des adjectifs composés.

a. a boy <u>who is 18 years old</u>
b. a story <u>that breaks the heart</u>
c. a girl <u>with green eyes</u>
d. a waiter <u>that is dressed well</u>
e. a cake <u>that looks good</u>

Fiche 8 Le comparatif et le superlatif

A Infériorité, égalité, superiorité

- Le comparatif permet de comparer deux éléments entre eux. Le superlatif permet de comparer un élément par rapport à tous les autres.

	Comparatif	Superlatif
Infériorité	***less*** + adjectif + ***than*** *This subject is **less** difficult **than** the others.* ***not as*** + adjectif + ***as*** *This subject is **not as** difficult **as** that one.*	***the least*** + adjectif *This subject is **the least** difficult in the whole school.*
Égalité	***as*** + adjectif + ***as*** *Surfing is **as** demanding **as** debating.*	

- La formation du comparatif et du superlatif diffère selon que l'adjectif est court (une syllabe) ou long (deux syllabes ou plus) et parfois selon sa terminaison.

	Comparatif	Superlatif
Supériorité	Adjectifs longs : ***more*** + adjectif + ***than*** *Pupils are **more** interested in surfing **than** in debating this year.* Adjectifs courts et adjectifs de deux syllabes ou plus terminés par *-er*, *-y*, *-ow* ou *-le* : ***the*** + adjectif + ***-er*** + ***than*** *This activity is eas**ier** than the others.*	Adjectifs longs : ***the most*** + adjectif *Surfing is **the most** appreciated subject.* Adjectifs courts et adjectifs de deux syllabes ou plus terminés par *-er*, *-y*, *-ow* ou *-le* : ***the*** + adjectif + ***-est*** *Snorkeling is **the** eas**iest** activity ever!*
	Si un adjectif court se termine par consonne + voyelle + consonne (= *big*), on double la consonne finale au comparatif et au superlatif. *This is a bi**gger** problem than I thought. I had **the** bi**gges**t laugh in my whole life.*	

- Les adverbes peuvent également s'utiliser au comparatif et au superlatif.
He trains as regularly as me but he runs much faster than me. In fact he runs the fastest of all the runners.

MIND THE TRICK!

- **Comparatifs et superlatifs irréguliers :**
good (adj ou adv) et *well* (adj ou adv) → *better, the best*
bad (adj ou adv) → *worse, the worst*
far (adv) → *further / farther, the furthest / the farthest*
old (adj) → *older / elder, the oldest / the eldest*

Attention ! En anglais, pour exprimer le **superlatif de supériorité de deux éléments uniquement**, on utilise le **comparatif**.
*young → her young**er** son (**of two** sons)*
*old → the eld**er** brother (**of two** brothers)*
*old → the eld**est** brother (**of three** brothers)*

B L'expression de l'accroissement ou de la diminution

- De plus en plus :
More and more students want to study in Australia.
- De moins en moins :
***Fewer and fewer** pupils prefer studying in their hometown.*
*They spend **less and less** time with their close relatives.*
- Plus / moins…, plus / moins :
***The** old**er** he grows, **the** wis**er** he becomes.*
***The** old**er** he grows, the **less** courageous he becomes.*
***The less** far you go, **the** few**er** points you will get.*

1 Formule des phrases à partir des éléments suivants.
a. High Gate school / + hard / Livingston school.
b. Studying abroad / + beneficial / staying here.
c. This boarding school / – far / we thought.
d. School in Australia / = interesting / England.

2 Traduis les énoncés suivants.
a. C'est l'école la plus connue de la ville.
b. Plus ils sont généreux, plus ils sont heureux.
c. De plus en plus d'adolescents aiment écrire des lettres.
d. Cette école est la plus éloignée de la capitale.

Fiche 9 Les pronoms

Les pronoms remplacent les noms auxquels ils font référence.

A Les pronoms personnels

Pronoms sujet	*I, you, he/she/it, we, you, they*
Pronoms complément	*me, you, him/her/it, us, you, them*

Ann met Andrew. → ***She*** *met* ***him***.
sujet complément

Attention ! Il n'y a qu'un seul type de **pronom sujet** en anglais (*I, you, he/she/it, we, you, they*), contrairement au français où le pronom sujet peut prendre les formes « je » ou « moi » selon les cas.
I *work every day.* **Je** travaille tous les jours.
You and I *have to stick together.* **Toi et moi**, nous devons être solidaires.
My brother and ***I*** *work in the same company*. Mon frère et **moi** travaillons dans la même entreprise.

MIND THE TRICK!

- ***You and I*** ou ***You and me***?
On utilise ***you and I*** quand ces pronoms sont sujets et qu'on peut les remplacer par ***we***.
You and I *have a lot to do.* → ***We*** *have a lot to do.*
On utilise ***you and me*** quand ces pronoms sont compléments et qu'on peut les remplacer par ***us***.
This is hard for ***you and me.*** → *This is hard for* ***us***.
- ***It*** est utilisé pour nommer les objets et les animaux. Mais on utilisera ***he/she*** pour parler d'un animal familier et ***she*** pour parler d'un bateau.

B Les pronoms réfléchis

- On les emploie lorsque le sujet et l'objet sont la même personne :

Pronoms réfléchis	*myself, yourself, himself/herself/itself, ourselves, yourselves, themselves*

She has hurt ***herself***. Elle s'est blessée.
≠ *She has hurt her (= her daughter).* Elle l'a blessée.

- On peut aussi les employer pour marquer une insistance : *Write it yourself!* Écris-le toi-même !

Attention ! Les verbes pronominaux sont différents en français et en anglais. Le pronom réfléchi n'est pas toujours nécessaire en anglais. La réflexion peut se traduire grâce à ***get*** : *get angry* se fâcher • *get married* se marier, etc, ou être déjà « sous-entendue » dans le verbe : *wake up* se réveiller • *sit down* s'asseoir • *hide* se cacher • *meet* se rencontrer • *relax* se relaxer, etc.

C Les pronoms réciproques

- On les emploie pour exprimer un échange entre deux personnes (***each other*** ou ***one another***) ou entre plusieurs personnes (***one another***).
Anne and Henry looked at each other. Anne et Henry se sont regardés.
The clans looked at one another. Les clans se sont regardés.

D Les pronoms indéfinis

- Ils sont composés de *some*, *any*, *no* et *every* d'une part et de *body*, *one*, *thing*, *where* d'autre part :
Somebody *has called you*. Quelqu'un t'a appelé.
This key is ***nowhere***! Cette clé est nulle part !
I knew ***nobody*** *at the party*. Je ne connaissais personne à la fête.
No one *forgets* ***their*** *first date*. Personne n'oublie son premier rendez-vous.
None of *the houses were sold*. Aucune des maisons n'a été vendue.

1 Remplace les éléments soulignés par un pronom personnel.
a. <u>Ali and Sarah</u> are my cousins.
b. They taught <u>Mark and me</u> how to make a good cheesecake.
c. They gave <u>the cat</u> a sweet name.
d. I visited <u>Emma and John</u> last Monday.
e. <u>The lift</u> is out of order.

2 Traduis les phrases suivantes.
a. Mon frère et moi sommes allés au MoMA hier.
b. Ils se sont rencontrés au cinéma.
c. Elles lui en ont donné une.
d. Elle lui a lavé les cheveux et les lui a coupés.
e. Elle se cache dans le garage.

3 Complète avec des pronoms réfléchis (*myself, etc.*) ou réciproques (*each other, one another*).
a. Guys, I have decided to lend you my car. Enjoy ...!
b. The twins introduced ... to the class.
c. Look at ...! You look exhausted!
d. Sally hugged her grandchildren and they looked at ... till the train left the station.
e. Philip and Sarah looked at ... and fell in love at first sight.

4 Traduis les phrases suivantes.
a. La tarte est sur la table. Servez-vous !
b. Ils se sont serré la main.
c. Le matin, je me réveille à 7 heures.
d. Les quatre frères se détestent.

Le groupe verbal

Fiche 10 Base verbale, infinitif et gérondif

A Formation

- La base verbale est la forme la plus simple du verbe : *go* • *cook* • *play*
- L'infinitif est la base verbale précédée de *to* : *to go* • *to cook* • *to play*
- Le gérondif, qui est un nom verbal, se forme grâce au suffixe *-ing* ajouté à la base verbale : *going* • *cooking* • *playing*
- Le participe présent, à ne pas confondre avec le gérondif, est la forme verbale V-*ing* qui permet de modifier l'aspect de l'action exprimée par le verbe : *I speak* → ***I'm*** *speak**ing*** (voir formes simples et formes en V-*ing*, fiches 12 et 13).

L'accentuation de *to* et *-ing*

To et *-ing* sont non accentués. L'accent porte sur la racine du verbe.
She cooks. → *She likes cooking.* • *She wants to come.* → *She's coming.*

B Emplois

1. Sens

- La base verbale exprime le **concept** du verbe d'une manière neutre.
  Verbes ou expressions **suivis de la base verbale** : *must* • *can*, etc. (modaux) • *help* • *let* • *make* • *had better* • *had rather*, etc.
- La préposition ***to*** de l'infinitif induit souvent une **visée**.
  Verbes **suivis de l'infinitif** : *want* • *decide* • *plan*, etc. (verbes de **volonté**) • *expect* • *ask* • *allow*, etc.
- La forme en ***-ing***, quant à elle, ajoute un commentaire sur l'activité du sujet.
  Verbes et expressions **suivis du gérondif** : *can't help* • *prefer* • *don't mind* • *look forward to* • *object to*, etc.

2. Base verbale ou participe présent ?

- Après les verbes de **perception** (*see* • *hear* • *smell*, etc.), on trouve les deux formes.
  I saw her run the race. (pas de commentaire)
  I saw her running the race. (insistance sur le déroulement de l'action)

3. Base verbale ou gérondif ?

- Après les verbes de **goût** (*like* • *love* • *enjoy* • *prefer* • *hate* • *detest*), on trouve le gérondif :
  I like playing soccer. J'aime jouer au football.
  Mais les expressions *would like* et *would love* sont suivies de l'infinitif : *I would like to discover rugby in New Zealand.* J'aimerais découvrir le rugby en Nouvelle-Zélande.

Attention ! Les verbes de goût peuvent être suivis de V-*ing* ou de *to* + BV. Pour mettre en valeur l'expérience ou l'action, on utilise V-*ing*. Pour insister sur l'habitude ou la préférence, on utilise *to* + BV.
*He **likes** tell**ing** jokes.* Il aime raconter des blagues. (On insiste sur l'action de raconter.)
*He **likes** to go to the market on Sundays.* Il aime aller au marché le dimanche (On insiste sur la préférence, l'habitude.)

4. Infinitif ou gérondif ?

- Après ***stop***, ***forget***, ***remember***, l'infinitif et le gérondif sont possibles, mais les énoncés n'ont pas le même sens.
  I've stopped smoking. J'ai arrêté de fumer. (cessation de l'activité)
  I stop to smoke. Je m'arrête pour fumer. (s'arrêter pour faire l'activité)
  I forgot (that) eating sweets is not good for your teeth. J'ai oublié que manger des bonbons n'était pas bon pour les dents.
  I forgot to buy some sweets. J'ai oublié d'acheter des bonbons.
  He remembers bringing the ball. Il se souvient d'avoir apporté le ballon.
  He must remember to bring the ball. Il doit se rappeler d'apporter le ballon.

1 Complète avec l'infinitif ou le gérondif.

a. He enjoys (*perform*) the Haka.
b. They are here. I saw them (*sign*) the attendance sheet.
c. She expects (*win*) the race hands down.
d. I was very tired but I heard the supporters (*chant*) my name and I won!

2 Complète avec la base verbale, l'infinitif ou le gérondif.

a. I am looking forward to (*hear*) from you.
b. I am planning (*go*) to New Zealand (*make*) a TV report on sheepshearing.
c. Sean helped me (*train*) and I won the race.
d. (*run*) is my passion. I can't help (*put*) on my trainers and (*leave*) home to run.
e. He is fond of (*cycle*). He wants (*take*) part in the Tour of Southland.

3 Traduis ces phrases.

a. She forgot to send a postcard.
b. She can't remember sending an email to him.
c. I remember locking the door.
d. They stopped running on the beach.
e. They stopped to admire the view.

4 Traduis ces phrases.

a. La voile est ma passion !
b. Ça ne me gène pas de nager dans l'eau froide.
c. Elle a hâte d'aller faire du vélo.
d. Le docteur ne t'autorise pas à faire du sport.
e. Ce soir, je préfère regarder la télévision.

Fiche 11 L'impératif

A Formation

▶ **À la forme affirmative**

– Aux 2es personnes du singulier et du pluriel, l'impératif se forme avec la **base verbale**.
Speak louder. Parle plus fort.
Listen carefully! Écoutez attentivement.
– À la 1re personne du pluriel, le verbe est précédé de ***let's*** ou ***let us***.
Let's watch the film now! Regardons le film maintenant !

▶ **À la forme négative**

– Aux 2es personnes du singulier et du pluriel, on ajoute ***not*** à l'auxiliaire ***do***.
Don't interrupt him. Ne lui coupe pas la parole.
Don't write. N'écrivez pas.
– À la 1re personne du pluriel, on ajoute ***not*** à ***let's*** ou ***let us***.
Let's not forget this exercise! N'oublions pas cet exercice !

B Emploi

▶ On utilise l'impératif pour donner un **ordre**, une **consigne** ou un **conseil**.
Read the text and circle the keydates. Lisez le texte et entourez les dates clés.

1 Mets ces énoncés à l'impératif.
a. You / pick out the keywords.
b. We / listen to the document once.
c. You / underline the stressed syllable.
d. We / bring the books to the library.

2 Mets ces énoncés à la forme négative.
a. Speak to your neighbour!
b. Take notes!
c. Let's leave now!
d. Let's share the results.

Fiche 12 Le présent simple et présent en *be* + V-*ing*

A Le présent simple

1. Formation

▶ Le présent simple se forme avec la **base verbale** à laquelle on ajoute un -***s*** à la 3e personne du singulier.
*They **live** in Harlem. He **lives** in Harlem.*

▶ Pour former une question, on utilise l'auxiliaire ***does*** pour la 3e personne du singulier et ***do*** pour toutes les autres personnes.
*Where **do** you **live**? Where **does** he **live**?*

▶ Pour former un énoncé négatif, on ajoute ***not*** à l'auxiliaire.
*I **do not** live in Manhattan. He **does not** live in Manhattan.*

▶ On contracte souvent les formes négatives : ***don't / doesn't***

MIND THE TRICK!

• ***Do*** est aussi un verbe. Pour les questions et les formes négatives, on aura donc besoin à la fois de **l'auxiliaire *do*** et du **verbe *do*** :
*I **do not do** research.* • ***Do** you **do** it every year?*

2. Emplois

Le présent simple est utilisé pour exprimer ce qui est stable et pour présenter des informations simples :

▶ énoncer une **vérité générale** :
Water boils at 100°C.

▶ **caractériser** quelqu'un ou quelque chose :
He lives in Harlem. He is a cook.

▶ exprimer un **goût** :
They enjoy dancing at Ginny's Supper Club.

▶ évoquer une **habitude** :
She goes to NYC every summer.

▶ raconter une **histoire** (présent de narration) :
He goes to the club, then meets the manager.

▶ présenter un événement à venir :
The show takes place at 9 o'clock tomorrow night.

B Le présent en *be* + V-*ing*

1. Formation

▶ On utilise l'auxiliaire ***be*** au présent + le verbe à la forme -***ing***.
*I **am** discover**ing** Harlem.*

▶ Pour former une question, on place ***be***, au présent, avant le sujet.
*What **are** you do**ing** in Harlem?*

▶ Pour former un énoncé négatif, on ajoute ***not*** à l'auxiliaire ***be***, conjugué au présent.
*They **are** not listen**ing** to jazz.*

2. Emplois

On utilise le présent en ***be*** + V-***ing*** :

▶ pour décrire une **action en cours de déroulement** :
*Sonia **is playing** the saxophone.*

▶ pour préciser la **position** de quelqu'un :
*She **is sitting** in the armchair.*

▶ pour faire un **commentaire** sur la personne dont on parle :
*He **is** always **bothering** her!* • *You'**re being** such a nice sister.*

MIND THE TRICK!

• Les verbes **exprimant un état** ne s'emploient généralement pas au présent en ***be*** + V-***ing***.
be • believe • feel • forget • hate • know • like • want...
I believe he can manage. Je pense qu'il peut y arriver.
I hate the way you talk to me! Je hais la façon dont tu me parles !

• ***Have, see, think*** ont deux sens :
Ils expriment un état : *have* avoir • *see* voir • *think* penser
Ils expriment une action : *have*, dans certaines expressions comme *have dinner* dîner • *see* se rencontrer • *think* envisager de
Quand ils expriment une action, ils peuvent s'utiliser au présent en *be* + V-*ing*.
I'm thinking of traveling next year. J'envisage de voyager l'année prochaine.
≠ *I think she's in the bathroom.* Je pense qu'elle est dans la salle de bain.

1 **Pose des questions portant sur les éléments soulignés.**

a. Sally enjoys singing in a choir.
b. She works as an accountant.
c. We usually go to the launderette.
d. He is explaining that he lives here.
e. The bell is ringing.
f. I am watching a documentary.

2 **Mets ces phrases à la forme négative.**

a. I walk in the park every Sunday.
b. I do my homework with my brother.
c. He opens a new restaurant in Harlem.
d. He is having a good time in this restaurant.
e. They are designing new clothes.

3 **Conjugue les verbes au présent simple ou au présent en *be* + V-*ing*.**

a. I (*often / go*) to Red Rooster. Today Marcus (*cook*) an original recipe. He (*want*) to celebrate the anniversary of the restaurant.
b. Harlem (*change*). New families (*regularly / move*) in. Rents (*rise*).
c. I can't bear him. He (*always / ask*) questions about my lifestyle. I (*enjoy*) music and I (*go*) to concerts every week. No matter what he (*think*).

4 **Traduis les phrases suivantes en anglais.**

a. Ils pensent déménager à Harlem.
b. Il est toujours en train de se plaindre.
c. Elle ne peut pas répondre au téléphone, elle prend un bain.

PRÉCIS GRAMMATICAL

Fiche 13 Le prétérit simple et le prétérit en *be* + V-*ing*

A Le prétérit simple

1. Formation

- Le prétérit simple des verbes réguliers se forme en ajoutant ***-ed*** à la **base verbale**. Les verbes irréguliers ont des formes particulières qui doivent être apprises par cœur (p. 248-249).
  *Agatha Christie **created** Miss Marple in 1930. She **wrote** The Murder at the Vicarage in 1930.*
- Pour former une question, on utilise l'auxiliaire ***did*** pour toutes les personnes.
  *Which character **did** Agatha Christie create in 1930?*
- Pour former un énoncé négatif, on ajoute ***not*** à l'auxiliaire.
  *Miss Marple **did not** exist. She is a fictional character.*

La prononciation de *-ed*

- Il est prononcé /t/ si le verbe se termine par le son /p/, /k/, /f/, /s/ ou /ʃ/ :
  stopped • worked • laughed • kissed • washed
- Il est prononcé /id/ après les sons /d/ et /t/ :
  needed • started
- Il est prononcé /d/ dans la plupart des autres cas :
  lived • banned • played • breathed

2. Emplois

- Le prétérit simple est utilisé pour exprimer un fait passé et terminé. Il est souvent associé à des repères temporels passés :
  ***Yesterday** the Harpers **invited** their neighbours to dinner.*

B Le prétérit en *be* + V-*ing*

1. Formation

- On utilise l'auxiliaire ***be* au prétérit** + V-*ing*.
  *He **was visiting** Leeds Castle.*
- Pour former une question, on place ***be***, conjugué au prétérit, avant le sujet.
  *What **was** he **doing** in Kent?*
- Pour former un énoncé négatif, on ajoute ***not*** à l'auxiliaire ***be***, conjugué au présent.
  *We **were not complaining** about it!*

La prononciation de *-ing*

Ce suffixe n'est pas accentué. L'accent porte sur la racine du verbe : *They were **play**ing bridge.*

2. Emplois

- On utilise le prétérit en *be* + V-*ing* pour **donner un avis,** une explication sur l'action. On insiste sur le fait que l'action est **en cours de déroulement**.

*He **was driving** through the countryside when he saw a UFO.* (Ici l'action en cours de déroulement *was driving* est interrompue par l'action ponctuelle *he saw*.)

1 **Mets ces énoncés à la forme négative (–) ou interrogative (?). La question porte sur l'élément souligné.**

a. They liked visiting haunted castles. (–)
b. He was looking for the culprit. (?)
c. The detective found some clues. (?)
d. The blackmailer was sending letters to everyone. (–)
e. Miss Marple did her duty. (–)
f. Agatha Raisin held the suspect. (?)

2 **Conjugue les verbes au prétérit simple ou en *be* + V-*ing*.**

a. When Miss Marple (*meet*) her neighbours, she (*notice*) that they (*not – get along*) very well.
b. While she (*go*) back home, she (*hear*) a loud noise and (*see*) a flash of lightning.
c. After work, they (*walk*) to the restaurant and (*have*) dinner. Meanwhile, a robber (*try*) to break their house.
d. As soon as he (*receive*) the letter, he (*phone*) the police. He (*not – know*) a blackmailer (*frighten*) the village.

Fiche 14 Le *present perfect*

A Formation

- Le *present perfect* se forme avec ***have*** conjugué au **présent** et le **participe passé** du verbe.
  *Lisa **has learnt** much from her grandparents.*
- Pour former une question, on place ***have*** conjugué au présent avant le sujet.
  *What **has** she **learnt**?*
- Pour former un énoncé négatif, on ajoute ***not*** à l'auxiliaire.
  *She **has not met** her family abroad.*

MIND THE TRICK!

- ***Have*** n'est pas qu'un auxiliaire, c'est aussi un verbe. Dans ce cas, pour les questions et les formes négatives, on a besoin des deux ***have*** (le premier *have* est l'auxiliaire, le second est le verbe : on peut le remplacer par *eat*) :
  *I **have** not **had** dinner with my relatives.*
  ***Have** you **had** dinner with your relatives?*

L'accentuation d'un verbe au *present perfect*

Have en tant qu'auxiliaire est une forme faible et *-ed* est un suffixe non accentué. L'accent porte sur la racine du verbe.
*She has disco**v**ered her grandparents' language.*

B Emplois

Le *present perfect* est utilisé pour :

- présenter les **résultats présents** d'une action passée ;
  They have learnt English.
- faire le **bilan** d'une situation passée ;
  His appearance has changed over the years.
- parler d'une action qui a **commencé dans le passé et se poursuit au moment où l'on parle**.
  They have lived in England for 25 years.

Attention ! Le *present perfect* ne se traduit pas systématiquement en français par le passé composé :
His appearance has changed. Son apparence a changé.
Il est souvent traduit par le présent :
This is the first time I have seen him. C'est la première fois que je le vois.

MIND THE TRICK!

Attention, si l'événement est rattaché à une date précise, on utilise le prétérit.

1 Mets les verbes entre parenthèses au prétérit ou au *present perfect*.

a. Last month I (*travel*) to India and I (*meet*) my relatives. I feel happy that I (*discover*) my parents' culture.
b. As a child I (*speak*) Polish beautifully. But, then I (*forget*) everything. I (*take*) lessons and I (*remember*) most of it.
c. Asians (*change*) British culture over the years. Diwali (*become*) an important event.

2 Traduis ces phrases.

a. As-tu vu ton oncle récemment ?
b. J'ai oublié ma valise.
c. Ils ont amélioré leur anglais pendant ce voyage.
d. Les prix dans ce restaurant indien ont augmenté.
e. C'est la première fois que tu viens chez nous !

Fiche 15 *Since, for, during, ago*

En anglais, il y a différentes façons d'exprimer l'origine et la durée d'une action. La structure des phrases est parfois différente de celles du français.

A Avec le *present perfect*

Lorsque **l'action a commencé dans le passé et continue dans le présent**, on utilise le ***present perfect*** et ***since*** ou ***for***, qui signifient alors « depuis ».

- ***Since*** est suivi d'une **date** ou d'un **moment précis** dans le passé :
  *I **have played** rugby **since I was five**.* Je joue au rugby **depuis que j'ai cinq ans**.
- ***For*** est suivi d'une **durée exprimée en quantité** (nombre d'années, de jours, de minutes, etc.) :
  *I **have played** rugby **for ten years**.* Je joue au rugby **depuis dix ans** (j'y joue toujours).

B Avec le prétérit

- Lorsque **l'action est terminée**, on utilise ***for*** et le **prétérit**. ***For*** introduit une durée exprimée en quantité (nombre d'années, de jours, de minutes, etc.) et signifie alors « pendant ».
  *I **played** rugby **for ten years**.* J'ai joué au rugby pendant dix ans (je n'y joue plus).
- ***During*** signifie lui aussi « pendant », mais il introduit une **période**. Il peut être utilisé avec le prétérit ou avec le présent :
  *I **discovered** zorbing **during the holidays**.* J'ai découvert le zorbing pendant les vacances.
  *My brother trains a lot **during the day**.* Mon frère s'entraîne beaucoup durant la journée.
- Pour exprimer la **longueur de temps écoulée depuis le début d'une action**, on utilise le prétérit et ***ago***, traduit par « il y a ». La durée est exprimée en quantité (nombre d'années, de jours, de minutes, etc.).
  *I **discovered** zorbing **five months ago**.* J'ai découvert le zorbing il y a cinq mois.

1 **Complète ces phrases avec *since, for, during* ou *ago*.**
a. The team has been playing in Wellington ... January.
b. The fans waited for him ... three hours.
c. The club is closed ... the Christmas holidays.
d. ... John discovered this sport, he has been training a lot.
e. He managed the club six years ... .
f. She was very happy ... this period.

2 **Conjugue ces verbes au prétérit ou au *present perfect*.**
I (*start*) playing rugby three years ago and (*train*) for two years but I (*find*) it too violent, so I (*give up*). Last year I (*turn*) to softball, which I (*enjoy*) since the first day. During our training sessions, we (*learn*) to play fair. Now, my sister (*join*) the club too. We (*take*) part in our first competition last weekend, that (*be*) fun! I believe I (*discover*) something very pleasant.

Fiche 16 Le *past perfect*

A Formation

- Le ***past perfect***, appelé aussi ***pluperfect***, se forme avec l'auxiliaire ***have* au prétérit** et le **participe passé du verbe**.
*She said that they **had bought** burgers.*
- Pour former une **question**, ***have***, conjugué au prétérit, est placé **avant le sujet**.
*What **had** they **bought**?*
- Pour former un énoncé **négatif**, on ajoute ***not*** à l'auxiliaire.
*They **had not bought** paninis.*

MIND THE TRICK!

- ***Have*** est aussi un verbe. Pour les questions et les formes négatives, on a besoin des deux ***have*** (auxiliaire et verbe) :
She had not had a break. • *Had she had a break?*

L'accentuation d'un verbe au *past perfect*

L'accent porte sur la racine du verbe.
*They'd prep**a**red the meal.*
Had en tant qu'auxiliaire est une forme faible et ***-ed*** est un suffixe non accentué. On les entend à peine.
Il est donc parfois difficile de faire la différence entre *had* (+ participe passé) et *would*. C'est le contexte qui t'aide à la compréhension.
*She didn't notice that they'**d** **prepared** the meal. (had)*
*They'**d** **prepare** the meal every time. (would)*

B Emploi

- Le *past perfect* permet d'effectuer un **bilan** par rapport à des **repères passés**. Il marque l'**antériorité** d'un fait par rapport à d'autres faits passés.
*When I arrived at the barbecue, they **had** already **started** to eat.* Quand je suis arrivée au barbecue, ils avaient déjà commencé à manger.
- Il est par exemple utilisé pour rapporter un **discours au passé**.
She said that they had prepared the barbecue. Elle a dit qu'ils avaient préparé le barbecue.
Le repère au passé est le moment où elle a parlé (*she said*). L'action s'est déroulée avant (*they had prepared the barbecue*). L'antériorité est marquée par l'emploi du *past perfect*.

Attention ! Le *past perfect* se traduit généralement par le plus-que-parfait. Mais il peut aussi se traduire par l'imparfait, notamment après l'expression ***it was the first time***.
It was the first time he had eaten an Asian burger.
C'était la première fois qu'il mangeait un hamburger asiatique.
On notera également la particularité de l'emploi du *past perfect* après ***after*** :
After he had grilled the meat, he cut the tomatoes.
Après avoir grillé la viande, il coupa les tomates.

1 **Mets ces phrases au passé.**
a. She is asking them if they invented an original burger.
b. They tell him that they tried a new food-truck.
c. Then she replies that she saw *Gone with the Wind*.
d. He has just said that he gave her a cooking lesson.

2 **Conjugue les verbes au prétérit ou au *past perfect*.**
a. I (*go*) to the food-truck with my friend. We (*order*) two Uncle Sam burgers. Jim (*never / try*) them.
b. She (*light*) the fire, (*put*) the meat on the barbecue and (*wait*). She (*forget*) the drinks, so her brother (*go*) to the nearest shop.

3 **Donne la forme pleine des *'d* (*had* ou *would*).**
a. They'**d** already met him.
b. She'**d** make a cake as she had promised it.
c. They told him that he'**d** succeeded in preparing an excellent meal.
d. They told him that he'**d** be the best cook in town.

4 **Traduis ces phrases.**
a. C'était la première fois que j'étais invité(e) à cette fête.
b. Après être allé au cinéma, il s'acheta un sandwich.
c. Il comprit qu'il avait inventé un hamburger fantastique.
d. Une fois qu'il eut goûté l'*Uncle Sam burger*, il ne put s'en passer.

Fiche 17 L'expression du futur

A Les formes et leur sens

Le futur n'est pas un temps en anglais. Il peut être exprimé de différentes manières selon le point de vue de l'énonciateur, donc selon le sens de l'énoncé.

Sens de l'énoncé	Forme
Simple information	Présent simple *She starts in September.*
Rappel de faits prévus	Présent en *be* + V-*ing* *I'm going to the music centre tomorrow. I told you I had to give a lesson.*
Prédiction de l'avenir grâce à une certitude personnelle	*Will* + BV *They won't come tonight.*
Situation qui est sur le point de se réaliser	*Be about to* + BV *Hurry up! The concert is about to start.*
Situation prévue et projetée dans l'avenir	*Be to* + BV *My job placement is to start next week.*
Prédiction de l'avenir grâce à des critères objectifs ou à une intention	*Be going to* + BV *Look at the sky. It's going to rain! I am going to organise a party.*
Situation susceptible de se produire	*Be likely to* + BV *The mayor is likely to come to our charity fair.*
Proposition polie	*Shall* + BV *Shall I call you next week?*

Attention ! Dans les subordonnées temporelles, on ne peut pas utiliser les modaux (*will*, *shall*).
__When I go to__ Chicago, I will meet my cousins. **Quand j'irai** à Chicago, je rencontrerai mes cousins.

MIND THE TRICK!

- Comme deux modaux ne peuvent pas être utilisés côte à côte, on utilisera ***be able to*** (et non *can*) pour exprimer la capacité dans le futur et ***have to*** (et non *must*) pour exprimer l'obligation dans le futur.
  He __will have to__ pay for a ticket. Il **devra** payer un billet.
  She __will be able to__ give this lesson. Elle **pourra** donner cette leçon.

1 Choisis la meilleure forme pour exprimer le futur.
- **a.** The film (*start*) at 9.00 pm.
- **b.** If they go on talking on the phone, they (*be*) late!
- **c.** Dear sir, (we / meet) again next week?
- **d.** I'm sure that they (*have*) children one day.
- **e.** Hurry up! Get ready! Grandma (*come*).

2 Traduis ces phrases.
- **a.** Il verra sa famille quand il reviendra d'Australie.
- **b.** Aide-le, il va tomber !
- **c.** Ils pourront les appeler dès qu'ils seront arrivés.
- **d.** Elle est sur le point de dire oui.

3 Mets les phrases suivantes au futur.
- **a.** They must take care of their mother.
- **b.** Andrea can teach them how to surf the net.
- **c.** We can sing for this charity.
- **d.** Alex must organise the charity fair.

Fiche 18 La voix passive

A La forme

- La voix passive se forme grâce à l'auxiliaire **be**, qui porte le temps et l'aspect, et au verbe au **participe passé**. Lorsque l'**agen**t est mentionné, il est introduit par la préposition ***by***. Mais, le plus souvent, il n'est pas mentionné.

Voix active	Voix passive
The city __builds__ a memorial.	*A memorial __is built__ __by__ the city.*
They __are building__ a memorial.	*A memorial __is being built__.*
They __built__ a memorial.	*A memorial __was built__.*
They __have built__ a memorial.	*A memorial __has been built__.*
They __will build__ a memorial.	*A memorial __will be built__.*

- La préposition des verbes prépositionnels reste après le verbe.
  They __were listening to__ the speech with emotion.
  → The speech __was being listened to__ with emotion.
- Cas des verbes à double complément : le complément indiquant une personne devient sujet et le complément indiquant un objet reste après le verbe.
  They gave __us__ an interview. → __We__ were given an interview.

B Les emplois

- La voix passive attire l'attention sur **l'objet ou la victime de l'action** et non sur l'auteur de l'action.
  A memorial was built. Un mémorial a été construit.

Attention ! Le passif est souvent traduit par « on » (à la voix active) en français.
I was asked to speak about slavery. On m'a demandé de parler de l'esclavage.

1 Réécris les énoncés à la voix passive.
- **a.** Harriet Tubman helped many slaves.
- **b.** They are showing *Twelve Years a Slave*.
- **c.** He will tell the slaves' stories.
- **d.** She lent me a book about the Underground Railroad.

2 Traduis les phrases.
- **a.** *Huckleberry Finn* a été publié en 1884.
- **b.** On va l'envoyer en prison.
- **c.** On m'a conseillé de voir *Revelations* d'Alvin Ailey.
- **d.** On s'est moqué de lui.

Fiche 19 Les modaux – introduction

A Sens

Les modaux ont deux utilisations :

1. Apporter une information sur le sujet :

*She **can** sing very well.*
*She **must** practise singing every day.*
} **modal 1 : capacité ou obligation** du sujet à chanter

2. Indiquer les chances de réalisation de l'action :

*She **can** still come.*
*She **must** be at school now.*
} **modal 2 : probabilité** de la venue, ou de la présence à l'école.

B Formation

- Les modaux sont **toujours suivis de la base verbale** (sans *to*) et ne portent pas de **-s** à la 3e personne du singulier.
- Pour poser une **question**, le modal est placé **avant le sujet** : ***Can** she sing?*
- Pour former une **négation**, on place ***not* après le modal** : *She **cannot** sing.*
- Certains modaux ont une **forme « passée »**.
  *can → **could** • will → **would** • may → **might** • shall → **should** • need → **needed***
  Must n'a pas de forme passée. On utilisera ***have to*** au prétérit. *must → **had to***
- Utilisée comme **modal 1**, la forme « passée » renvoie au **passé** :
  *She **could sing** very well when she was a child.*
  Elle **chantait** très bien quand elle était enfant.
- Utilisée comme **modal 2**, la forme « passée » exprime l'**hypothétique** :
  *She **could come**.* **Il se pourrait** qu'elle vienne.

La prononciation et l'accentuation des modaux

- On ne prononce pas le ***l*** de *could*, *would* et *should*.
- Les modaux ne sont accentués ni à la forme affirmative (sauf dans les réponses courtes) ni dans les questions en *wh-*.
  ***When** can you come?* /kən/
  Ils sont accentués dans les *yes-no questions*, à la forme négative, dans les tags, les réponses courtes et à la fin des énoncés.
  *Yes, I **can**.* /kæn/

Fiche 20 Les modaux – capacité, possibilité, volonté, habitude

Ces modaux apportent une information sur le sujet.

- ***Can • could*** **: capacité physique ou intellectuelle, ou possibilité**
  She can run very fast. Elle peut/est capable de courir très vite.
  He could read when he was four. Il savait lire à quatre ans.
  We can come and see you at 5 pm. Nous pouvons venir te voir à 5 heures.
- ***Cannot • could not*** **: incapacité**
  They cannot climb the hill. Ils ne peuvent pas grimper la côte.
  We could not go in without the key. Nous n'avons pas pu entrer sans la clé.
- Pour renforcer l'idée de performance ou de défaut d'aptitude, on utilise ***be able to***.
  *This artist **is able to** draw very quickly.* Cet artiste est capable de dessiner très vite.
  *We **were not able to** cross the river; it was too deep.* Nous n'avons pas été capables de traverser la rivière, elle était trop profonde.
  Be able to permet aussi d'exprimer la capacité ou l'incapacité au futur (on ne peut pas associer *will* et *can*.)
  *Soon my baby **will be able to** stand up.* Bientôt, mon bébé pourra / sera capable de se tenir debout.
- ***Will • would*** **: volonté, intention, habitude.**
  I will come with you. Je vais venir avec toi.
  He would go to the theatre at weekends. Il avait l'habitude d'aller au théâtre le week-end.

Attention ! En général, on ne traduit pas ***can*** devant un verbe de sensation :
I can see you but I can't hear you. Je te vois, mais je ne t'entends pas.

MIND THE TRICK!

- Ne pas confondre les **deux emplois de *would*** :
  – il peut exprimer **l'habitude dans le passé** : *I would go there with you when you were a child.* J'avais l'habitude d'y aller avec toi quand tu étais petit.
  – il permet aussi d'exprimer **le conditionnel** :
  I would go with you if I had time. Je t'accompagnerais si j'avais le temps.

1 Complète les énoncés avec *can*, *could*, *will* ou *would*. Ajoute *not* si nécessaire.

a. When I lived in New York, I ... often run in Central Park.
b. I solved her problem, she ... restart her computer.
c. When he was 6, he ... play the violin very well.
d. She has changed her mind. She ... marry him.

2 Traduis les phrases suivantes à l'aide d'un modal.

a. Nous ne pouvons pas compter sur lui.
b. L'année prochaine, Joe va faire le tour du monde.
c. Ils regardaient la télé quand ils rentraient.
d. Il ne sait pas changer une roue (*wheel*) de voiture.

Fiche 21 Les modaux – obligation, interdiction, permission, conseil et reproche

A *Must, mustn't, should, shouldn't, could, may, might*

Ces modaux indiquent que l'énonciateur essaie d'agir sur le sujet, en exerçant une pression plus ou moins forte.

- **Obligation : *must***
  *My children **must** do their homework before watching TV.* Mes enfants doivent faire leurs devoirs avant de regarder la télé.
- **Interdiction : *mustn't***
  Our kids mustn't watch violent movies. Nos enfants n'ont pas le droit de regarder des films violents.
- **Conseil : *should***
  Kim should read this novel. Kim devrait lire ce roman.
- **Reproche : *shouldn't have + V-en***
  You shouldn't have left your brother by himself. Tu n'aurais pas dû laisser ton frère tout seul.
- **Permission : *could • may***
  May I come and see the play? Puis-je venir voir la pièce ?
- **Suggestion, hypothèse : *might***
  You might ask him first. Tu devrais d'abord lui demander.

Pour exprimer ces modalités au futur ou au passé, on a recours aux équivalents des modaux.

B Les équivalents des modaux

Lorsqu'une contrainte, une situation, une règle est imposée de l'extérieur, on utilise les équivalents des modaux.

- **Obligation :**
  Have to (contrainte extérieure)
  It's raining, the pupils have to stay inside. Il pleut, les élèves doivent rester à l'intérieur.
  Need to (obligation liée à un besoin)
  He needs to see his parents. Il doit voir ses parents.
- **Permission :**
  Be allowed to
  I was allowed to use my mobile phone to record my oral presentation. J'ai été autorisé à utiliser mon téléphone portable pour enregistrer ma présentation orale.
- **Interdiction :**
  Not to be allowed to, be forbidden
  They are not allowed to use their mobile phones. Ils ne sont pas autorisés à utiliser leur portable.
  Mobile phones are forbidden. Les téléphones portables sont interdits.
- **Conseil :**
  Ought to (devoir moral)
  You ought to help the younger pupils. Tu devrais aider les élèves (les) plus jeunes.
  Need + V-ing
  The lawn needs mowing. La pelouse a besoin d'être tondue. (= Il faudrait tondre la pelouse.)

1 Complète les énoncés avec *must, mustn't, should* ou *shouldn't*.

a. You ... go and see this film. It's amazing!
b. You ... wash your hands before preparing the meal.
c. He ... have access to our documents. He doesn't belong to the team.
d. They ... have abandoned him.

2 Reformule les énoncés à l'aide d'un modal.

a. The actors ought to meet their fans.
b. I was not allowed to go on the film set.
c. They have to show their passes.
d. They need to go to the bank.

3 Complète à l'aide de *must, need, have to* ou *should*.

a. You ... fasten your seatbelt when you drive a car.
b. You ... think about it! It's important!
c. He will ... take a taxi when he arrives at the airport, it's too far to walk.
d. You ... take a jacket. It's cool outside.
e. My son's hair ... cutting, it's really too long now.

4 Traduis les énoncés en prêtant attention au verbe « devoir ».

a. Il aurait dû l'inviter.
b. Je dois arrêter de manger des chips devant la télé.
c. Le gâteau doit cuire plus.
d. Tu dois montrer ta carte d'identité pour rentrer.

Fiche 22 Les modaux – la probabilité

Ces modaux donnent une indication sur les **chances de réalisation** d'un fait.

- Lorsque le fait évoqué est **présent ou futur**, on emploie le **modal suivi de la base verbale**.
- Lorsque le fait évoqué est **passé**, on emploie le **modal suivi de *have* + V-*en***.

MIND THE TRICK!

- Ne confonds pas les modaux et les adverbes, même s'ils expriment tous deux la probabilité.
  Maybe he is tired. (adverbe)
  He may be tired. (modal)

Certitude	***must*** *They must be gossiping!* Je suis sûr qu'ils sont en train de jaser !
Possibilité logique	***can*** *This can happen tonight!* Ça peut arriver ce soir !
Possibilité logique mais avec une **chance de réalisation moindre**	***could*** *That could happen tonight!* Ça pourrait arriver ce soir ! *She could have been delayed by the traffic.* Elle a pu être retardée par la circulation.
Possibilité (50 % de chances)	***may*** *Miss Marple may guess who the culprit is.* Il se peut que Miss Marple devine qui est le coupable. *He may be listening to our conversation.* Il est possible qu'il soit en train d'écouter notre conversation. *She may have killed him with her quiche.* Il se peut qu'elle l'ait tué avec sa quiche.
Probabilité restreinte (peu de chances)	***might*** *He might be interested by this offer.* Il pourrait être intéressé par cette proposition. *He's late, he might have missed the bus...* Il est en retard. Il a peut-être raté le bus...

1 Complète les phrases avec *must, could, may* ou *might*.
a. She ... be lying. Her version isn't very convincing.
b. He ... not pass his exams. He found them very difficult.
c. They ... not have seen the thief. It was dark.
d. It's 5 o'clock. She ... be having tea, as usual.

2 Reformule les énoncés à l'aide d'un modal.
a. Perhaps they met the murderer at the baker's.
b. Surely he's gone to the town fair.
c. Maybe he was discovered by Miss Marple.
d. She is probably telling the detectives the whole story.

Fiche 23 L'expression du conditionnel

A Le conditionnel articulé avec l'hypothèse

Le conditionnel est utilisé pour exprimer un fait ou une action soumis à une condition. On l'exprime grâce au modal ***would***. On l'emploie dans diverses structures.

- **hypothèse incertaine** (introduite par le **prétérit**) :

If **+ prétérit modal,** ***would*** **+ BV**

If you ***had*** *your degree, you* ***would*** *go to Berkeley.* Si tu avais ton diplôme, tu irais à Berkeley.

- **hypothèse non réalisée** (introduite par le ***past perfect***) :

If **+** ***past perfect*** **modal,** ***would have*** **+ V-*en***

If I ***had been*** *adventurous, I* ***would have started*** *a digital business.* Si j'avais été audacieux, j'aurais lancé une entreprise numérique.

MIND THE TRICK!

• L'auxiliaire ***be*** au **prétérit modal** est ***were*** à la 1re et 3e pers. du sing.
If I ***were*** *adventurous, I* ***would start*** *a digital business.* Si j'étais audacieux, je lancerais une entreprise numérique.

B Le futur dans le passé

- *He said that he* ***would start*** *a new life in California.*
Il a dit qu'il commencerait une nouvelle vie en Californie. (Attention à la concordance des temps dans le discours indirect.)

C L'expression d'un souhait

- *I* ***would like to*** *move to California.* J'aimerais déménager en Californie.
- Le souhait peut également être exprimé grâce à la structure ***I wish*** + **prétérit**, que l'on peut traduire en français par l'expression « j'aimerais... » :
I wish I had a bigger flat. J'aimerais avoir un appartement plus grand.
- Ou avec ***I wish + could / would*** :
I ***wish*** *I* ***could*** *do it.* J'aimerais pouvoir le faire (capacité).
I ***wish*** *you* ***would*** *help me.* J'aimerais que tu m'aides (volonté).

1 En utilisant le verbe entre parenthèses, complète avec *could* + BV, *would* + BV ou *would* + *have* + V-*en*.
a. If they listened to their banker, they ... (*open*) their shop.
b. I wish she ... (*change*) her mind.
c. I wish they ... (*build*) our house but they're too busy.
d. She asked him if he... (*accept*) the mission.
e. If they had had more time, they ... (*visit*) the States.

2 Traduis les phrases suivantes.
a. S'il savait parler anglais, il partirait immédiatement.
b. J'aimerais pouvoir voyager davantage.
c. Il a dit que la Californie lui offrirait des opportunités.
d. S'ils avaient connu ses difficultés, ils auraient été plus compréhensifs.
e. J'aimerais qu'il vienne me voir plus souvent en Californie.

Fiche 24 Les adverbes

A Adverbes en -*ly*

▶ La plupart des adverbes, notamment de manière, sont formés à partir d'un adjectif. On ajoute le suffixe **-*ly*** à la forme adjectivale.
*He came **immediately**.* Il vint immédiatement.
*They were driving very **carefully**.* Ils conduisaient très prudemment.

MIND THE TRICK!

- Si l'adjectif se termine par **-*le***, on supprime le ***e*** et l'on n'ajoute que **-*y*** : *simple* → ***simply***
- Tous les mots qui se terminent par **-*ly*** ne sont pas des adverbes : *cowardly • friendly • lonely • lovely* sont des adjectifs. Si l'on peut dire "*in a ... way*", c'est qu'il s'agit d'un adjectif et non d'un adverbe : *in a friendly way* de manière amicale.

Attention ! Certains adjectifs ont une forme adverbiale irrégulière : *good* → *well*

B Adverbes identiques à l'adjectif

▶ Quelques adverbes ont la même forme que l'adjectif : *high • low • better • fast • late • early • weekly*
He is paid weekly. Il est payé à la semaine. (adverbe) / *a weekly TV show* un show télévisé hebdomadaire (adjectif)
It was late in the afternoon. (adverbe) / *You're always late!* (adjectif)

C Autres adverbes

▶ Certains adverbes, de temps notamment, ne sont formés à partir d'aucun adjectif.
never • tomorrow • soon • now • always • often...
He never told me the truth. • They will arrive soon.

D Sens, emploi et position

▶ Les adverbes apportent une **précision**, une nuance sur un élément de la phrase. Ils peuvent modifier :
– un verbe : *He eats **slowly**.* Il mange **doucement**.
– un adjectif : *This house is **very** warm.* Cette maison est **très** chaleureuse.
– un autre adverbe : *He walks **very** slowly.* Il marche **très** lentement.
– une proposition entière : ***Finally**, he decided to stay.* **Finalement**, il décida de rester.

▶ Ils donnent des indications dans divers domaines : le lieu, le temps, la fréquence, le degré, la liaison, la manière, l'opinion de l'énonciateur, etc.

▶ Leur **position** dans la phrase peut varier :

Notion	Adverbes	Position (en général)
lieu	*here, there, behind, nearby, etc.*	Fin d'énoncé (ou plus rarement en début d'énoncé). *He lives **nearby**.*
temps	*now, today, tomorrow, soon, afterwards, etc.*	Début ou fin de proposition. *It's going to rain **tomorrow**.* ***Now**, take your books.*
fréquence	*always, often, sometimes, rarely, never, etc.*	Entre le sujet et le verbe (ou plus rarement en début d'énoncé). *I **never** swim at weekends.*
degré	*very, too, enough, almost, hardly, etc.*	*Very, too, almost, hardly* : avant l'adjectif *It is **too** hot.* *Enough* : après l'adjectif *That's not good **enough**!*
liaison	*anyway, secondly, thus, then, etc.*	*Début de proposition :* ***First** he was late, **secondly** he was rude.* *Début ou fin de proposition :* ***Anyway**, we'll be here. I will stay here **anyway**.*
manière	*softly, violently, aggressively, pleasantly, etc.*	Après le verbe : *Speak **loudly**!* Mais avant l'adjectif : *a **poorly** ventilated area*
opinion de l'énonciateur	*probably, certainly, sure(ly) , etc.*	Début d'énoncé. ***Sure**, they will bring their own tools.* Entre l'auxiliaire et le verbe. *They will **probably** come with their own tools.*

1 Dis si les mots soulignés sont des adverbes ou des adjectifs.

a. We were impressed. He spoke very well.
b. This man is cowardly. He has not come.
c. She often plays soccer with her neighbours.
d. Paul behaved bravely when he saved the cat.

2 Place l'adverbe au bon endroit.

a. He tore his sleeve. (*violently*)
b. He will be told off. (*certainly*)
c. His mother will buy him a new jacket. (*tomorrow*)
d. He will take his brother's bag as it is big. (*enough*)

3 Traduis les énoncés suivants.

a. Il va souvent au musée le dimanche.
b. Ils se sont assez entraînés pour participer à la course.
c. Ils courent très vite, mais ils ne vont probablement pas gagner.
d. Il y a un stade derrière, mais ils n'y vont jamais.

4 Traduis les énoncés suivants.

a. It's so unfair!
b. They worked hard today!
c. They hardly worked during the whole week!
d. They passed the exam brilliantly.
e. I will certainly fail even though I worked hard.

Fiche 25 Les verbes prépositionnels et les verbes à particule adverbiale

- Certains verbes sont suivis d'une préposition qui introduit le **complément d'objet.** Cette préposition de modifie pas le sens du verbe : on parle alors de **verbe prépositionnel**.
*They are playing games, they are not listening **to** their teacher.*
Listen to est un verbe à préposition.
- Certains verbes peuvent être accompagnés d'une particule, qui **modifie leur sens.** On parle alors de **verbe à particule adverbiale**.
*He got **away***. Il s'échappa. • *He got **up***. Il se leva.
Get away et ***get up*** sont des verbes à particule adverbiale.

La prononciation des verbes à particule

Les verbes à particules s'écrivent en deux mots, mais se prononcent comme s'il s'agissait d'un seul mot. Ne marque pas de pause entre le verbe et la particule.
*Don't **give up**!*

Verbe prépositionnel	Verbe à particule
• La préposition introduit le **complément d'objet.** *He is **looking at** the map.*	• Le verbe à particule peut être construit **avec un complément d'objet.** *He **gave up** the idea.* Lorsque le complément est un **pronom**, il se place **avant la particule**. *He **gave it up**.*
• Lorsque le verbe n'a **pas de complément**, la **préposition disparaît**. ***Look!** The bus stop is here!*	
• La préposition est **maintenue après le verbe** dans les questions, les relatives et à la voix passive : *What are you **looking at**?* *This is the map he was **looking at**.* *They were being **looked at**.*	• Le verbe à particule peut se construire **sans complément. La particule est nécessaire** et **ne peut pas être retirée** dans les questions, les relatives ni à la voix passive. *He **gave up**.* *Why are you **giving up**?* *That is the project I **gave up**.* *They won't be **given up**.*

1 Dis si le verbe en gras est un verbe à préposition ou un verbe à particule adverbiale.

a. Please, **wait for** me!
b. **I'm putting on** my coat.
c. They will **sail across** the channel.
d. His grandmother **looked after** him.

2 Complète les énoncés à l'aide de la bonne particule adverbiale.

a. To go there you need to climb ... the stairs.
b. Take ... your shoes when you are in the house.
c. Turn the music ..., I can't hear you.
d. They will get ... very well and become friends very soon.

3 Traduis les énoncés suivants.

a. The child is looking for the right answer.
b. I'm looking at the painting.
c. She is looking down on him.
d. I will look through the papers.

4 Traduis les énoncés suivant à l'aide d'un verbe prépositionnel ou d'un verbe à particule. Choisis entre les deux propositions.

a. Tu dois surveiller ta petite sœur. (*look for / after*)
b. À qui parles-tu ? (*talk to / about*)
c. La voiture est tombée en panne (*break down / off*)
d. Je reviens vers toi dès que possible. (*get back / down*)

De la phrase simple à la phrase complexe

Fiche 26 L'affirmation et la négation

A L'affirmation

▶ Les énoncés affirmatifs suivent l'ordre **sujet** + **verbe** + **complément**.
She likes music. • *I brought my guitar.*

▶ Dans un énoncé affirmatif, on peut utiliser l'auxiliaire ***do / does*** (***did*** au prétérit) pour donner du poids à ce que l'on dit. Ce « ***do*** » est emphatique.
He said that he would come, and he did come. (confirmation)
He said that I did not like music, but I do like music. (contradiction)
Do keep in touch. (souhait ardent)

L'accentuation du *do* emphatique
Le ***do*** emphatique est accentué pour renforcer le point de vue de celui qui parle.

B La négation

▶ Les énoncés négatifs se forment grâce à un auxiliaire. C'est sur cet auxiliaire que porte la négation.
I am not playing. • *I do not play the violin.* • *She doesn't play the guitar.*

Attention !
- Lorsqu'on utilise ***no*** et ses composés (*nowhere, nobody, no one, nothing*) ou ***never***, le verbe est à la forme affirmative. **Not** n'apparaît pas, tandis qu'en français, on utilise « ne ».
I play no instrument. Je ne joue d'aucun instrument.
I play nothing. Je ne joue de rien.
I never play the violin. Je ne joue jamais du violon.
- En revanche, on garde la négation avec *any* et ses composés.
I do not play any instrument. Je ne joue d'aucun instrument.
I do not play anything. Je ne joue de rien.

1 Énonce le contraire.
a. She does not attend a ballet school.
b. They did not meet yesterday.
c. He always goes to the club on Fridays.
d. I did not succeed in shooting the goal.

2 Traduis les énoncés à l'aide d'une tournure emphatique.
a. – Elle n'a pas pris de parapluie.
– Mais si, elle en a pris un.
b. Fais vraiment attention, la route est dangereuse !
c. Il a dit qu'il lui achèterait un vélo et il l'a bien acheté.
d. Essaie encore !

3 Mets les énoncés à la forme négative.
a. I will learn how to knit.
b. I brought my guitar.
c. She enjoys spending time alone.
d. They are listening to the match on the radio.

4 Complète les énoncés avec un composé de *any* ou de *no*.
a. ... came to her party. She was disappointed.
b. This hotel is in the middle of ... .
c. He is embarrassed. He has not brought ... .
d. He did not speak to ... at the restaurant.

Fiche 27 L'exclamation

▶ **Les énoncés exclamatifs avec *what***
What + groupe nominal (= quel + GN)
Ce groupe nominal est introduit par l'article ***a/an*** s'il est au singulier.
***What** a difficult sport!* Quel sport difficile !
***What** difficult sports!* Quels sports difficiles !

▶ **Les énoncés avec *how***
How + adjectif ou ***How*** + adverbe (= comme + adjectif)
***How** difficult rugby is!* Comme le rugby est difficile !

▶ **Les énoncés avec *so* et *such***
So + adjectif (= si + adjectif)
*Zorbing is **so** impressive!* Le zorbing est si impressionnant !

Such + groupe nominal (= si + adjectif, un tel + GN, une telle + GN)
Ce groupe nominal est introduit par l'article *a/an* s'il est au singulier.
*Zorbing is **such** an impressive sport!* Le zorbing est un sport si impressionnant ! • *She is **such** an inspiration to me!* Elle est une telle source d'inspiration pour moi !

1 Transforme ces phrases en énoncés exclamatifs.
a. New Zealand is a breathtaking country. (*what*)
b. Sheepshearing is a fascinating activity. (*how*)
c. The bikers are brave. (*how*)
d. The fans are supportive. (*what*)

2 Complète les phrases avec *such* ou *so*.
a. It was (*a great trip*)! We are (*delighted*)!
b. We spent hours in the museum, they have (*a huge collection*)!
c. I can't believe you told her that. You are (*a liar*)!
d. Mum and I will come back again to this restaurant. It was (*delicious*)!

Fiche 28 Les questions

A Les questions en *yes-no*

- Ce sont des questions qui appellent une réponse en oui ou non. On les appelle aussi des **questions fermées.**
  Elles se construisent selon le schéma : **auxiliaire** (*be, do, did, have* ou modal) + **sujet** + **verbe**.
  Can you speak your father's language? Yes, I can. / No, I cannot / can't.
- L'anglais utilise beaucoup les phrases interro-négatives, notamment pour inviter ou suggérer. La négation porte sur l'auxiliaire.
  Don't you think we could help him? Ne penses-tu pas que nous pourrions l'aider ?

B Les questions en *wh-*

- Ce sont des questions qui appellent une réponse autre que oui ou non. Elles sont introduites par un pronom interrogatif.
  On les appelle aussi **questions ouvertes** ou ***wh- questions***, parce que plusieurs pronoms interrogatifs commencent par ***wh-*** (les questions en ***how*** en font aussi partie).

Pronom interrogatif	Sens : type d'information recherchée	Construction
What	La nature d'un objet	***What** do you need?* (COD) De quoi as-tu besoin ? ***What** is nostalgia?* (sujet) Qu'est-ce que la nostalgie ? ***What** languages do you speak?* (parmi toutes les langues) Quelles langues parles-tu ?
Which	Lequel (parmi plusieurs)	*Your parents speak German and Russian. You learn English. **Which** languages do you speak?* (parmi celles citées) Tes parents parlent allemand et russe. Tu apprends l'anglais. Quelles langues parles-tu ?
Who	L'identité d'une personne	***Who** came yesterday?* (sujet) Qui est venu hier ? ***Who** do you live with?* (complément) Avec qui vis-tu ?
Whose	L'identité d'une personne à qui appartient une chose	***Whose** book is it?* À qui appartient ce livre ?
Where	Le lieu	***Where** were you born?* Où es-tu née ?
When	La date	***When** did your parents arrive in the UK?* Quand tes parents sont-ils arrivés au Royaume-Uni ? ***Since when** have you been waiting here?* Depuis quand attends-tu ici ?
Why	La cause	***Why** did they leave India?* Pourquoi ont-ils quitté l'Inde ?
How	La manière	***How** did they travel?* Comment ont-ils voyagé ?

- **Les questions en *how* :**

How deep / tall / old... (+ adjectif ou + adverbe)	La mesure	***How old** are you?* Quel âge as-tu ? ***How tall** is he?* Quelle est sa taille ?
How far	La distance	***How far** is the airport?* À quelle distance se trouve l'aéroport ?
How often	La fréquence	***How often** do they go back to India?* À quelle fréquence retournent-ils en Inde ?
How long	La durée	***How long** have you been in England?* Depuis combien de temps es-tu en Angleterre ?
How much / How many	La quantité	***How much** money did you have?* (indénombrable) Combien d'argent avais-tu ? ***How many** brothers and sisters do you have?* (dénombrable) Combien de frères et sœurs as-tu ?

Attention ! En français, c'est souvent l'intonation seule qui indique qu'il s'agit d'une question : Tu as pris des cours de Polonais ?
En anglais, l'inversion est nécessaire : *Have you taken Polish lessons?*

- L'intonation des **questions fermées** est **montante**.
  Do you speak Chinese? ↗
- L'intonation des **questions ouvertes** est **descendante**.
  What language do you speak? ↘

1 Pose les questions sur les éléments soulignés. Attention aux prépositions.
a. They emigrated to England <u>to start a new life</u>.
b. They moved <u>into a small flat</u> in 1967.
c. They have worked in this shop <u>since 1968</u>.
d. This company is <u>their brother's</u>.

2 Complète les questions suivantes.
a. How ... does it take to fly from India?
b. How ... does it cost to go to India?
c. How ... is your suitcase? You may have to pay luggage fees.
d. How ... suitcases can I bring on the plane?

3 Complète les énoncés à l'aide de *what* ou de *which*.
a. You left India. ... do you miss the most?
b. You practise soccer and cricket. ... one do you prefer?
c. ... happened to you when you arrived in London?
d. ... of the two brothers did they hire?

4 Dis si l'intonation est montante ou descendante.
a. Have they talked to their parents?
b. Why don't they want to speak?
c. Who accepted it?
d. Do you want to live there?

Fiche 29 *Question tags* et réponses courtes

A Les *question tags*

- Pour obtenir une confirmation, on utilise un ***question tag***.
  *He is listening, **isn't he**?* Il écoute bien, n'est-ce pas ?
- Le *tag* reprend l'auxiliaire de l'énoncé et le pronom sujet en une question. Lorsque l'énoncé est affirmatif, le *tag* est interro-négatif. Lorsque l'énoncé est négatif, le *tag* est interrogatif.
  The children will stay, won't they?
  The children won't stay, will they?
  Sean drives a lot, doesn't he?
  Sean does not drive a lot, does he?

L'intonation des *questions tags*
Pour cette demande de confirmation, l'intonation est généralement descendante.

B Les réponses courtes

- Pour répondre à une question en *yes-no*, l'anglais utilise l'**auxiliaire** (avec ou sans *not*) précédé du **pronom**.
  "Do you read the scientific press?" "I do. / I do not (don't)."
  "Can you come?" "Yes, I can." / "No, I cannot (can't)."
- D'autres réponses courtes peuvent être faites grâce à ***so***, équivalent de « moi aussi » (*so* + auxiliaire + pronom) :
  "I love biology." "So do I."
  – Lorsque l'énoncé est négatif, on utilise ***neither*** :
  "She cannot bear pollution." "Neither can I." Moi, non plus
  – ***So*** peut également être équivalent de « je le pense, je l'espère » en référence à ce qui vient d'être dit :
  "Does he like his eco-school?" "I think so." / "I don't think so." Je le pense. / Je ne le pense pas.
  "I hope so." Je l'espère.

1 Complète les énoncés avec un *tag*.
a. The organisation will soon launch the Run, Refuel, Recycle campaign, ...?
b. Beavers have a key role to play, ...?
c. Paul and Felicia don't agree, ...?
d. She has studied in an eco-school, ...?
e. They cannot go to the Centre for Alternative Energy, ...?

2 Donne une réponse courte aux énoncés suivants.
a. Can beavers build dams? (+)
b. Will she take part in the project? (+)
c. Has the wind farm opened? (–)
d. Does Wales promote renewable energies? (*hope*) (+)
e. The mining site has become a museum. (*think*) (–)

3 Réponds par l'équivalent de « moi aussi » ou de « moi non plus ».
a. She recycles waste.
b. He didn't use his car yesterday.
c. They will buy solar panels.
d. She cannot help the children build their windmill.
e. She is collecting money.

4 Traduis ces énoncés.
a. Il va donner une présentation sur les énergies vertes, n'est-ce pas ?
b. – Allez-vous alerter les médias ? – Oui, bien-sûr.
c. – Ils ne peuvent pas manifester. – Moi, non plus.
d. – Je suppose que tu n'y es pas allée. – Mais si !
e. Il avait dit qu'il aiderait l'association et il l'a vraiment fait !

Fiche 30 La proposition infinitive

La proposition infinitive est utilisée pour exprimer la pression ou la contrainte qu'exerce quelqu'un sur quelqu'un d'autre.

A La proposition infinitive (verbes de volonté, d'offre, de demande)

- La structure est :
  sujet + **V** de la prop. principale + (sujet de la prop. infinitive) + ***to*** + **BV** de la prop. infinitive
  I want to stay. Je veux rester.
- Le verbe de la proposition infinitive peut être accompagné d'un sujet :
  – un groupe nominal → *I want my friends* ***to stay****.*
  – un pronom personnel (*me, you, him/her/it, you, us, them*)
  → *I want them* ***to stay****.*
  – ou ne pas être accompagné d'un sujet. → *I want* ***to stay****.*
- La proposition infinitive peut se mettre à la forme négative. La négation ***not*** se place avant ***to*** :
  I would like him ***not*** *to stay.* J'aimerais qu'il ne reste pas.
- Verbes suivis d'une proposition infinitive :
  allow • advise • ask • encourage • expect • like • force • get • oblige • order • prefer • tell • want, etc.
- Sont également suivis d'une proposition infinitive :
  – les verbes *allow • advise*, etc.
  – les expressions avec *would* : *would like • would want*

B La proposition infinitive introduite par *for*

1. Après un adjectif exprimant le jugement

- Elle permet d'argumenter, en exprimant la possibilité, l'impossibilité ou le jugement.
- La structure est :
  adjectif + ***for*** + **sujet** de la prop. infinitive + ***to*** + **BV**
  It's unreasonable ***for*** *you* ***to*** *go out today, you look very ill.*
  Il n'est pas raisonnable que tu sortes, tu as l'air très malade.
  It's easier ***for*** *the clarinet teacher* ***to*** *divide his classes into several groups.*
  C'est plus facile pour le professeur de clarinette de diviser ses classes en plusieurs groupes.
  It will be absolutely impossible ***for*** *me* ***to*** *arrive before 9 p.m. tonight.*
  Il me sera absolument impossible d'arriver avant 9 h ce soir.

2. Pour exprimer un but

- *I invited Paul* ***for*** *him* ***to*** *take his mind off his problems.*
  J'ai invité Paul pour qu'il se change les idées.
  Did you buy that book ***for*** *him* ***to*** *read during the holidays?*
  As-tu acheté ce livre pour qu'il le lise pendant les vacances ?

1 Complète ces phrases.

a. Do you expect (*I / come*) to the ceremony?
b. I want (*they / write*) a speech.
c. The slave owners forced (*they / work*) hard.
d. She encouraged (*we / read*) *The Underground Railroad*.
e. I allowed (*he / watch*) *Twelve Years a Slave*.

2 Réécris ces phrases à l'aide d'une proposition infinitive.

a. You have no right to enter this part of the museum.
→ It is forbidden...
b. I've never seen an actor being so moved by his character.
→ It is unusual...
c. My grand-father couldn't join us at the ceremony.
→ It was impossible...
d. We would learn a lot if we could meet a historian.
→ It could be enriching...

Fiche 31 Les structures causatives : « faire faire » et « laisser faire »

- Les structures causatives permettent d'exprimer l'interaction entre deux sujets. Dans ces structures, le sujet est à l'origine de l'action, mais n'en est pas l'auteur : il fait faire ou laisse faire l'action par autrui.
- Elles se construisent avec les verbes *make • have • let*, qui jouent alors le rôle d'un auxiliaire, selon la structure suivante :

sujet + V + objet + infinitif sans *to*

- Le sujet de l'infinitif peut être un groupe nominal ou un pronom personnel complément (*me, you, him/her/it, you, us, them*).
  You should ***let your children go out****. You should* ***let them go!***
- ***Make*** **: forte relation de cause à effet ou contrainte forte**
  He ***made*** *her laugh.* Il l'a fait rire.
  She ***made*** *him admit he was wrong.* Elle l'a fait admettre qu'il avait tort.
- ***Have*** **: cause à effet sans contrainte**
  She ***had*** *him repair her car.* Elle lui a fait réparer sa voiture.
- ***Let*** **: autorisation**
  He ***let*** *me go.* Il m'a laissé partir.

MIND THE TRICK!

- ***Have*** peut être suivi du participe passé. Dans ce cas, l'action n'est pas demandée par le sujet, mais ce dernier en subit les conséquences :
  I ***had*** *my car* ***stolen****.* Je me suis fait voler ma voiture.

Corrigés des exercices du précis

Fiche 1

1 **a.** Dénombrable **b.** Indénombrable **c.** Indénombrable **d.** Indénombrable

2 **a.** buffaloes **b.** boxes **c.** teeth **d.** paths **e.** children **f.** leaves **g.** sheep **h.** glasses **i.** wives **j.** phenomena

3 **a.** J'aimerais des informations sur le voyage.
b. Quel moyen de transport vas-tu / allez-vous prendre ?
c. Ils vont étudier la politique.
d. Nous avons dû faire face à une série d'événements.

4 **a.** Women got the right to vote in Great Britain in 1918.
b. He has made spectacular progress.
c. I saw wolves, horses, and fish at the zoo.
d. Alice could not see her feet.

Fiche 2

1 **a.** a grown-up **b.** a haircut **c.** a fish tank **d.** a bus stop

2 **sun:** sunglasses – sunbathe – sunlight – sunset
out: cut-out – time-out – black-out – burnout

3 **a.** stepmother – La belle-mère de Cendrillon était méchante avec elle.
b. grandmother – Le petit chaperon rouge a rendu visite à sa grand-mère.
c. mother-in-law – La princesse a rencontré sa belle-mère seulement une semaine avant le mariage.
d. mother-to-be – La future maman a peint une licorne dans la chambre du bébé.

4 **a.** une lampe de bureau **b.** un clavier **c.** une chaise de bureau **d.** un repose-pied **e.** un ordinateur fixe **f.** un taille-crayon **g.** des carnets **h.** un stylo-plume

Fiche 3

1 **a.** that **b.** these **c.** this **d.** that **e.** those

2 **a.** These flowers are so beautiful!
b. This car is not mine. My car is over there.
c. I don't trust that man.
d. At that time, there were cassettes.
e. I like this idea pretty well!

3 **a.** Je ne m'attendais pas à cela !
b. Ces bagages ne sont pas les miens.
c. Ne prends pas ce plat. Prends celui-ci.
d. Je suis bien conscient(e) de cela !

4 **a.** pronom **b.** adjectif **c.** pronom **d.** adjectif

Fiche 4

1 **a.** an **b.** an **c.** a **d.** a

2 **a.** Ø Kenya is a country where Ø innovation is everywhere.
b. The Maasai are a tribe that protects Ø African wildlife.
c. The flower industry may be a danger for the environment.
d. Ø Prince Harry likes helping Ø humanitarian associations.

3 the Netherlands – Ø Italy – the United Kingdom – Ø Great Britain – Ø South Africa – Ø India

4 **a.** She came without a suitcase.
b. The man who has saved the turtle is a vet.
c. They go to Kenya once a year.
d. She did not use the Internet there.
e. He plays the lungo, a traditional Kenyan musical instrument.

Fiche 5

1 **a.** My grandma's new neighbours
b. Today's young people
c. Anna's guitar – Eric Clapton's (one).
d. The brothers' songs

2 **a.** our **b.** my – yours **c.** his/her **d.** their

3 **a.** He shook his/her hand.
b. She brushed her teeth.
c. He hurt his knee.
d. She is brushing her daughter's hair.

4 **a.** his **b.** hers **c.** theirs **d.** him ours

Fiche 6

1 **a.** some – any **b.** some **c.** any – some **d.** some – any

2 **a.** little **b.** a little **c.** a few **d.** few

3 **a.** every **b.** all – each / all **c.** every **d.** all / each

4 **a.** many **b.** little **c.** a few **d.** little **e.** few

5 **a.** the whole **b.** all / the whole **c.** the whole **d.** all

6 **a.** Either he will move to the Silicon Valley or he will leave for San Francisco / go to San Francisco.
b. Neither Jenny nor Amber want to become actresses.
c. Most travellers stop in Palm Springs.
d. He devoted his whole life / all his life to extreme sports.

Fiche 7

1 **a.** a fabulous sea activity
b. a tiny old red car
c. a traditional blue woollen skirt
d. a cheerful 15-year-old brown-haired roommate

2 **a.** a 18-year-old boy
b. a heartbreaking story
c. a green-eyed girl
d. a well-dressed waiter
e. a good-looking cake

Fiche 8

1 **a.** High Gate school is harder than Livingston school.
b. Studying abroad is more beneficial than staying here.
c. This boarding school is less far than we thought.
d. School in Australia is as interesting as in England.

2 **a.** It is the best-known school in the city.
b. The more generous they are, the happier they feel.
c. More and more teenagers like writing letters.
d. This school is the furthest from the capital city.

Fiche 9

1 **a.** they **b.** us **c.** him/her **d.** them **e.** it

2 **a.** My brother and I went to the MoMA yesterday.
b. They met at the cinema.
c. They gave him/her one.
d. She washed his/her hair and she cut it.
e. She is hiding in the garage.

3 **a.** yourselves **b.** themselves **c.** yourself **d.** one another
e. each other

4 **a.** The tart is on the table. Help yourself! / Help yourselves!
b. They shook hands.
c. I wake up at 7.00 a.m. / I wake up at seven (o'clock) in the morning.
d. The four brothers hate one another.

Fiche 10

1 **a.** performing **b.** signing **c.** to win **d.** chanting

2 **a.** hearing **b.** to go – to make **c.** train **d.** running – putting – leaving **e.** cycling – to take

3 **a.** Elle a oublié d'envoyer une carte postale.
b. Elle ne se souvient pas de lui avoir envoyé un mail.
c. Je me souviens d'avoir fermé la porte à clé.
d. Ils ont arrêté de courir sur la plage.
e. Ils se sont arrêtés pour admirer la vue.

4 **a.** Sailing is my passion!
b. I don't mind swimming in cold water.
c. She is looking forward to going biking.
d. The doctor does not allow you to do sport.
e. Tonight, I prefer watching TV.

Fiche 11

1 **a.** Pick out the keywords.
b. Let's listen to the document once.
c. Underline the stressed syllable.
d. Let's bring the books to the library.

2 **a.** Don't speak to your neighbour!
b. Don't take notes!
c. Let's not leave now!
d. Let's not share the results.

Fiche 12

1 **a.** Who enjoys singing in a choir?
b. What does she do for a living? / What does she work as? / What's her job?
c. Where do we usually go?
d. What is he explaining?
e. What is ringing?
f. What are you watching?

2 **a.** I don't / do not walk in the park every Sunday.
b. I don't / do not do my homework with my brother.
c. He doesn't / does not open a new restaurant in Harlem.
d. He isn't / is not having a good time in this restaurant.
e. They aren't / are not designing new clothes.

3 **a.** often go – is cooking – wants
b. is changing – regularly move – are rising
c. is always asking – enjoy – go – thinks

4 **a.** They are thinking of moving to Harlem.
b. He is always complaining.
c. She cannot answer the phone; she is having / taking a bath.

Fiche 13

1 **a.** They did not like visiting haunted castles.
b. What / Who was he looking for?
c. What did the detective find?
d. The blackmailer was not sending letters to everyone.
e. Miss Marple did not do her duty.
f. What did Agatha Raisin do?

2 **a.** met – noticed – were not getting along
b. was going – heard – saw
c. walked – had – was trying
d. received – phoned – did not know – was frightening

Fiche 14

1 **a.** travelled – met – have discovered
b. spoke – forgot – took – remembered
c. have changed – has become

2 **a.** Have you seen your uncle recently?
b. I have forgotten my suitcase.
c. They improved their English during this trip.
d. Prices have increased in this Indian restaurant.
e. It is the first time that you have come to our house!

Fiche 15

1 **a.** since **b.** for **c.** during / for **d.** since **e.** ago **f.** during

2 started – trained – found – gave up
turned – have enjoyed
have learnt – has joined
took – was
have discovered

Fiche 16

1 **a.** She was asking them if they had invented an original burger.
b. They told him that they had tried a new food-truck.
c. Then she replied that she had seen *Gone with the Wind*.
d. He had just said that he had given her a cooking lesson.

2 **a.** went – ordered – had never tried
b. lit – put – waited – had forgotten – went

3 **a.** had **b.** would **c.** had **d.** would

4 **a.** It was the first time (that) I had been invited to this celebration / party.
b. After he had gone to the cinema, he bought himself a burger.
c. He understood that he had invented a fantastic burger.
d. Once he had tasted the Uncle Sam burger, he could not do without it.

Fiche 17

1 **a.** starts / is to **b.** will be **c.** shall we meet **d.** will have
e. is about to come / is coming

2 **a.** He will see his family when he comes back from Australia.
b. Help him, he is about to / is going to fall.
c. They will be able to call them as soon as they arrive.
d. She is about to say yes.

3 **a.** They will have to take care of their mother.
b. Andrea will be able to teach them how to surf the net.
c. We will be able to sing for this charity.
d. Alex will have to organise the charity fair.

Fiche 18

1 **a.** Many slaves were helped by Harriet Tubman.
b. *Twelve Years a Slave* is being shown.
c. The slaves' stories will be told.
d. I was lent a book about the Underground Railroad.

2 **a.** *Huckleberry Finn* was published in 1884.
b. He will be sent to prison.
c. I was advised to see *Revelations* by Alvin Ailey.
d. He was laughed at.

Fiche 20

1 **a.** would **b.** can **c.** could **d.** will (not)

2 **a.** We cannot rely on him.
b. Joe will take a trip around the world next year.
c. They would watch TV when they went back home.
d. He cannot change a car wheel.

Fiche 21

1 **a.** should / must **b.** must / should **c.** mustn't **d.** shouldn't

2 **a.** should meet **b.** could not go **c.** must show **d.** must go

3 **a.** have to / must **b.** must / have to **c.** have to **d.** should **e.** needs

4 **a.** He should have invited him / her.
b. I must stop eating crisps while watching TV.
c. The cake needs to cook longer.
d. You have to show your ID card to enter / to get in.

Fiche 22

1 **a.** may **b.** might **c.** could **d.** must

2 **a.** They may have met the murderer at the baker's.
b. He must have gone to the town fair.
c. He may / might have been discovered by Miss Marple.
d. She may be telling the detectives the whole story.

Fiche 23

1 **a.** would open **b.** would change **c.** could build **d.** would accept **e.** would have visited

2 **a.** If he could speak English, he would go / leave immediately.
b. I would like to travel more often.
c. He said that California would give him some opportunities.
d. If they had known his/her difficulties, they would have been more understanding.
e. I would like him to come and see me more often in California.

Fiche 24

1 **a.** adverbe – adverbe **b.** adjectif **c.** adverbe **d.** adverbe

2 **a.** He tore his sleeve violently.
b. He will certainly be told off.
c. Tomorrow his mother will buy him a new jacket. / His mother will buy him a new jacket tomorrow.
d. He will take his brother's bag as it is big enough.

3 **a.** He often goes to the museum on Sundays.
b. They have trained enough to take part in the race.
c. They run very fast, but they will probably not win.
d. There is a stadium behind, but they never go there.

4 **a.** C'est si injuste !
b. Ils ont travaillé dur aujourd'hui.
c. Ils ont à peine travaillé de toute la semaine !
d. Ils ont réussi l'examen brillamment.
e. Je vais certainement échouer même si j'ai travaillé dur.

Fiche 25

1 **a.** préposition **b.** particule **c.** préposition **d.** particule

2 **a.** up **b.** off **c.** down **d.** along / on

3 **a.** L'enfant cherche la bonne réponse.
b. Je regarde la peinture.
c. Elle le regarde de haut.
d. Je vais parcourir les papiers.

4 **a.** You must look after your younger sister.
b. Who are you talking to?
c. The car broke down.
d. I will get back to you as soon as possible.

Fiche 26

1 **a.** She attends a ballet school.
b. They met yesterday.
c. He never goes to the club on Fridays.
d. I succeeded in shooting the goal.

2 **a.** She did not take an umbrella. – Yes, she did.
b. Do be careful ; the road is dangerous!
c. He said that he would buy him a bike and he did buy one.
d. Do try again.

3 **a.** I will not learn to knit.
b. I did not bring my guitar.
c. She does not enjoy spending time alone.
d. They are not listening to the match on the radio.

4 **a.** no one **b.** nowhere **c.** anything **d.** anybody

Fiche 27

1 **a.** What a breathtaking country New Zealand is!
b. How fascinating sheepshearing is!
c. How brave the bikers are!
d. What supportive fans!

2 **a.** It was such a great trip! – We are so delighted!
b. They have such a huge collection!
c. You are such a liar!
d. It was so delicious!

Fiche 28

1 **a.** What did they emigrate to England for?
b. Where did they move in 1967?
c. Since when have they worked in this shop?
d. Whose company is this?

2 **a.** long **b.** much **c.** heavy **d.** many

3 **a.** What **b.** Which **c.** What **d.** Which

4 **a.** montante **b.** descendante **c.** descendante **d.** montante

Fiche 29

1. **a.** won't it / they? **b.** don't they? **c.** do they? **d.** hasn't she? **e.** can they?
2. **a.** Yes, they can. **b.** Yes, she will. **c.** No, it hasn't. **d.** I hope so. **e.** I don't think so.
3. **a.** So do I. **b.** Neither did I. **c.** So will I. **d.** Neither can I. **e.** So am I.
4. **a.** He is going to give a presentation on green energies, isn't he?
   b. Are you going to alert the media? Yes, of course.
   c. They cannot demonstrate. Neither can I.
   d. I suppose you didn't go. Yes I did!
   e. He said that he would help the association and he did it!

Fiche 30

1. **a.** Do you expect me to come to the ceremony?
   b. I want them to write a speech.
   c. The slave owners forced them to work hard.
   d. She encouraged us to read *The Underground Railroad*.
   e. I allowed him to watch *Twelve Years a Slave*.
2. **a.** It is forbidden to enter this part of the museum.
   b. It is unusual to see an actor being so moved by his character.
   c. It was impossible for my grand-father to join us at the ceremony.
   d. It could be enriching to meet a historian.

Fiche 31

1. **a.** Our teacher made us study a lot to prepare the visit to the museum. – Notre professeur nous a beaucoup fait travailler pour préparer la visite au musée.
   b. The president's speech made the ministers understand why the crisis was serious. – Le discours du président a fait comprendre aux ministres pourquoi la crise était grave.
   c. The abolition of slavery in America made European society change. – L'abolition de l'esclavage en Amérique a fait changer la société européenne.
   d. They never let me know what was happening. – Ils ne m'ont jamais dit ce qui se passait.
2. **a.** The film made me cry.
   b. He took them to visit the international museum of slavery.
   c. He never lets them go into his house.
   d. He made his father believe that the work was finished.
   e. The film made us think about liberty and human rights.

Fiche 32

1. **a.** Consequently **b.** Meanwhile **c.** Yet **d.** Indeed
2. **a.** That's why **b.** As a matter of fact **c.** In addition **d.** Otherwise

Fiche 33

1. **a.** which **b.** where **c.** whose **d.** who
2. **a.** what **b.** Ø **c.** which **d.** what

Fiche 34

1. **a.** until / unless **b.** if **c.** unless **d.** as soon as
2. **a.** He won't win the marathon unless he changes his coach.
   b. They will be able to participate in the Games provided they find a sponsor.
   c. As soon as she gets some / the money, she will create an association.
   d. Whenever he goes back to his country, he is upset / moved.

Fiche 35

1. **a.** She gives her time so as to / in order to help children.
   b. As he was very nervous, he was allowed to leave the room.
   c. What does she give him money for?
   d. He was blamed for being late again.
   e. Since you don't want to leave, I will (go out).
2. **a.** Comme il a gagné la compétition, il est considéré comme un héros.
   b. Afin de gagner la course, elle a embauché un coach.
   c. Puisque tu as manqué le dernier cours, je ne te reproche pas de ne pas comprendre ceci.
   d. Elle a écrit au Comité Olympique pour participer aux Jeux.

Fiche 36

1. **a.** Nigeria has a bobsleigh team whereas it never snows.
   b. Even if she has never met him, she believes he is a good person.
   c. As she won the final, her family was very proud.
   d. Although he has no sponsor, he is the best.
   e. While they were training, the coach received a phone call.
   f. They never won although they trained hard.
2. **a.** He learnt everything by heart while he does not like this author.
   b. Even if she was tired, she went running every evening.
   c. While she likes ballet, she prefers soccer / football.
   d. Contrary to / unlike his sister, he spends his time riding his bike.

Fiche 37

1. **a.** "I will find Snow White in this wood," he said.
   b. "Is Snow White more beautiful than me?" the witch asked.
   c. Her father told her daughter, "Take my horse!"
   d. She said to the prince, "I have been waiting for you for a long time."
2. **a.** He said that they were watching the new version of *Beauty and the Beast*.
   b. The children asked if they could go to the amusement park the day after / the following day.
   c. The mother said that she had taken the tickets the day before / the previous day.
3. **a.** wondered **b.** asked **c.** told **d.** assured **e.** said
4. **a.** Helen blamed the story for being too classical.
   b. She suggested that I / we turn my / our story into something new.
   c. She advised them / us to reverse the roles.
   d. I admitted that Helen was right.

LEXIQUE Anglais-Français

A

achieve *v* *atteindre, accomplir*
achiever *n* *quelqu'un qui réussit*
addicted to *adj* *accro à*
adrenaline rush *n* *montée d'adrénaline*
adventurous *adj* *téméraire*
advisory committee *n* *conseil consultatif*
advocate *v* *préconiser, recommander*
aim at/for *v* *viser quelque chose*
ancestor *n* *ancêtre*
anti-poaching *adj* *antibraconnage*
appalling *adj* *effrayant*
apply for *v* *postuler à*
argue *v* *débattre, discuter*
aspire to *v* *aspirer à*
athletic *adj* *athlétique*
attend *v* *assister à*
attend a workshop *v* *participer à un atelier*
attend to someone *v* *s'occuper de, servir quelqu'un*
attract *v* *attirer*
ATV (all-terrain vehicle) *n* *véhicule tout terrain, 4x4*
auction *n* *vente aux enchères*
audience *n* *public*
awe *n* *terreur*

B

baby-boomers *n* *personnes de la génération du baby-boom, nées entre 1945 et 1965*
beast *n* *bête*
belong to *n* *appartenir à, faire partie de*
bilingual *adj* *bilingue*
binge-watch *v* *regarder tous les épisodes d'une série d'une traite*
binoculars *n* *jumelles*
blame *v* *accuser*
bleachers *ns* *gradins*
blend in *v* *s'intégrer à*
bloodcurdling *adj* *à glacer le sang*
boarding school *n* *internat*
bold *adj* *courageux*
bond with *v* *se lier à*
book a tour *v* *réserver une visite guidée*
borough *n* *arrondissement de New York*
brand new *adj* *flambant neuf*
brave *adj* *courageux*
break *n* *récréation, pause*
break a record *v* *battre un record*
break up *v* *rompre*
breathtaking *adj* *incroyable, à couper le souffle*
bright *adj* *brillant, lumineux*
bring together *v* *réunir, éduquer*
bring up *v* *évoquer, soulever*
brownstone building *n* *immeuble en grès rouge*
bun *n* *petit pain*
bungy-jumping *n* *saut à l'élastique*
burger joint *n* *restaurant de burgers*
burglary *n* *cambriolage*

C

campaign *v* *faire campagne*
campsite *n* *camping*
campus *n* *campus*
capital city *n* *capitale*
careful *adj* *prudent*
careless *adj* *imprudent, négligent*
carry out a programme *v* *mettre en place un programme, une politique*
cast *n* *acteurs et actrices d'un film*
cast a spell *v* *lancer un sort*
celebrate *v* *célébrer*
cheer *v* *applaudir, acclamer*
chef *n* *chef (cuisinier)*
chief *n* *chef (leader)*
chief executive officer (CEO) *n* *PDG*
churchyard *n* *cimetière*
city centre *n* *centre-ville*
clash *n* *violent désaccord*
classmate *n* *camarade de classe*
cliffhanger *n* *suspense à la fin d'un épisode*
close or distant relative *n* *parent proche ou éloigné*
close-knit *adj* *très uni, soudé*
clue *n* *indice*
coal *n* *charbon*
coast, coastline *n* *côte, littoral*
college *n* *université*
colourful *adj* *coloré*
commemorate *v* *commémorer*
committed *adj* *engagé*
community *n* *communauté*
compete *v* *disputer (un championnat)*
competitive *adj* *compétitif*
competitor *n* *concurrent*
comply with *v* *se conformer à*
computer savvy *adj* *doué en informatique*
confederate states *n* *États confédérés, États du Sud*
conform to *v* *se conformer à*
confused *adj* *embarrassé*
connect with *v* *nouer des liens avec*
contestant *n* *concurrent*
contribute to *v* *contribuer à*
cook *v* *cuisiner*
cope with *v* *gérer, s'occuper de*
corpse *n* *cadavre*
cost-saving *adj* *économique*
countryside *n* *campagne*
courageous *adj* *courageux*
creak *v* *grincer*
creative *adj* *créatif*
creepy *adj* *effrayant*
criticise *v* *critiquer*
crop *n* *culture, récolte*
crowd *n* *foule*
cry *n* *cri*
cry *v* *pleurer*
culprit *n* *coupable*
curious *adj* *curieux*
cut down *v* *réduire, couper*

D

damage *v* *endommager*
daring *adj* *courageux, audacieux*
dark *adj* *sombre*
deal with the past *v* *faire face à son passé*
debate *v* *débattre*
defend a cause *v* *défendre une cause*
defiant *adj* *rebelle*
demanding *adj* *exigeant*
denounce *v* *dénoncer*
develop skills *v* *développer des compétences*
devoted to *adj* *dévoué à*
disrespectful *adj* *irrespectueux*
distort *v* *détourner*
download *v* *télécharger*
drama *n* *drame*
drive-through *n* *drive*
dwarf/dwarves *n* *nain(s)*

E

eager to *adj* *impatient de*
eco-friendly *adj* *respectueux de l'environnement*
eco-school *n* *école écologique*
eco-tourism *n* *tourisme écologique*

eerie adj *étrange, inquiétant*
the elderly n *les personnes âgées*
embarrassed adj *gêné*
embedded in adj *intégré dans*
embody v *incarner*
employee n *employé*
enact a law v *promulguer une loi*
encourage v *encourager*
endangered adj *menacé d'extinction*
enhance v *améliorer*
enrich v *enrichir*
enthusiastic about adj *enthousiaste à propos de*
equality n *égalité*
event n *événement*
eventful adj *mouvementé*
everlasting adj *éternel*
evidence n *preuve*
evil adj *maléfique*
evolve v *évoluer*
excursion n *sortie (scolaire)*
executive n *cadre*
exhibition n *exposition*
expand v *étendre*
exploit someone v *exploiter quelqu'un*
extended family n *famille élargie*
extra n *figurant*
extreme sport n *sport extrême*

F

failure n *échec*
fairy n *fée*
fame n *célébrité*
famous adj *célèbre*
fantasy adj *fantastique*
far-away kingdom n *royaume lointain*
fascinated by adj *fasciné par*
fashionable adj *à la mode*
fear of heights n *peur des hauteurs*
fearful adj *craintif*
fearless adj *intrépide*
fictional adj *fictionnel*
field athlete n *athlète*
field trip v *sortie (scolaire)*
field worker n *travailleur sur le terrain*
fight for, fight against v *se battre pour/contre*
film director n *réalisateur*
film location n *lieu de tournage*
film studio n *studio de cinéma*
fit in v *s'intégrer*
flavour n *saveur*
fluent adj *parlant couramment une langue*
footstep n *bruit de pas*
foreign culture n *culture étrangère*
foreign-born adj *né à l'étranger*
forensics n *police scientifique*
formal n *bal de fin d'année*
fossil fuel n *énergie fossile*
foster v *promouvoir*
freeze v *geler*
French fries n *frites*
friendly adj *amical*
frightening adj *effrayant*
fund n *fonds*

G

gather v *réunir*
gathering n *réunion*
get a certificate of education v *obtenir l'équivalent du bac en Australie*
get involved in v *s'impliquer dans*
get lost v *se perdre*
ghost n *fantôme*
give orders v *donner des ordres*
glued to the screen adj *collé à l'écran*
go on a journey v *partir en voyage*
go on a quest v *se lancer dans une quête*
godmother n *marraine*
good deed n *bonne action*
goosebumps n *chair de poule*
graduate v *obtenir son diplôme*
grandstand n *tribunes*
grateful adj *reconnaissant*
gratitude n *gratitude*
greenhouse n *serre*
grow a plant v *faire pousser une plante*
guarantee v *garantir*
guard n *garde, gardien*
guilty adj *coupable*

H

hair-raising adj *effrayant*
hallway n *couloir*
handcuff n *menotte*
handle v *gérer*
have an impact on v *avoir un impact sur*
have goosebumps v *avoir la chair de poule*
headboy/-girl n *représentant(e) des élèves*
headmaster/-mistress n *directeur/-trice d'établissement scolaire*
headquarters n *quartier général, siège social*
healthy adj *sain, diététique*
heartbreaking adj *déchirant*
high school n *lycée*
hilarious adj *hilarant*
historical adj *historique*
hold one's breath v *retenir sa respiration*
honour v *honorer*
hooked on adj *accro, captivé*
hope for v *espérer*
hospitable adj *hospitalier*
host n *hôte*
hostel n *auberge de jeunesse*
house captain n *délégué des élèves*
huge adj *immense*

I

identify with v *s'identifier à*
ill-at-ease adj *mal à l'aise*
implement v *mettre en place*
import v *importer*
impressive adj *impressionnant*
improve v *améliorer*
inclusiveness n *non-exclusion*
inequality n *inégalité*
influence v *influencer*
influential adj *influent*
innovative adj *innovant*
inquiry n *enquête, investigation*
inspiring adj *qui est source d'inspiration*
integrate v *intégrer*
interact with v *interagir avec*
intern n *stagiaire*
interrogate v *interroger*
invest in v *investir dans*
investigation n *enquête*
involved in adj *impliqué dans*
irony n *ironie*
isolated adj *isolé*
isolation n *isolement*
issue n *problème, sujet en question*
ivory n *ivoire*

J

join a club v *rejoindre un club*
journey n *voyage*
junior pupil n *élève de première année en Australie*

K

keep memories alive v *conserver le souvenir*
keep the memory of v *perpétuer le souvenir de*

L

lane n *chemin*
language barrier n *barrière linguistique*
laptop n *ordinateur portable*
lead a project v *mener un projet*
lead role n *rôle principal*
legislate v *légiférer*
lenient adj *indulgent*
lifeguard, lifesaver n *maître-nageur(se)*
litter n *ordures*
living conditions n *conditions de vie*
locally-grown adj *de provenance locale*
look after v *veiller sur*
lunch time n *heure du déjeuner*

M

maid n *(une) domestique*
main role n *rôle principal*
make connections with v *nouer des relations avec*
make ends meet v *joindre les deux bouts*
make one's dream come true v *rendre son rêve réalité*
market (place) n *marché (place du)*
mass tourism n *tourisme de masse*
meaningful n *enrichissant*
meat-free adj *sans viande*
medal n *médaille*
meet people v *rencontrer de nouvelles personnes*
meet up with v *retrouver, avoir un rendez-vous avec*
memorial n *monument commémoratif*
millennial n *jeune né(e) dans les années 1980 et 1990*
mischief n *méfaits, troubles*
mistreat v *maltraiter*
misunderstanding n *malentendu*
mixed up adj *déboussolé*
modernise v *moderniser*
money-making adj *lucratif*
mother tongue n *langue maternelle*
multilingual adj *polyglotte*
mural n *peinture murale*
mythical adj *mythique*

N

narrow-minded adj *étroit d'esprit*
native tongue n *langue maternelle*
natural habitat n *habitat naturel*
nature park n *parc naturel*
neighbourhood n *quartier*
network n *réseau*
nightmare n *cauchemar*
northern adj *du nord*
nuclear family n *famille nucléaire*
nursery school n *école maternelle*

O

obsessed adj *obsédé*
office n *bureau*
on the run loc *en cavale*
on time loc *à l'heure*
Once upon a time loc *Il était une fois*
onion n *oignon*
opportunity n *occasion*
the oppressed n *les opprimés*
the oppressor n *l'oppresseur*
organic adj *bio*
organised adj *organisé*
outstanding adj *incroyable*
overcome v *surmonter*

P

paradoxical adj *paradoxal*
part of loc *partie de*
participate in v *participer à*
pass on knowledge v *transmettre un savoir*
pass the final exams v *obtenir son diplôme*
passenger n *passager*
patty n *steak haché*
pay (a) tribute to v *rendre hommage à*
pensioner n *retraité*
period n *heure de cours*
permissive adj *permissif, indulgent*
pick cotton v *cueillir le coton*
pilot n *premier épisode d'une série*
plot n *intrigue*
poach v *braconner*
poetry n *poésie*
politeness n *politesse*
practice n *entraînement*
practise v *s'entraîner*
praise v *faire l'éloge de*
preserve v *préserver*
Prince Charming n *Prince charmant*
proficient adj *très compétent*
prom v *bal de fin d'année*
promote v *promouvoir*
protest n *manifestation*
protest v *protester*
proud adj *fier*
provide care for v *s'occuper de*
pursuit of happiness n *recherche du bonheur*

Q

qualify for v *se qualifier pour*

R

raise awareness v *éveiller les consciences, sensibiliser*
ranger n *garde-forestier*
rank n *rang*
rate n *taux*
rattling n *cliquetis, bruit de ferraille*
rebellious adj *rebelle*
recess n *récréation*
reckless adj *imprudent, irréfléchi*
recognition n *reconnaissance*
recommend v *recommander*
reconcile v *(se) réconcilier*
record-breaking adj *qui bat tous les records*
reduce v *réduire*
reinvent v *réinventer*
relate to v *se sentir concerné par*
relish v *savourer, apprécier*
remote adj *lointain*
replace v *remettre, remplacer*
reproach v *reprocher*
reservation n *réserve*
resilient adj *résistant*
resort, holiday centre n *station/centre de vacances*
result in v *provoquer*
retirement home n *maison de retraite*
reveal the end v *dévoiler la fin*
review n *critique de presse*
revitalise v *revitaliser*
rewriting n *réécriture*
rhino n *rhinocéros*
rivalry v *rivalité*
roam v *errer, vagabonder*
roommate n *colocataire*
root n *racine*
rooted in adj *ancré dans*

S

schedule *n* *emploi du temps*
school grounds *n* *campus*
school hall *n* *salle polyvalente*
screech *v* *hurler*
screenwriter *n* *scénariste*
search *v* *rechercher*
seashore *n* *côte, littoral*
seek revenge *v* *vouloir se venger*
segregation *n* *ségrégation*
self-conscious *adj* *gêné, complexé*
sell *v* *vendre*
senior pupil *n* *élève de terminale*
seniors *n* *personnes âgées*
sense *n* *sens*
sense of fulfilment *n* *sentiment d'accomplissement, de réussite*
serve *v* *servir*
servitude *n* *servitude*
set a record *v* *établir un record*
setting *n* *décor*
shackles *n* *chaînes*
shade *n* *ombre*
shadow *n* *ombre*
share *v* *partager*
share testimonies *v* *partager des témoignages*
sheepshearing *n* *tonte de moutons*
shivers of fear *n* *frissons de terreur*
shocked *adj* *choqué*
shore *n* *rivage*
showcase *v* *présenter, mettre en valeur*
sight *n* *vue*
single-parent family *n* *famille monoparentale*
sitcom *n* *sitcom, comédie*
slave *n* *esclave*
slum *n* *bidonville*
socialise *v* *voir du monde*
solar *adj* *solaire*
solidarity *n* *solidarité*
sort *v* *trier*
southern *adj* *du sud*
species *n* *espèce*
spending *n* *dépense*
split up *v* *scinder, rompre*
spoil *v* *révéler un élément d'intrigue*
sportsman/sportswoman *n* *sportif/sportive*
sprinter *n* *sprinter*
squeak *v* *couiner*
stadium *n* *stade*
staff *n* *personnel*
stand for *v* *représenter*
stanza *n* *strophe*
stick together *v* *rester ensemble*
stimulate *v* *stimuler*
storyline *n* *intrigue*
stream *v* *regarder en ligne*
strength *n* *force*
strengthen relationships *v* *consolider ses relations*
stroll *v* *se promener*
study *v* *étudier*
submissive *adj* *soumis, docile*
submit an application for *v* *postuler à*
success *n* *succès*
suffer *v* *souffrir*
support *v* *soutenir, promouvoir*
supportive *adj* *qui soutient*

T

take an exam *v* *passer un examen*
take part in *v* *participer à*
take up a challenge *v* *relever un défi*
talented *adj* *talentueux*
tattoo *n* *tatouage*
teen show *n* *série pour adolescents*
terrifying *adj* *terrifiant*
testify *v* *témoigner*
thankful *adj* *reconnaissant*
theft *n* *vol*
threatened *adj* *menacé (d'extinction)*
throw a curse *v* *jeter une malédiction*
tidal *adj* *de marée*
timetable *n* *emploi du temps*
togetherness *n* *sentiment d'appartenance*
topping *n* *garniture*
torn apart *adj* *déchiré*
tour guide *n* *guide touristique*
tournament *n* *tournoi*
town hall *n* *mairie*
track *n* *piste d'athlétisme*
train *v* *s'entraîner*
training session *n* *session d'entraînement*
transform *v* *transformer*
trash *n* *ordures*
trendy *adj* *chic, branché*
tribe *n* *tribu*
trip *n* *voyage*
trophy *n* *trophée*
turtle *n* *tortue*
twist a plot *v* *détourner l'intrigue*

U

unionist *adj* *unioniste*
unite *v* *s'unir, réunir*
united *adj* *uni*
unknown *adj* *inconnu*

V

values *n* *valeurs*
vegan *adj* *vegan*

W

wait on someone *v* *servir quelqu'un*
waiter, waitress *n* *serveur(se)*
wander *v* *errer, vagabonder*
waste *v* *gaspiller*
weakness *n* *faiblesse*
wealth *n* *richesse*
welcoming *adj* *accueillant*
whip *n* *fouet*
wicked witch *n* *méchante sorcière*
wildlife *n* *flore et faune sauvage*
withdraw *v* *retirer*
witness *v* *être témoin de*
wizard *n* *sorcier*
work ethic *n* *déontologie*

Y

yell *v* *hurler*

Z

zebra *n* *zèbre*

A

à couper le souffle *adj* *breathtaking*
à glacer le sang *adj* *bloodcurdling*
à l'heure *loc* *on time*
à la mode *adj* *fashionable*
accomplir *v* *achieve*
accro à *adj* *addicted to, hooked on*
accueillant *adj* *welcoming*
accuser *v* *blame*
améliorer *v* *enhance, improve*
amical *adj* *friendly*
ancêtre *n* *ancestor*
ancré dans *adj* *rooted in*
antibraconnage *adj* *anti-poaching*
appartenir à *n* *belong to*
apprécier *v* *relish*
arrondissement de New York *n* *borough*
aspirer à *v* *aspire to*
assister à *v* *attend*
atelier *v* *workshop*
athlète *n* *field athlete*
athlétique *adj* *athletic*
atteindre *v* *achieve*
attirer *v* *attract*
auberge de jeunesse *n* *hostel*
audacieux *adj* *daring*
avoir un impact sur *v* *have an impact on*
avoir un rendez-vous avec *v* *meet up with*

B

baccalauréat en Australie *n* *certificate of education*
bal de fin d'année *v* *formal, prom*
barrière linguistique *n* *language barrier*
battre un record *v* *break a record*
bête *n* *beast*
bêtise *n* *mistake, misbehaviour*
bidonville *n* *slum*
bilingue *adj* *bilingual*
bio *adj* *organic*
bonne action *n* *good deed*
braconner *v* *poach*
branché *adj* *trendy*
brillant *adj* *bright*
bruit de ferraille *n* *rattling*
bruit de pas *n* *footstep*
bureau *n* *office*

C

cadavre *n* *corpse*
cadre *n* *executive*
camarade de classe *n* *classmate*
cambriolage *n* *burglary*
campagne (paysage) *n* *countryside*
campagne (politique) *n* *campaign*
camping *n* *campsite*
campus *n* *campus*
campus *n* *school grounds*
capitale *n* *capital city*
captivé *adj* *hooked on*
casting *n* *cast*
cauchemar *n* *nightmare*
célèbre *adj* *famous*
célébrer *v* *celebrate*
célébrité *n* *fame*
centre/station de vacances *n* *resort, holiday centre*
centre-ville *n* *city centre*
chaînes *n* *shackles*
chair de poule *v* *goosebumps*
charbon *n* *coal*
chef (cuisinier) *n* *chef*
chef (leader) *n* *chief*
chemin *n* *lane*
chic *adj* *trendy*
choqué *adj* *shocked*
cimetière *n* *churchyard*
cliquetis *n* *rattling*
collé à l'écran *adj* *glued to the screen*
colocataire *n* *roommate*
coloré *adj* *colourful*
comédie *n* *comedy, sitcom*
commémorer *v* *commemorate*
communauté *n* *community*
(très) compétent *adj* *proficient*
complexé *adj* *self-conscious*
concurrent *n* *competitor, contestant*
conditions de vie *n* *living conditions*
confus *adj* *embarrassed*
conseil consultatif *n* *advisory committee*
conserver le souvenir *v* *keep memories alive*
consolider des relations *v* *strengthen relationships*
contribuer à *v* *contribute to*
côte *n* *coast, seashore*
couiner *v* *squeak*
couloir *n* *hallway, corridor*
coupable *adj* *guilty*
coupable *n* *culprit*
courageux *adj* *bold, brave, courageous, daring*
craintif *adj* *fearful*
créatif *adj* *creative*
crèche *n* *crèche, daycare*
cri *n* *cry, scream, shout*
critique de presse *n* *review*
critiquer *v* *criticise*
cueillir le coton *v* *pick cotton*
cuisiner *v* *cook*
culture (agriculture) *n* *crop*
culture étrangère *n* *foreign culture*
curieux *adj* *curious*

D

de marée *adj* *tidal*
de provenance locale *adj* *locally-grown*
débattre *v* *debate, argue*
déboussolé *adj* *mixed up*
déchirant *adj* *heartbreaking*
déchiré *adj* *torn apart*
décor *n* *setting*
défendre une cause *v* *defend a cause*
délégué de classe *n* *house captain, headboy/-girl*
dénoncer *v* *denounce*
déontologie *n* *work ethic*
dépense *n* *spending*
détourner l'intrigue *v* *twist a plot*
détourner *v* *distort*
développer des compétences *v* *develop skills*
dévoiler la fin *v* *reveal the end*
dévoué à *adj* *devoted to*
diététique *adj* *healthy*
directeur/-trice d'établissement scolaire *n* *headmaster/-mistress*
discuter *v* *discuss, debate*
disputer (un championnat) *v* *compete*
distribution (cinéma) *n* *cast*
docile *adj* *submissive*
domestique *n* *maid (female), servant*
donner des ordres *v* *give orders*
doué en informatique *adj* *computer savvy*
drame *n* *drama*
drive *n* *drive-through*
du nord *adj* *northern*
du sud *adj* *southern*

E

échec *n* *failure*
école écologique *n* *eco-school*

école maternelle n *nursery school*
économique adj *cost-saving*
effrayant adj *frightening, hair-raising, appalling, creepy*
effroyable adj *frightful, horrifying*
égalité n *equality*
élève de première année n *junior pupil (Australia)*
élève de terminale n *senior pupil*
emploi du temps n *schedule, timetable*
employé n *employee*
en cavale loc *on the run*
encourager v *cheer, encourage*
endommager v *damage*
énergie fossile n *fossil fuel*
engagé adj *committed*
enquête n *inquiry, investigation*
enrichir v *enrich*
enthousiaste à propos de adj *enthusiastic about*
entraînement n *practice, training*
errer v *roam, wander*
espèce n *species*
espérer v *hope for*
établir un record v *set a record*
Etats confédérés (du Sud) n *confederate states*
étendre v *expand*
éternel adj *everlasting*
étrange adj *eerie*
être témoin de v *witness*
étroit d'esprit adj *narrow-minded*
étudier v *study*
éveiller les consciences v *raise awareness*
événement n *event*
évoluer v *evolve*
évoquer, soulever v *bring up*
exigeant adj *demanding*
expérience enrichissante n *meaningful experience*
exploiter quelqu'un v *exploit someone*
exposition n *exhibition*

F

faiblesse n *weakness*
faire campagne v *campaign*
faire face à son passé v *deal with the past*
faire l'éloge de v *praise*
faire partie de n *belong to*
faire pousser une plante v *grow a plant*
famille élargie n *extended family*
famille monoparentale n *single-parent family*
famille nucléaire n *nuclear family*
fantastique n *fantasy*
fantôme n *ghost*
fasciné par adj *fascinated by*
la faune et la flore sauvages n *wildlife*
fée n *fairy*
fictionnel adj *fictional*
fier adj *proud*
figurant n *extra*
flambant neuf adj *brand new*
fonds n *fund*
force n *strength*
fouet n *whip*
foule n *crowd*
frissons de terreur n *shivers of fear*
frites n *French fries*

G

garde, gardien n *guard*
garde-forestier n *ranger*
garniture n *topping*
gaspiller v *waste*
geler v *freeze*
gêné adj *embarrassed, self-conscious*
gérer v *handle, cope with*
gradins n *bleachers (ns)*
gratitude n *gratitude*
grincer v *creak*
guarantir v *guarantee*
guide n *guide*
guide touristique n *tour guide*

H

habitat naturel n *natural habitat*
heure de cours n *period*
heure du déjeuner n *lunch time*
hilarant adj *hilarious*
historique adj *historical*
honorer v *honour*
hospitalier adj *hospitable*
hôte n *host*
hurler v *screech, yell*

I

Il était une fois loc *Once upon a time*
immense adj *huge*
immeuble en grès rouge n *brownstone building*
impatient de adj *eager to*
impliqué dans adj *involved in*
importer v *import*
impressionnant adj *impressive*
imprudent adj *careless, reckless*
incarner v *embody*
inclusion n *inclusiveness*
inconnu adj *unknown*
incroyable adj *breathtaking, incredible, outstanding*
indice n *clue*
indulgent adj *lenient, permissive*
inégalité n *inequality*
influencer v *influence*
influent adj *influential*
innovant adj *innovative*
inquiétant adj *eerie*
intégré dans adj *embedded in*
intégrer v *integrate*
interagir avec v *interact with*
internat n *boarding school*
interroger v *interrogate*
intrépide adj *fearless*
intrigue n *plot, storyline*
investigation n *inquiry*
investir dans v *invest in*
ironie n *irony*
irréfléchi adj *reckless, careless*
irrespectueux adj *disrespectful*
isolé adj *isolated*
isolement n *isolation*
ivoire n *ivory*

J

jeter une malédiction v *curse*
jeune né(e) entre 1981 et 1997 n *millennial*
joindre les deux bouts v *make ends meet*
jumelles n *binoculars*

L

lancer un sort v *cast a spell*
langue maternelle n *mother/native tongue*
légiférer v *legislate*
lieu de tournage n *film location*
littoral n *coastline, seashore*
lointain adj *remote*
lucratif adj *lucrative, money-making*
lumineux adj *bright*
lycée n *high school*

M

mairie *n* *town hall*
maison de retraite *n* *retirement home*
maître-nageur *n* *lifeguard, lifesaver*
mal à l'aise *adj* *ill-at-ease*
maléfique *adj* *evil*
malentendu *n* *misunderstanding*
maltraiter *v* *mistreat*
manifestation *n* *protest*
marché (place du) *n* *market (place)*
marraine *n* *godmother*
méchante sorcière *n* *wicked witch*
médaille *n* *medal*
menacé (d'extinction) *adj* *endangered, threatened*
mener un projet *v* *lead a project*
menotte *n* *handcuff*
mettre en place (un programme) *v* *carry out, implement (a programme)*
mettre en valeur *v* *showcase*
moderniser *v* *modernise*
montée d'adrenaline *n* *adrenaline rush*
monument commémoratif *n* *memorial*
mouvementé *adj* *eventful*
musée *n* *museum*
mythique *adj* *mythical*

N

nain(s) *n* *dwarf/dwarves*
né(e) à l'étranger *adj* *foreign-born*
négligent *adj* *reckless, careless*
nouer des liens avec *v* *connect with*
nouer des relations avec *v* *make connections with*

O

obsédé *adj* *obsessed*
obtenir son diplôme *v* *graduate, pass the final exams*
occasion *n* *opportunity*
oignon *n* *onion*
ombre *n* *shade, shadow*
l'oppresseur *n* *the oppressor*
les opprimés *n* *the oppressed*
ordinateur portable *n* *laptop*
ordures *n* *litter, trash*
organisé *adj* *organised*
origine *n* *origin*

P

paradoxal *adj* *paradoxical*
parc naturel *n* *nature park*
parent proche ou éloigné *n* *close or distant relative*
parlant couramment une langue *adj* *fluent*
partager des témoignages *v* *share testimonies*
partager *v* *share*
participer (à un atelier) *v* *attend (a workshop)*
participer à *v* *participate in, take part in*
partie de *loc* *part of*
partir en voyage *v* *go on a journey*
passager *n* *passenger*
passer un examen *v* *take an exam*
pause *n* *break*
PDG (président directeur général) *n* *chief executive officer (CEO)*
peinture murale *n* *mural*
permissif *adj* *permissive*
perpétuer le souvenir de *v* *keep the memory of*
personnel *n* *crew, staff, team*
personnes âgées *n* *the elderly, seniors*
personnes de la génération du baby-boom, nées entre 1945 et 1965 *n* *baby-boomers*
petit pain *n* *bun*
peur des hauteurs *n* *fear of heights*
piste d'athétisme *n* *track*
pleurer *v* *cry*
poésie *n* *poetry*
police scientifique *n* *forensics*
politesse *n* *politeness*
polyglotte *adj* *multilingual*
postuler à *v* *apply for, submit an application for*
préconiser, recommander *v* *advocate*
premier épisode d'une série *n* *pilot*
présenter *v* *showcase*
préserver *v* *preserve*
preuve *n* *evidence*
Prince charmant *n* *Prince Charming*
problème, sujet en question *n* *issue*
promouvoir *v* *foster, promote*
promulguer une loi *v* *enact a law*
protester *v* *protest*
provoquer *v* *result in*
prudent *adj* *careful*
public *n* *audience*

Q

quartier général, siège social *n* *headquarters*
quartier *n* *neighbourhood*
quelqu'un qui réussit *n* *achiever*
qui bat tous les records *adj* *record-breaking*
qui est source d'inspiration *adj* *inspiring*
qui soutient *adj* *supportive*

R

racine *n* *root*
rang *n* *rank*
réalisateur *n* *film director*
rebelle *adj* *defiant,rebellious*
recherche du bonheur *n* *pursuit of happiness*
rechercher *v* *search*
récolte *n* *crop*
recommander *v* *recommend*
reconnaissance *n* *recognition*
reconnaissant *adj* *grateful, thankful*
récréation *n* *break, recess*
réduire *v* *cut down, reduce*
réécriture *n* *rewriting*
regarder en ligne *v* *stream*
regarder tous les épisodes d'une série d'une traite *v* *binge-watch*
réinventer *v* *reinvent*
rejoindre un club *v* *join a club*
relever un défi *v* *take up a challenge*
remettre *v* *replace*
rencontrer de nouvelles personnes *v* *meet people*
rendre hommage à *v* *pay (a) tribute to*
rendre son rêve réalité *v* *make one's dream come true*
représenter *v* *stand for*
reprocher *v* *reproach*
réseau *n* *network*
réserve *n* *reservation*
réserver une visite guidée *v* *book a tour*
résistant *adj* *resilient*
respectueux de l'environnement *adj* *eco-friendly*
ressentir *v* *feel*
restaurant de burgers *n* *burger joint*
rester ensemble *v* *stick together*
retenir sa respiration *v* *hold one's breath*
retirer *v* *withdraw*
retraité *n* *pensioner, retired person*
retrouver *v* *meet up with*
réunion *n* *gathering*
réunir *v* *bring together, gather, unite*

révéler un élément d'intrigue v *spoil*
revitaliser v *revitalise*
rhinocéros n *rhino*
richesse n *wealth*
rivage n *shore*
rivalité v *rivalry*
rôle principal n *lead/main role*
rompre v *break up, split up*
royaume lointain n *far-away kingdom*

S

s'entraîner v *practise, train*
s'identifier à v *identify with*
s'impliquer dans v *get involved in*
s'inscrire à (un club) v *join (a club)*
s'intégrer v *blend in, fit in*
s'occuper de v *attend to someone, cope with, handle, provide care for*
s'unir v *unite*
sain adj *healthy*
salle polyvalente n *school hall*
sans viande adj *meat-free*
saut à l'élastique n *bungy-jumping*
saveur n *flavour*
savourer v *relish*
scénariste n *screenwriter*
scinder v *split up*
se battre pour/contre v *fight for, fight against*
se confomer à v *comply with, conform to*
se lancer dans une quête v *go on a quest*
se lier à v *bond with*
se perdre v *get lost*
se promener v *stroll*
se qualifer pour v *qualify for*
se réconcilier v *reconcile*
se sentir concerné par v *relate to*
ségrégation n *segregation*
sens n *sense*
sentiment d'accomplissement, de réussite n *sense of fulfilment*
sentiment d'appartenance n *togetherness*
série pour adolescents n *teen show*
serre n *greenhouse*
serveur n *waiter*
servir quelqu'un v *attend to someone, wait on someone*
servir v *serve*
servitude n *servitude*
session d'entraînement n *training session*
siège social n *headquarters*
sitcom, comédie n *sitcom*
solaire adj *solar*
solidarité n *solidarity*
sombre adj *dark*
sorcier n *wizard*
sortie (scolaire) n *excursion, field trip*
soudé adj *close-knit*
souffrir v *suffer*
soulever (un problème) v *bring up (a problem)*
soumis adj *submissive*
soutenir v *support*
sport extrême n *extreme sport*
sportif/-ve n *sportsman/sportswoman*
stade n *stadium*
stagiaire n *intern*
steak hâché n *patty*
stimuler v *stimulate*
strophe n *stanza*
studio de cinéma n *film studio*
succès n *success*
sujet n *issue*
surmonter v *overcome*
suspense à la fin d'un épisode n *cliffhanger*

T

talentueux adj *talented*
tatouage n *tattoo*
taux n *rate*
télécharger v *download*
téméraire adj *adventurous*
témoigner v *testify*
terrain d'athétisme n *track*
terreur n *awe*
terrifiant adj *terrifying*
tonte de moutons n *sheepshearing*
tortue n *turtle*
tourisme de masse n *mass tourism*
tourisme écologique n *eco-tourism*
tournoi n *tournament*
transformer v *transform*
transmettre un savoir v *pass on knowledge*
travailleur sur le terrain n *field worker*
tribu n *tribe*
tribunes n *grandstand*
trier v *sort*
trophée n *trophy*

U

uni adj *close-knit, united*
unioniste adj *unionist*
université n *college*

V

vagabonder v *roam, wander*
valeurs n *values*
vegan adj *vegan*
véhicule tout terrain, 4x4 n *ATV (all-terrain vehicle)*
veiller sur v *look after*
vendre v *sell*
vente aux enchères n *auction*
violent désaccord n *clash*
viser quelque chose v *aim at/for*
voir du monde v *socialise*
vol n *theft*
vouloir se venger v *seek revenge*
voyage n *journey, trip*
vue n *sight*

Z

zèbre n *zebra*

Édition : Anne Andrault, Anna François, Marie Lucas
Relecture : Victoria Britten, Seonaid Cruickshank
Iconographie : Valérie Delchambre
Conception de la couverture : Massimo Miola, Elise Launay
Conception de la maquette : Massimo Miola, Elise Launay, Simon Géliot
Cartographie : AFDEC, Philippe Chauvet
Illustrations : Alain Boyer, Philippe Chauvet, Tiffanie Uldry
Infographies : Philippe Chauvet, Marie Van der Marlière (pages *Boost your English*)
Mise en pages : Anne-Danielle Naname, Laure Gros
Composition du précis grammatical : Soft Office
ONISEP, p. 12-15, 262-263. Rédaction : Séverine Maestri, Michel Muller.
Coordination : Emmanuel Percq. Edition : Isabelle Dussouet
Apprendre c'est facile, p. 14-15, © Éditions Nathan 2018
L'éditeur et les auteurs remercient Catherine Baudry, professeure d'anglais à Saint-Denis (93) pour sa relecture pédagogique.

L'ENSEIGNEMENT DE SPÉCIALITÉ
ANGLAIS

LANGUES, LITTÉRATURES ET CULTURES ÉTRANGÈRES

1 Pouvez-vous nous décrire ce nouvel enseignement de spécialité ?

Cet enseignement initie plus encore les élèves à l'autonomie, au travail de recherche et au développement de l'esprit critique. Il prépare à l'enseignement supérieur mais il n'est pas un enseignement universitaire. **Il combine harmonieusement langue, littérature et culture** et **développe la maîtrise de la langue écrite et de la langue orale** (niveau B2 attendu en fin de première et niveau C1 visé en fin de terminale). Il vise également à **développer le goût de lire** par l'étude d'œuvres intégrales, de textes littéraires, de textes de nature historique, civilisationnelle, scientifique, historique, ou d'articles de presse.

2 Cette spécialité propose-t-elle une pédagogie ou des pratiques particulières ?

L'approche actionnelle et la **pédagogie de projet** sont au cœur des pratiques afin de **donner du sens aux apprentissages**. Le recours aux **outils numérique**s est vivement encouragé pour multiplier l'exposition à la langue de manière variée, favoriser l'entrainement individuel, **associer numérique et créativité**, ou encore mettre en relation les élèves avec des **interlocuteurs internationaux**.

3 À quel(le)s élèves s'adresse cette spécialité ?

Elle ne s'adresse pas aux seuls futurs spécialistes ni aux seuls littéraires mais à **tous les élèves qui veulent développer leurs compétences** linguistiques et culturelles, leurs compétences de **communication à l'écrit et à l'oral**. Ceci dans l'objectif d'une poursuite d'études, d'une visée professionnelle ou simplement par intérêt culturel ou curiosité.
J'ajouterais que la maîtrise de l'anglais sera un atout pour bon nombre de carrières.

Quelques exemples d'études facilitées par cette spécialité

www.horizons2021.fr

- **Licences :** Sciences du langage, Information et communication, LLCE (langues, littératures et civilisation étrangères et régionales), LEA (Langues étrangères appliquées) Lettres, Langues, Sciences politiques,
- **Classes préparatoire**s littéraires, commerciales, Instituts d'études politiques, Écoles de commerce,
- **BTS** Communication, Édition, Tourisme, Management, Commerce, Négociation et relation client, Gestion,
- **DUT** Information-communication, Gestion des entreprises et des administrations, Gestion logistique et transport,

Il existe près d'une centaine de BTS et une vingtaine de DUT dans les domaines de la production et des services.
Les bacheliers professionnels (BTS) et technologiques (DUT) sont prioritaires sur ces formations.

Young women and kangaroo, Lucky Bay, Cape Le Grand National Park, Esperance, Western Australia, Australia

Riverdale Park and skyline of Toronto, Canada

Crédits photographiques

Couverture : h Benedek/iStock ; **b** Andrew Watson/Photolibrary/Getty
6 h, reprise **de 16** ; **mh, reprise de 32 h** ; **mb, reprise de 42 g** ; **b, reprise de 45 hg** ; **7 h** ProdDB/Allpix/Aurimages ; **mh, reprise de 68** ; **mb** DR ; **b** Banksy ; **8 h, reprise de 90 h** ; **mh,** reprise **de 106 m** ; **mb, reprise de 115** ; **b** Charles McQuilan/Getty/AFP ; **9 h, reprise de 135 b** ; **mh** Vagabondi Travel Mag ; **mb, reprise de 148 h** ; **b, reprise de 161 b** ; **10 h, reprise de 168** ; **mh** Daz Stock/Shutterstock ; **mb, reprise de 186** ; **b, reprise de 198** ; **16, reprise 23 hd** Brandan "B-mike" Odums and Marthalicia Matarrita for Education is Not A Crime, produced by Street Art Anarchy ; **17 d** Inside Out/Susan Modaress ; **18, reprise 23 hg** The Granger Coll./Bridgeman Images ; **19 h** The Art Institute of Chicago, Ill/Bridgeman Images ; **19 b** Bettmann/Getty ; **20 h et b** Camilo José Vergara ; **21 h** Lars Niki/Getty/AFP ; **21 m, reprise 25 et 218** Kibonen ; **22 h** Spotmatik Ltd/Shutterstock ; **26, reprise 23 md** : Hulton Archive/Getty ; **27** New York Habitat ; **28** Helen Nezdropa/Fairfax Media/Getty ; **29 h** Anthony Johnson/Fairfax Media/Getty ; **29 b** Linda Hannig ; **30** St Peters Lutheran College, Brisbane, Australia ; **32 h** *hamiltoncollege.vic.edu.au* ; **32 b** Ivanhoe Girls' Grammar School ; **33 h et b, reprise 38** *high-school-australia.com*/Adie Bush/Cultura/AGE ; **34 h** High Resolves ; **b** One Vision Production ; **39** VCAA ; **40 b** Southeastern Guide Dogs ; **44** Studio Canal – Working Title Films/Coll. Christophe L ; **41, 42, 43** Cameron Covell ; **45 hg** *visitbritain.com* ; **hd** Front cover of *The Secret of High Eldersham* by Miles Burton reproduced courtesy of British Library Publishing ; **m** Berkley, 2011 ; **b** Sara Rosett, Amazon Digital Services LLC, 2014 ; **46** creacart/iStock ; **47 g, hd, bd** SWNS ; **48, reprise 53 et 231** Agatha Christie, *Murder at the vicarage*, HarperCollins Publishers Ltd, 1930, DR . **49** *Agatha Raisin and the Quiche of Death*, Sky One, 2014 ; **50, reprise 210** Jelltex ; **55** Photo12/Alamy ; **56** 20th Century Fox Television/Coll. Christophe L ; **57 h** Lightfield Studios/Shutterstock ; **57 b** Oscar Mayer ; **58** The Advertising Archive/Bridgeman Images ; **59 h** 20th Century Fox Television – Picture Day Production/Coll. Christophe L ; **59 b, 65** Honey Maid ; **60** Sturti/iStock ; **61 b** CBS NEWS ; **62 h** Cyber-Seniors ; **b** Kindermusik ; **66 h** Cyber-Seniors ; **b** Kindermusik ; **67** Al Jazeera English ; **68** The 80s Cruise ; **69 h** *the80scruise.com*/Entertainment Cruise Productions ; **b** Fine Brothers Entertainment ; **70 hg** Warner Bros – Amblin Entertainment/Coll. Christophe L ; **hd** Universal Pictures/RnB/Coll. Christophe L ; **b** Lucasfilm/Coll. Christophe L ; **71** Simon Brown/Katie A. King/Coll. Christophe L ; **72** David Parry/PA/Abaca Press ; **73 h** Dinendra Haria/Rex/Shutterstock/Sipa ; **b, reprise 79 hd** Arena Productions/Coll. Christophe L ; **74 h** Poisson Rouge Pictures – BFI/Coll. Christophe L ; **m** The Oxford Film Company/Coll. Christophe L ; **75** Jane Lindholm/VPR ; **76, reprise 81** Piotr Maleck/Panos/Rea ; **77** Olivia Harris/Reuters ; **78 hg** Jonathan Kim/Image Bank/Getty ; **hd** Photo12/Alamy ; **78, 82** Mentorn Media ; **79 hg** Ray Tang/LNP/Rex/Shutterstock/Sipa ; **bg** Frances Lincoln Children's Books, 2009 ; **bc** *cosmopolitanreview.com* ; **83 g** Michael Bowles/Rex/Shutterstock/Sipa ; **d** Stuart C. Wilson/WPA Pool/Getty/AFP ; **84** Paranoid Pictures/Coll. Christophe L ; **85 h** Simon Chapman/LNP/Rex/Shutterstock/Sipa ; **b** Hussein Zak/Sipa ; **86 h** Banksy, 2013 ; **b** Ray Tang/LNP/Rex/Shutterstock/Sipa ; **87** Banksy, compte Instagram ; **88, reprise 97** Fiona Goodall/Getty/AFP ; **89 h, reprise 95 h** Michael Thomas/Photosport NZ/Panoramic ; **b, reprise 98** Photo12/Alamy ; **90 h, reprise 95 md et 214 h** Photo12/Alamy ; **b, reprise 95 b** Masanori Udagawa/Photo Wellington ; **91 h, reprise 95 mg** Photo12/Alamy ; **b** Juan Mabromata/AFP ; **92** Doug Pearson/Jon Arnold Images/AGE ; **93 h et bg** Phil Walter/Getty/AFP ; **md** Photo12/Alamy ; **bd** Simon Baker/Reuters ; **94 g** What Now ; **d** Coll. Archives Larbor ; **99** Study Auckland – ATEED ; **100** GSI/Abaca Press ; **101 h** *visitsequoia.com* ; **b** Christoph Dernbach/DPA/AFP ; **102 h** Compass Coalition ; **b** California State Parks ; **103 h** Aquarium of the Bay, San Francisco ; **b** *nyaquarium.com* ; **104 h** BBQ – DFY/Aurimages ; **b** Joel Ryan/Invision/AP/Sipa ; **105 h** *itsocial.fr* ; **mg** Wayhome Studio/Shutterstock ; **md, reprise 109** Vulp/Shutterstock ; **bg** Jacob Lund/Shutterstock ; **bd** Mimage Photography/Shutterstock ; **107 m** Tony Avelar/Bloomberg/Getty ; **109** Marina Mogilko ; **113 h** Tourism Canada ; **b** Blaire Russell, 2016 ; **114, 115** Nadja Kwandibens/*redworks.ca* ; **116** Netflix/Coll. Christophe L ; **117 h** NBC – 20th Century Fox Television/Coll. Christophe L ; **mg** Netflix/Coll. Christophe L ; **md, 126** The Booktube Girl ; **118, reprise 125** San Diego Union tribune/Zuma/Rea ; **119 b** onepoll.us ; **120 h** Tiia Öhman/*fangirlquest.com* ; **b** i-D ; **121 h** Photo12/Alamy ; **b** DR ; **122** ABC – Sony Pictures Television/Coll. Christophe L ; **127** The Crazy Gorilla Inc. ; **128** Maja Hitij/Bongarts/AFP ; **129 h** Friedemann Vogel/Getty/AFP ; **b** Eranga Jayawardena/AP/Sipa ; **130 g** Suleiman Mbatiah/Nation Media Group ; **d** Fabrice Coffrini/AFP ; **131 h** ENDA ; **bg et bd reprise 246** Ben Curtis/AP/Sipa ; **132** Jean-Pierre Muller/AFP ; **133** Clive Rose/Getty/AFP ; **134** Alexander Hassenstein/Getty/AFP ; **135 fond** Paragorn Dangsombron/Shutterstock ; **h** Von der Laage Gladys Chai/AC/Rex/Shutterstock/Sipa ; **b, reprise 137** Miles Wilis/Getty/AFP ; **137** Miles Wilis/Getty/AFP ; **139** Alibaba Group ; **140, 141 b** Vagabondi Travel Mag ; **141 h** Photo12/Alamy ; **142 h** Film Frucht ; **m** Lightfield Studio/Shutterstock ; **143 h** Wes Davies ; **b** Young & Free Alberta ; **144** GilbertdeStoke/Fotosearch/AGE ; **145 hg** Nicj Upton/Nature PL/EB Photos ; **hd** Welsh Beaver Project ; **bd** Recycle for Wales/Brecon Carreg Mineral Water ; **146 h** Robert Harding/Hémis.fr ; **b** Jon Arnold Images/Hémis.fr ; **147 h** The Welsh Government – Crown Copyright ; **b, reprise 151 hg et 153, 154** Photo12/Alamy ; **148 h** Photo12/Alamy ; **b** Marine Energy Wales ; **149 h** Keep Wales Tidy ; **b, reprise 151 bg, 153** Photo12/Alamy ; **150** Paul Box/Report Digital/Rea ; **151 fond** Robert Harding/Hémis.fr ; **hd** Photo12/Alamy ; **bd** Photo12/Alamy ; **155** The Wildlife Trust of South and West Wales ; **156, reprise 165** *cheeseandburger.com* ; **157** First We Feast ; **158** Jorge Corona and Emily Mathis Corona ; **159 h** Selnick International Pictures/Coll. Christophe L ; **b** Al Jazeera English ; **160** Business Casual ; **161 h** McDonald's ; **b** The Impossible Burger ; **162, 163 d** Gojima ; **166** Photo12/Alamy ; **167** Scott Entertainment ; **168** Paros Chandaria/Caters News/Sipa ; **169 h** Magical Kenya / David Lloyd ; **bg, reprise 177** Akesak/iStock ; **bd** Bobby Neptune ; **170 m, b** Deutsche Welle ; **171 g** TropicDreams/Shutterstock ; **d** UIG/AGE ; **172 h** Fotosearch/AGE ; **b** MEAACT Kenya ; **173, 178** Sauti Kuu Foundation ; **174 h et m** Ben Curtis/AP/Sipa ; **b** Tony Karumba/AFP ; **179** Deutsche Welle ; **180 h** Daz Stock/Shutterstock ; **mh, reprise 181, 182, 183, 184, 185** Lightstone Media/iStock ; **mb, reprise 181, 182, 183, 184, 185** Emmily/Shutterstock ; **bg** August_802/Shutterstock ; **bm** Spiderstock/iStock ; **bd** Benstevens/iStock ; **181 mgh, reprise 183** Yio/iStock ; **mbg** Panagiotis Bakogiannis/iStock ; **bg et bm, reprise 183, 184, 185** Lotus Studio/Shutterstock ; **bd** Akintevs/iStock ; **182 hm** Volodymyr Tverdokhlib/Shutterstock ; **hmb** Artisteer/iStock ; **183 b** Socha/iStock ; **184 m** Skodonnel/iStock ; **185 md** Photo12/Alamy ; **b** Pahlam/iStock ; **186, reprise 193 h** Larry Busacca/Getty/AFP ; **187 h, reprise 195** Gary Malerba/AP/Sipa ; **b** Regency Enterprises – River Road Entertainment/Coll. Christophe L ; **188, 189 h, 189 m, 193** *The Adventures of Huckleberry Finn*, retold by ; Tom Ratliff, illustrated by Penko Gelev, Graffex, Book House, 2008 ; **189 b** Erika SOS Books ; **190 h, 196** A Kid Explains History ; **m** Bill Day, Tallahassee, FL/Cagle Cartoons ; **b, reprise 193 mhd** Elk County Historical Society ; **191, reprise 193 mbg** Sophie Bassouls/Leemage ; **192 h** The Whitney Plantation ; **b** *ebony.com* ; **193 b** Frederic Legrand, COMEO/Shutterstock ; **197** PBS ; **198, reprise 207** 2012 American Broadcasting Companies/Coll. Christophe L ; **199 h** Theo Wargo/Getty/AFP ; **bg** Netflix/Coll. Christophe L ; **bd** Chris Carlson/ChrisCarlsonArt ; **200** Metro Goldwyn Mayer Pictures/Coll. Christophe L ; **201 h** Mandeville Films, Walt Disney Pictures/Coll. Christophe L ; **b** Fotosearch/AGE ; **202 h et bg** Tim Manley, *Alice in Tumblr-Land and Other Fairy Tales for a New Generation*, Penguin Books, 2013 ; **bd** Brooklyn Book Fair ; **203** How It Should Have Ended Kids ; **204** Warner Bros/Coll. Christophe L ; **209** Black Hollywood Live ; **213** affiche Stranger Things ; **214 m** Trans World Sport

Crédits des textes

19 Reprinted by permission of Harold Ober Associates. © 1994 by the Langston Hughes Estate ; **20** *nymag.com*, Christopher Bonanos, 2017, DR ; *nytimes.com*, Michael Henry Adams, 2016, DR ; **22** *harlem.projectplay.us*, DR ; **22** *116thfestival.com* ; **27** *huffingtonpost.com*, Stacy Parker Le Melle, 2017, DR ; **30** From *A New Type of Education* in *My First Lesson: Stories Inspired by Laurinda*, by Keely Brown ; © Keely Brown, 2016 ; Reprinted by permission of Black Inc., an imprint of Schwartz Publishing ; **31** © 2017 - St Helena Secondary College ; **32** *hamiltoncollege.vic.edu.au* ; **33** *high-school-australia.com* ; **34** *tweeddailynews.com.au*, Liana Turner, 2017, DR ; **39 b** M. R. Deguara, *The Neverland of Highschool*, (*The Adventures of Big Chook Book 2*), eXtasy Books, 2015 ; **46** *theguardian.com*, DR ; **47** © Telegraph Media Group Limited 2016 ; **48** Reprinted by permission of HarperCollins Publishers Ltd © (1930) (Agatha Christie) ; **49** M. C Beaton, *Agatha Raisin and the Quiche of Death*, St Martin's Press, MacMillan Publishers, 1992, DR ; **50** © Telegraph Media Group Limited 2008 ; **55** MailOnline ; **58** Fast Company, "How my American Dream is different from my parents", 2018 ; **60** Rainbow Rowell, *Fangirl*, St Martin's Press, MacMillan Publishers, 2013, DR ; **61** *Fox News Live*, DR ; **67** "Not a 'Modern Family' At All", appears courtesy of Susan McWilliams Barndt ; **69** *the80scruise.com*, DR ; **70** *theatlantic.com*, Garin Pirnia, 2015, DR ; **74** *theguardian.com* ; **75 hg** Na'ima B. Robert, *From Somalia with love*, Lincoln Children's Books, imprint of the Quarto Group, 2008 ; **76** Astrid, Mihaela, Anokhee, Rangin, Anwar, Dilo, Shirin, *Grapes in my Father's Yard* ; **76 b** Joanna Czechowska, "After my polish grandmother died, I did not speak her native language for 40 years", *theguardian.com*, 2009 ; **83** *the-talks.com*, "Rita Ora: 'I didn't have the answers'", 2014 ; **87** *theguardian.com*, Jonathan Jones, 2018 ; **90 b** Stuff Limited ; **92** Archana Singh, Brand Strategist and Travel Journalist at Travel See Write ; **99** Ellie Ross, "Action packed: a packrafting trip in New Zealand", *theguardian.com*, 2016 ; **103** Scripps Institution of Oceanography at UC San Diego ; **106** *cnbc.com*, Marguerite Ward, 2017, DR ; **109** Marina Mogilko **111** Roxie Sarhangi, "My Failed Acting Career – and Why It Wasn't a Failure at all", Huffington Post, 2013 ; **114** *redworks.ca*, DR ; **118** *deseretnews.com*, Chandra Johnson, 2016 ; **119** XLIBRIS, Kelly Ann Gonzales, 2014 ; **121** *dailynews.com*, Lee Moran, 2013 ; **122** *themighty.com*, Amanda Steele, 2018 ; **127** *washingtonpost.com*, Maia Silber, 2017, DR ; **130** *sportskeeda.com*, Shuvro Ghosha, 2016 ; **132** © Telegraph Media Group Limited 2013 ; **134** *nytimes.com*, Motoko Rich and Emmanuel Akinwotu, 2018, DR ; **139** *dailymail.co.uk*, 2017, DR ; **140** WWOOF Canada ; **146** Pembrokeshire Coast National Park, 2015 DR ; **148** Imogen Calderwood, "The biggest onshore wind farm in Wales", *www.globalcitizen.org*, 2017 DR ; **150** Natural resources Wales ; **155** *www.eco-schools.org.uk* DR ; **158** *southernliving.com*, Robert Moss, 2017, DR ; **160** "Why do burgers continue to get more & more popular?", *zzzippy.com*, DR ; **161** *www.fortune.com*, Nathasha Bach, 2018, DR ; **162** *foodservicenews.com.au*, 2017, DR ; **167** Carrie Dennett, "The new generation of veggie burgers", *Seattle Times*, 2018 ; **171** "How to have a turtle-friendly holiday on Kenya's coast", *theguardian.com*, 2011 ; **172** *traveller.com.au* ; **173** *sautikuufoundation.org* ; **179** "From Nairobi To Mombasa", *theworldweekly.com*, 2018 DR ; **188-189** Book House, an imprint of the Salariya Book Company, Graffex, Tom Ratliff and Penko Gelev, 2008 DR ; **191** Colson Whitehead, Little Brown Book Group Ltd ; **197** Houghton Mifflin Harcourt, Ann Rinaldi, *Hang a Thousand Trees with Ribbons: The Story of Phillis Wheatley*, HMH Books for Young Readers, 2005, DR ; **201** Steve Meacham, *traveller.com.au* ; **203** Sarah Mlynowski, Orchard Books, Hachette Children's Books, 2015 ; **204** *springfieldspringfield.co.uk*, 2011, DR ; **209** Liz Brazwell, Disney Press, 2016

Crédits sonores

21 TODAY ; **27** New York Habitat ; **50** Haunted Earth Films & TV ; **55** Sky TV ; **57** ABC News ; **67** Al Jazeera English ; **93** BBC Worldwide Limited ; **104** WTOP Entertainment/Editor Jason Fraley ; **117** The Booktube Girl ; **155** The Wildlife Trust of South and West Wales ; **157** First We Feast ; **167** Scott Entertainment ; **189** Erika SOS Books ; **199** TV Insider ; **201** Flicks And The City/Disney ; **202** Jen Lee Productions ; **208** Black Hollywood Live

N° editeur : 10257542 - Dépôt legal : Août 2019 - Achevé d'imprimer en Italie, en Août 2019 par Rotolito S.p.A.

VERS QUELS MÉTIERS ?

Melissa, planneuse stratégique dans une agence de communication

- **L3 LEA** (langues étrangères appliquées) à l'université de Nice Sophia Antipolis
- **M2** en stratégie de communication à l'ECS (European Communication School)

Pourquoi avez-vous choisi des études d'anglais ?

Étant issue d'une famille franco-italienne et ayant depuis mon enfance le goût des langues, j'ai toujours espéré exercer un métier dans lequel elles seraient importantes.

En quoi l'anglais vous sert-il dans votre métier ?

Il me sert à faire de la veille internationale en communication. Je visite souvent les sites des agences internationales qui sont bien sûr en anglais. Des clients nous demandent parfois de créer un site bilingue, je vais évaluer si les traductions sont non seulement correctes, mais aussi conformes à la culture et aux habitudes du pays visé. L'anglais est très présent dans le domaine de la communication.

Florian, agent de transit international pour une entreprise agro-alimentaire

- **DUT** Techniques de commercialisation à l'université de Saint-Nazaire
- **Licence pro** logistique et transports internationaux à l'université de Saint-Nazaire
- **DU** Langue anglaise spécialisée et certification (DULASC) à l'université de Paris-Diderot

Quelle importance a eu l'anglais dans vos études ?

Je souhaitais travailler à l'international, j'ai toujours veillé à conserver un excellent niveau d'anglais que j'ai choisi de renforcer après ma licence professionnelle.

En quoi l'anglais vous sert-il dans votre métier ?

Au port du Havre, je dois d'abord faciliter les formalités de douanes de marchandises venant du monde entier, puis m'assurer que leur contrôle sanitaire aura lieu dans les délais requis.
Je gère les relations avec les transporteurs qui vont livrer les marchandises dans toute l'Europe en limitant le temps de stationnement car cela coûte très cher. La plupart de ces échanges se font en anglais qui est la langue du commerce international.

Laurette, technico-commerciale dans une entreprise de télécommunications

- **Licence** LLCER (Langues, littératures, civilisations étrangères et régionales) à l'université de Paris-Nanterre
- **Master 2** en traduction audiovisuelle à l'université de Paris-Nanterre

Pourquoi avez-vous choisi des études de langues ?

Ma matière préférée était l'anglais, je me suis donc naturellement inscrite en licence d'anglais. Je souhaitais au départ être enseignante, puis je me suis lancée dans le doublage. J'ai travaillé quelque temps dans la traduction technique avant de me lancer dans le secteur des télécoms.

En quoi l'anglais vous sert-il dans votre métier ?

J'accompagne une équipe de cinq à six commerciaux, dont je suis la garante technique.
Mais il m'arrive aussi d'aider des collègues à communiquer directement en anglais avec des entreprises internationales. Mon anglais m'est aussi utile pour répondre à des appels d'offres et en comprendre les subtilités.

Portraits et témoignages à retrouver dans leur intégralité sur le site nathan.fr/orientation

www.orientation-lycees.fr

onisep

Bien entendu, il existe de multiples autres métiers possibles !